# The Logic of Ish

# The Logic of Ish

## The First Temple is the Mind
## The First Prayer is a Question

*With Foreword by*
Prof. Jeffery D. Long

Mrittunjoy Guha Majumdar

MLBD PUBLICATIONS

**Motilal Banarsidass Publications**

**MOTILAL BANARSIDASS**
**PUBLICATIONS**
4741/23, Ansari Road, Daryaganj, New Delhi - 110002 (India)
Email: mlbd@mlbd.com | sales@mlbd.com
exports@mlbd.com | publications@mlbd.com
Website: www.mlbd.com



**The Logic of Ish**
***by***
**Mrittunjoy Guha Majumdar**

*First Edition Published in 2026*



Published in India by Motilal Banarsidass Publications

ISBN : 978-93-7513-282-0 (PB)
978-93-7513-890-7 (HB)

Printed and bound in India

# Contents

# Foreword

*by Prof. Jeffery D. Long*

In many intellectual circles, there is a widely held view that philosophical theology–a once-revered discipline which has exercised such great minds as St. Anselm, St. Thomas Aquinas, and Gottfried Wilhelm Liebniz–is dead, slain by the likes of David Hume, Immanuel Kant, and a host of 'new' atheists. In this elegantly argued volume, Mrittunjoy Guha Majumdar shows us how philosophical theology can proceed in the twenty-first century. What is even more exciting is that he does this while also accomplishing (at least) two other tasks: namely, taking seriously the many criticisms to which the discipline of philosophical theology has been subject over the last few centuries, and drawing our attention to the fact that a conversation was already underway in ancient India that anticipates and is incredibly relevant to our contemporary era.

In regard to the latter accomplishment, by drawing on the arguments of the venerable Nyāya and Vedānta traditions of India, his work is an outstanding example of what Swami Medhananda calls "cross-cultural philosophy of religion." Importantly, genuine cross-cultural philosophy of religion is not simply a well-intentioned exercise in border crossing–a fundamentally Eurocentric exercise that seeks to come across as more cosmopolitan by pulling elements of non-Western philosophies into its reflections. Genuine cross-cultural philosophy of religion is, first and foremost, *philosophy*. It is driven not so much by a desire to be (or worse, appear) cross-cultural as by basic philosophical questions. The cross-cultural element enters not so much as an end in itself (salutary and desirable though this goal is) but in the service of the question at hand. In short, a wide variety philosophical traditions are drawn upon precisely because they are relevant to the argument, because they have light to shine upon it.

In this volume, Mrittunjoy deftly shows us that the work of ancient Indian logicians–in particular, Udayanācārya–is deeply relevant to a question that refuses to go away, despite the efforts of a wide range of skeptics to refute it: the question of theism. As Dr. Guha Majumdar rightly says, the Nyāya system of philosophy which Udayana represents is too often characterized as a dry set of syllogisms. But as presented here, we see Udayana as pushing the boundaries of what it is possible for reason to accomplish. The discussion of Udayana and his response to Indian anti-theists (mostly Buddhists and Jains) is deftly woven into a conversation about Western philosophy and the current state of the theistic conversation. Even quantum physics is shown to fit within this conversation.

In short, this book is an admirable demonstration of what cross-cultural philosophy of religion can be. It is to be hoped that it will serve as an example and open this conversation even further. For the question of theism, as Dr. Guha Majumdar ably argues, is not a simple question of fact, nor a matter for dry, abstract theorization. Rather, it touches upon humanity's deepest longings and helps to ground central moral intuitions which transcend cultural boundaries. This book is thus important on many levels. It should be widely read and disseminated.

*Chapter*

*One*

# The Temple of the Mind

The first temple is the mind, and its first prayer is a question. For over two thousand years, Indian philosophers of the *Nyāya* school have pursued questions related to the nature of reality with relentless precision. Where others sought the divine in *Mantras*, rituals, or *śabdapramāṇa* – testimony of the Veda, *Nyāya* thinkers believed the path to *Īśvara*—the supreme being—must run through logic, debate, and reason. In an age when belief was often inherited, they dared to ask: *Can we prove the existence of God?* This audacious vision gave birth to one of humanity's great intellectual traditions: a rational theology that rivals anything in the West for its depth and originality. Long before Thomas Aquinas wrote his *Five Ways* or Leibniz posed his famous question, *"Why is there something rather than nothing?"*, Indian logicians like Akṣapāda Gautama, Vātsyāyana, and Udayanācārya were crafting arguments that combined fierce logic with a profound sense of wonder. To appreciate their achievement, we must first strip away centuries of misunderstanding. *Nyāya* has too often been reduced to a sterile school of syllogisms—a mere proto-analytic philosophy of ancient India—its deeper metaphysical and theistic ambitions overlooked. But this misses the heart of its project. For *Nyāya*, logic was never an end in itself. It was a tool—a means to pierce the illusions of the world and uncover its ultimate cause. Their reasoning was rigorous enough to satisfy a skeptic, yet suffused with a theistic vision that saw *Īśvara* not as a dogma but as the inevitable conclusion of sound argument. The foundational text of this tradition—the *Nyāya Sūtras*, in verses IV.1.19 – IV.1.21, presents dialectics related to *Īśvara*,

> सिद्धान्तसूत्र : ईश्वरः कारणम्, पुरुषकर्माफल्यदर्शनात्
> पूर्वपक्षसूत्र : न, पुरुषकर्माभावे फ्लानिष्पत्तः
> सिद्धान्तसूत्र : तत्कारितत्वादहेतुः
>
> *Translation*: The proposition (*sūtra*) is: *Īśvara* is the cause, since we see sometimes human action lacks fruits (results). The retort (*sūtra*) arises: This is not so since, as a matter of fact, no fruit is accomplished without human action. (Counter) propoposition (*sūtra*) is: Not so, since it is influenced by *Īśvara*.

Causality has been the centre-point of dialogues and dialectics on the presence and existence of *Īśvara*. We can trace the evolution of *Nyāya*'s rational theology from its earliest formulation in the *Nyāya Sūtras*, through Vātsyāyana's 5th-century commentaries, to its pinnacle in Udayanācārya's *Nyāyakusumāñjali* (literally 'A Handful of Flowers for *Nyāya*'). Along the way, we will encounter five ingenious arguments for God's existence—some startlingly modern in their reasoning, others deeply rooted in India's metaphysical traditions. What makes this journey compelling is not just the brilliance of the arguments but their method. Udayanācārya and his predecessors engaged rival worldviews—Buddhist *Śūnyatā*, Jain pluralism, *Mīmāṃsā* ritualism—not with polemics but with intellectual generosity and razor-sharp analysis. Their goal was simple yet profound: to show that reason alone, unaided by revelation or blind faith, could lead to the divine. But what is 'God' in this context? For the *Nyāya* tradition, *Īśvara* is not the tribal deity of a single people nor the inscrutable God of negative theology, but the cosmic intelligence whose existence explains the order, intelligibility, and moral fabric of the universe. Unlike the personal gods of myth and devotion, this *Īśvara* is a necessary postulate of reason—a being inferred as the ground of causality, morality, and the very possibility of knowledge. It is a vision of the divine that seeks neither to coerce belief nor to silence doubt, but to invite inquiry: a God (although this term does not quite do justice to the concept of *Īśvara*) not of fear but of understanding. Today, as science and philosophy wrestle with the origins of the cosmos, consciousness, and moral order, the *Nyāya* project feels uncannily prescient. Could an ancient Indian philosopher have something to teach us about the search for God in a universe of quarks and galaxies? Could we take forward Udayanācārya's arguments for the modern age, to help find God without faith?

This is the story of how reason became a bridge to the *beyond*.

To appreciate the unique position occupied by Indian rational theology, it is imperative to clarify the distinction between rational inquiry and its revelatory counterpart. Revealed theology (*āgamika-vidyā*) grounds its epistemic authority in scriptural testimony (*śruti*), divine disclosure, or mystical experience—domains traditionally regarded as transcending the bounds of human reason. Within the Indian context, this encompasses the vast corpus of Vedic literature, the Upaniṣadic contemplations, and the variegated sectarian texts of the *āgama* traditions, each claiming derivation from supra-human sources. The *śruti* tradition—literally *'that which is heard'*—epitomizes this modality by asserting that certain truths lie beyond the purview of inferential reasoning and are accessible only through authoritative transmission. Sri Ādi

Śaṅkarācārya's seminal text *Vivekacūḍāmaṇi* (verse 294) says,

> अहंपदार्थस्त्वहमादिसाक्षी
> नित्यं सुषुप्तावपि भावदर्शनात्।
> ब्रूते ह्यजो नित्य इति श्रुतिः स्वयं
> तत्प्रत्यगात्मा सदसद्विलक्षणः।।
>
> *Translation*: But the real 'I' is that which witnesses the ego and the rest. It exists always, even in the state of profound sleep. The *śruti* itself says, *'It is birthless, eternal'*, etc. Therefore the *Paramātman* is different from the gross and subtle bodies.

This verse underscores the *śruti>s* claim that ultimate reality (*Paramātman*) transcends empirical cognition and remains self-revealed, reinforcing the primacy of revelation over discursive reason in matters of metaphysical truth. The question then is how can we reason this out? Is that even possible? Rational theology—what we can call *tārkika Īśvara-vāda*—seeks to establish the existence and attributes of the divine through *tarka* (reason), *anumāna* (inference), and empirical observation (*pratyakṣa*). It does not necessarily reject the validity of revelation, nor does it posit itself as antagonistic to it; rather, it maintains that reason, operating autonomously, is competent to discern and defend metaphysical truths concerning ultimate reality. This approach presupposes that the faculties of human cognition, guided by the rigors of logic (*Nyāya*), are capable of penetrating to the ontological foundations of existence—including the question of a divine ground or principle.

The contrast, however, proves far more subtle in the Indian philosophical milieu than a simple opposition between faith and reason would suggest. Unlike certain strands of Western thought where the dichotomy between reason and revelation has been sharply drawn, Indian traditions often exhibit a hermeneutic of synthesis. In the *Nyāya* tradition, the role of reason is twofold: it serves both as an independent avenue to metaphysical insight and as an exegetical instrument to clarify and defend truths already intimated in *śruti*. This dual function exemplifies the Indian tendency toward *pramāṇa-samvāda*—a harmonization of multiple epistemic instruments—rather than privileging any one absolutely. *Nyāya*'s methodological commitments rest on several key presuppositions: that the universe manifests an intelligible order susceptible to rational analysis; that logical principles such as causality (*kārya-kāraṇa-bhāva*), inference (*anumāna*), and non-contradiction (*avirodha*) hold universally, even in metaphysical domains; that empirical observation, properly interpreted, can yield insight into transcendental realities; and that philosophical reasoning possesses sufficient probative force to ground not only intellectual assent but also religious praxis. This stance situates *Nyāya* rational theology in a distinctive median position. Unlike radical empiricism, it affirms that reason can extrapolate beyond sense-data to posit unobservable causes and principles. Unlike fideism, it insists that belief in the divine ought to be rationally warranted, eschewing blind assent in favour of demonstrative argumentation. In this way, *Nyāya*'s *tārkika* project exhibits both rigor and restraint: it aspires neither to supplant revelation nor to defer uncritically to it, but to chart a path where reason and faith may converge without collapse.

At the heart of this intellectual enterprise lies *Nyāya*'s theory of knowledge (*pramāṇa-śāstra*). Early *Nyāya* delineated four valid means of knowledge (*pramāṇa*): perception (*pratyakṣa*), inference (*anumāna*), comparison (*upamāna*), and verbal testimony (*śabda*). In addressing theological questions, the tradition privileges inference, supported by empirical observation. This methodological orientation stems from an epistemological realism: while *Īśvara* may not be directly apprehensible to the senses, *tat*'s existence may be reliably inferred from observable effects—such as cosmic order, causality, and moral regularities—through valid reasoning. Here I have used *tat* (तत्) as the possessive determiner/adjective instead of *His* (as is often used in western traditions), because not only is gender not annotated to the fundamental reality in Dharmic traditions but the divine feminine has as important, if not more, a role in the unfolding of reality. The inferential structure deployed in *Nyāya's* theological arguments adheres to its distinctive five-membered syllogism (*pañcāvayava-vākya*): *Pratijñā* (Proposition) – The universe has a creator, *Hetu* (Reason) – because it exhibits the characteristics of an artifact, *Udāharaṇa* (Example) – whatever exhibits such characteristics has a maker like a pot, *Upanaya* (Application) – this universe exhibits such characteristics, and *Nigamana* (Conclusion) – therefore, it has a creator. In the *Nyāyasūtras* 1.1.33-39, we have

> साध्यनिर्देशः प्रतिज्ञा
> उदाहरणसाधर्म्यात् साध्यसाधनं हेतुः
> तथा वैधर्म्यात्
> साध्यसाधर्म्यात् तद्धर्मभावी दृष्टान्तः उदाहरणम्
> तद्विपर्ययात् वा विपरीतम्
> उदाहरणापेक्षः तथा इति उपसंहारः न तथा इति वा साध्यस्य उपनयः
> हेत्वपदेशात् प्रतिज्ञायाः पुनर्वचनम् निगमनम्
>
> *Translation*: The statement of what is to be proven is the proposition (*pratijñā*). The reason (*hetu*) is that which establishes the *sādhya* through similarity with the example. Similarly, (*hetu* is established) through dissimilarity.

> The example (*udāharaṇa*) is that which, being similar to the *sādhya*, possesses the relevant property. Or, through the opposite, the contrary (example) is shown. The application (*upanaya*) is the affirmation 'just so' or denial 'not so' of the *sādhya* in the subject, based on the example. The conclusion (*nigamana*) is the repetition of the proposition along with the statement of the reason.

This elegant logical form not only exemplifies *Nyāya*'s concern for epistemic rigor but also underscores its commitment to intelligibility in theological discourse. This five-part syllogism is the hallmark of *Nyāya* logic, distinguishing it from the simpler three-part syllogism found in Aristotelian logic. But even this is not closed to criticism and even refutation. For instance, Ācārya Ānandajñāna offers a detailed critique of the *pañcāvayava-vākya*, questioning the basic definitions of each part. He shows that they often lead to logical problems like *avyāpti* (too narrow), *ativyāpti* (too broad), and *ātmāśraya* (self-dependence). For example, he challenges the idea that the desire to prove something (*pratipipādayiṣā*) can be clearly located in the speaker, listener, or moderator, and argues that even the examples and conclusions rely on already flawed concepts. By refuting each part, Ācārya Ānandajñāna ultimately destabilizes the entire structure of formal reasoning in these schools. This is significant because it questions the very foundation of rational debate as practiced in classical Indian philosophy. In the course of our meditation and explorations, we will assess our expansion of Udayanācārya's arguments not only to the modern context but also assess their validity against the criticism of luminaries such as Ācārya Ānandajñāna.

## From Gautama to Udayana

The evolution of rational theology within *Nyāya* traverses nearly a millennium, from Gautama's foundational

*Nyāyasūtras* (c. 2nd century CE), through Vātsyāyana's 5th-century exegesis, to Udayanācārya's sophisticated synthesis in the *Nyāyakusumāñjali* (c. 11th century CE). This trajectory reflects both internal dialectical refinement and external engagements with rival schools. Buddhists challenged the *Nyāya* conception of a permanent self and a governing deity, invoking arguments grounded in impermanence (*anityatā*) and dependent origination (*pratītya-samutpāda*). For instance, in *Dhammapada* (verse 277), we have

> अनिच्चा वत सङ्खारा, उप्पादवयधम्मिनो।
> उप्पज्जित्वा निरुज्झन्ति, तेसं वूपसमो सुखो॥
>
> *Translation*: All conditioned things are impermanent—arising and passing away. Having arisen, they cease; their stilling is true bliss.

The *Sāṅkhya* system, while accepting multiple *puruṣas* (selves), denied a supreme creator, attributing cosmic evolution to the inherent dynamics of *prakṛti* (nature). But this was not the only strand: Ācārya Vijñānabhikṣu, a 16th-century philosopher, affirmed a theistic *Sāṅkhya* by introducing *Īśvara* as a distinct, omniscient *puruṣa*, contrasting earlier non-theistic *Sāṅkhya* views. Jain pluralism and *Mīmāṃsā* ritualism posed additional challenges, forcing *Nyāya* thinkers to develop a robust intellectual apparatus capable of defending theism against formidable interlocutors. Ācārya Vācaspati Miśra, in his commentary *Nyāyavārttikatātparyaṭīkā* on Uddyotakara's *Nyāyavārttika,* refuted Jain pluralism by arguing that independent, omniscient selves cannot coordinate truth without a unifying *Īśvara*, and challenged *Mīmāṃsā* ritualism by asserting that only a conscious divine agent—not inert Vedic words—can ensure the Veda's authority and purposeful authorship. It is in Udayanācārya's *Nyāyakusumāñjali*—

literally '*A Handful of Flowers for Nyāya*'—that the tradition's rational theology reaches its zenith. There, Udayanācārya marshals five distinct arguments for *Īśvara's* existence, weaving together metaphysical, cosmological, and moral considerations in a manner both rigorously logical and spiritually resonant. His project remains one of the most compelling attempts in world philosophy to demonstrate that reason, unaided by revelation, can lead to a vision of the divine. The *Nyāyasūtras* attributed to Ācārya Gautama establishes the fundamental framework for all subsequent *Nyāya* philosophy but addresses theological questions only indirectly. Ācārya Gautama's primary concern lies with establishing a systematic methodology for valid knowledge (*pramāṇa*) and sound argument (*vāda*). However, the text's opening *sūtra*—"*tattvajñānān niḥśreyasādhigama*" (the attainment of the highest good follows from knowledge of reality)—implicitly assumes a teleological universe where correct knowledge leads to spiritual liberation.

The theological implications of Ācārya Gautama's system emerge more clearly in his treatment of the soul (*ātman*) and liberation (*mokṣa*). The text argues that individual souls are distinct, eternal, and capable of both bondage and liberation. This metaphysical framework presupposes a moral universe where actions produce appropriate consequences (*karma*), though Ācārya Gautama does not explicitly argue for a divine administrator of this moral order. The systematic ambiguity regarding divine involvement reflects the text's focus on logical methodology rather than metaphysical speculation. Ācārya Gautama's contribution to rational theology lies primarily in establishing the epistemological and logical foundations that later thinkers would apply to theological questions. His analysis of inference (*anumāna*), in particular, provides the technical apparatus for subsequent arguments about divine existence. He talks of three kinds of in the *Nyāyasūtra* (verse 1.1.5),

अथ तत्पूर्वकं त्रिविधं अनुमानं पूर्ववत् शेषवत् सामान्यतोदृष्टं च

*Translation*: Now, following that, the three kinds of inference are: inference based on prior observation (*pūrvavat*), inference based on residual effect (*śeṣavat*), and inference based on general observation (*sāmānyatodṛṣṭa*).

The distinction between inference for oneself (*svārthānumāna*) and inference for others (*parārthānumāna*) becomes crucial for theological discourse later, as highlighted by Ācārya Annaṃbhaṭṭa in the *Tarkasaṃgraha*, since arguments about divine existence typically aim to convince others rather than simply clarify one's own understanding. The *Nyāyasūtra*'s treatment of verbal testimony (*śabda*) also proves significant for later theological development. While Ācārya Gautama accepts the authority of reliable speakers (आप्तोपदेशः शब्दः – *Nyāyasūtra* verse 1.1.7), he does not grant absolute authority to any text or tradition. Even the authority of *Mantras* is seen to be established on the word of reliable sources, in verse 2.1.69,

मन्त्रायुर्वेदप्रामाण्यवत् च तत्प्रामाण्यम्, आप्तप्रामाण्यात्

*Translation*: Just as the authority (validity) of *mantras* and Ayurveda is accepted, so too is its authority — because of the authority of a trustworthy source (*āpta*).

This position allows later *Nyāya* thinkers to maintain respect for Vedic authority while insisting that rational analysis remains the ultimate criterion for truth. The tension between these commitments generates much of the creative energy in subsequent *Nyāya* theology.

Ācārya Vātsyāyana's *Nyāyabhāṣya* (c. 4th-5th century CE) represents the first systematic commentary on Ācārya Gautama's *Nyāyasūtra* and marks a crucial stage in the development of *Nyāya* rational theology. While maintaining fidelity to the foundational text, Ācārya Vātsyāyana clarifies ambiguous passages, responds to objections from competing schools, and begins the process of theological elaboration that reaches maturity in Udayanācārya. His most significant theological contribution lies in his explicit defence of divine existence against Buddhist and *Sāṅkhya* objections. Unlike Ācārya Gautama, who largely left the question of (a)theism unanswered, Ācārya Vātsyāyana feels compelled to argue for theism. This shift reflects an altered philosophical environment, where Buddhist schools had developed sophisticated critiques of theistic assumptions, and *Sāṅkhya* had proposed alternative explanations for cosmic order that eliminated divine involvement. The *Nyāyabhāṣya* presents several arguments for divine existence, though these remain relatively undeveloped compared to later treatments. Ācārya Vātsyāyana argues that the world's order and regularity require intelligent causation (व्याहतव्यूहानामवयवानां पूर्वव्यूहनिवृत्तौ व्यूहान्तरात् द्रव्यनिष्पत्तिर्नाभावात् – *Nyāyabhāṣya* 4.1.18), that moral consequences (*karma*) require divine administration, and that the Vedic revelation implies an authoritative source. These arguments establish the basic structure for all subsequent *Nyāya* theology, though they await systematic development. Ācārya Vātsyāyana's response to Buddhist critiques proves particularly important for understanding the rational character of *Nyāya* theology. Buddhist schools, especially the *Yogācāra*, had argued that the concept of a permanent, unchanging creator contradicts the universal principle of impermanence (*anicca*). They also questioned how an immaterial being could influence material processes and how divine perfection could be compatible with worldly involvement. Ācārya Vātsyāyana's responses, while not fully satisfactory by later standards, demonstrate the tradition's commitment to meeting objections through rational argument rather than dogmatic assertion. In fact, as a consequence of the presence of Buddhism, the philosophy of *Nyāya* evolved. The maturity of Ācārya Vātsyāyana's thinking can be seen by his knowledge of the concept of universal concomitance, as seen in Satkari Mookerjee's *The Buddhist Philosophy of Universal Flux* (chapter 24),

> *"Though the Nyāyasūtra does not contain any reference to this all-important factor of inference and there is room for supposition that the argument in Nyāya is based on analogy, there are indications that Vātsyāyana was conscious of the necessity of universal concomitance."*

The epistemological discussions in the *Nyāyabhāṣya* also advance the rational theological program by clarifying the relationship between different sources of knowledge. Ācārya Vātsyāyana maintains that inference can establish truths not accessible through direct perception, including metaphysical truths about the soul and its liberation. He says, in the *Nyāyabhāṣya* 1.1.5,

> तत्पूर्वकमित्यनेन लिङ्गलिङ्गिनोः संबन्धदर्शनं लिङ्गदर्शनं चाभिसंबध्यते
> लिङ्गलिङ्गिनोः संबध्द्योर्दर्शनेन लिङ्गस्मृतिरभिसंबध्यते
> स्मृत्या लिङ्गदर्शनेन चाऽप्रत्यक्षः अर्थः अनुमीयते
>
> *Translation*: When something is said to be preceded by another, it means that one must have seen both the connection between a sign and what it indicates, and the sign itself. By observing this connection, one remembers the sign. Using this memory along with the present observation of the sign, one arrives at knowledge of something not directly seen.

This position supports the possibility of rational theology while acknowledging the limitations of sensory experience for transcendent matters. Ācārya Vātsyāyana's treatment of scriptural authority (*āgama*) reveals the subtle balance characteristic of *Nyāya* rational theology. While accepting the authority of Vedic revelation, he insists that such authority must be rationally defensible. The Vedas carry authority because they originate from a reliable source (ultimately, the divine), but this claim itself requires rational justification. This circular structure—reason supports revelation, which supports reason—generates ongoing tension within the tradition but also prevents either pure rationalism or pure fideism. The period between Ācārya Vātsyāyana and Udayanācārya witnessed significant development in *Nyāya* theology, though much of this occurs in texts that are either lost or available only in fragments. The names of Uddyotakara and Vācaspati Miśra, among other intermediate figures, suggest a continuous tradition of commentary and refinement, though the details remain obscure. What can be reconstructed suggests that this intermediate period saw increasing sophistication in theological argumentation, driven partly by continued Buddhist challenges and partly by internal development within the *Nyāya* tradition. For instance, the characterization of the mind by Uddyotakara in *Nyāyavārttika* (1.1.4) is noteworthy,

> कार्यधर्मावेतौ भौतिकमभौतिकं च, न कार्यं मनः, तस्मान्न भौतिकं नाप्यभौतिकमिति
>
> *Translation*: These two — the material and the non-material — are both properties of effects. But the mind is not an effect. Therefore, it is neither material nor non-material.

The rise of Advaita Vedānta during this period also created new challenges, as Sri Ādi Śaṅkarācārya offered approaches to ultimate reality that combined rational argument with scriptural exegesis in ways that differed from the *Nyāya* approach. He subverted the very categories *Nyāyikas* premised their formulation on: *guṇa*, *dravya*, *sambandha* and *pramāṇa*—and dismantled epistemic realism from within, using rigorous metaphysical minimalism.

The philosophical environment of medieval India created pressure for increasingly precise theological formulations. The great debates at centers like Nalanda and the patronage of philosophical disputation by various rulers meant that theological positions required sophisticated defence. This context helps explain the remarkable precision and complexity of Udayanācārya's mature synthesis. Udayanācārya represents the culmination of *Nyāya* rational theology and one of the most sophisticated philosophical theologians in any tradition. Swāmi Vivekānanda once wrote to John Henry Wright, saying,

> *"He who is the Brahman of the Vedantins, Īśvara of the Naiyayikas, Purusha of the Sankhyas, cause of the Mimamsakas, law of the Buddhists, absolute zero of the Atheists, and love infinite unto those that love, may [He] take us all under His merciful protection": Udayanācārya—a great philosopher of the Nyaya or Dualistic school. And this is the Benediction pronounced at the very beginning of his wonderful book Kusumanjali (A handful of flowers), in which he attempts to establish the existence of a personal creator and moral ruler of infinite love independently of revelation.*

Udayanācārya's *Nyāyakusumāñjali* presents the most systematic and comprehensive rational arguments for divine existence in classical Indian philosophy. The text demonstrates both the possibilities and the limitations of rational theology while engaging seriously with the most sophisticated objections from Buddhist, *Sāṅkhya*, and other schools. Udayanācārya's approach differs from his predecessors in several crucial respects. First, he provides far more detailed and systematic arguments, addressing objections with unprecedented thoroughness. Second, he integrates insights from other philosophical traditions, including *Sāṅkhya* metaphysics and Buddhist logic, while maintaining distinctively *Nyāya* commitments. Third, he develops a more nuanced understanding of the relationship between rational demonstration and religious practice, acknowledging that theological knowledge serves soteriological as well as purely intellectual purposes. The *Nyāyakusumāñjali* presents five main arguments for divine existence, each addressing different aspects of the question and responding to different objections. The argument from design infers divine intelligence from the order and complexity of the natural world. The argument from moral governance contends that moral consequences require divine administration. The argument from scriptural authority maintains that revealed texts imply an authoritative source. The argument from religious experience appeals to the testimony of accomplished yogins and saints. The argument from logical necessity attempts to show that divine existence follows from basic metaphysical principles.

Each argument employs the sophisticated logical apparatus developed within the *Nyāya* tradition, including detailed analysis of inferential relationships (*vyāpti*), consideration of alternative explanations (*vipakṣa*), and response to potential counterexamples (*vyāghāta*). The technical precision of these arguments reflects centuries of philosophical development and creates formidable challenges for critics. Udayanācārya's theological vision extends beyond mere existence arguments to encompass divine attributes and their relationship to the world. He argues that the divine possesses consciousness (*caitanya*), will (*icchā*), effort (*prayatna*), and knowledge (*jñāna*) while maintaining transcendence of ordinary limitations. This combination of immanence and transcendence requires careful philosophical articulation, which Udayanācārya provides through subtle distinctions and qualifications. The systematic character of Udayanācārya's approach appears in his integration of theological arguments with broader metaphysical and epistemological commitments. Divine existence is not an isolated conclusion but part of a comprehensive worldview that includes theories of causation, knowledge, moral action, and spiritual liberation. This integration gives *Nyāya* rational theology its distinctive character as a philosophical system rather than merely a collection of arguments.

## Philosophical Crossroads

The *Nyāyakusumāñjali* emerged from a specific historical and intellectual context that shaped both its content and its approach. Understanding this context proves essential for appreciating the text's significance within the broader development of Indian rational theology and its relevance for contemporary philosophical discussions. Udayanācārya composed the *Nyāyakusumāñjali* during the eleventh century, a period of remarkable intellectual ferment in Indian philosophy. The preceding centuries had witnessed the systematic development of major philosophical schools, each offering comprehensive worldviews supported by sophisticated arguments. Buddhism had reached new heights of logical precision in the work of Ācārya Dignāga and Ācārya Dharmakīrti, while Advaita Vedānta had achieved systematic formulation under Sri Ādi Śaṅkarācārya and his immediate successors. *Sāṅkhya* had developed detailed accounts of cosmic evolution that excluded divine involvement, and various sectarian traditions had produced extensive theological literatures. This philosophical diversity created both opportunities and challenges for rational theology. On one hand, the general acceptance of rational discourse as a legitimate means of establishing truth created an environment where theological arguments could receive serious consideration. On the other hand, the sophistication of competing positions required increasingly precise and comprehensive responses from theistic philosophers. The political context also influenced theological development. The period saw the rise of various kingdoms that patronized philosophical debate and learning, creating institutional support for intellectual work. Royal courts often hosted debates between representatives of different schools, creating pressure for clear and convincing formulations of basic positions. In 11th-century India, philosophical debates concerning Advaita Vedānta and Viśiṣṭādvaita Vedānta were prominent among scholars, with figures such as Sri Rāmānujācārya—who had studied with the Advaitin Ācārya Yādava Prakāśa—developing positions opposed to classical Advaita non-dualism. While later hagiographies and tradition describe such confrontations occurring in the courts of the Cholas and Hoysalas, direct evidence of formal public debates is limited, though royal patronage under rulers like Hoysala Vishnuvardhana did bolster the Sri Vaishnava cause. In Kashmir, the philosopher Ācārya Abhinavagupta, under royal patronage, refined Pratyabhijñā Śaivism into a distinctive non-dualism that critically engaged with both Sri Ādi Śaṅkarācārya's Advaita and Buddhist idealism. In the Deccan, Mīmāṃsaka and Naiyāyika scholars—often supported by Chalukya rulers—responded to a variety of rival schools, both theistic and non-theistic. However, the exact nature of these interactions and the extent of direct royal involvement are mediated by later tradition and should be interpreted cautiously. The *Nyāyakusumāñjali* reflects this environment in its careful attention to potential objections and its systematic response to alternative viewpoints.

The religious context of medieval India presented additional complexities for rational theology. While the Vedic tradition provided a general theistic framework, the proliferation of sectarian movements created questions about the specific nature of divine reality. Vaishnavism, Shaivism, and Shaktism each offered distinctive theological perspectives, often supported by their own philosophical arguments. Udayanācārya's approach attempts to establish generic theism while remaining compatible with various sectarian specifications. The immediate intellectual context for the *Nyāyakusumāñjali* includes several centuries of debate between *Nyāya* and its philosophical opponents, particularly Buddhism. Buddhist thinkers had developed increasingly sophisticated critiques of theistic assumptions, forcing *Nyāya* defenders to refine their positions and arguments. For instance, the *Nyāyabindu* by Ācārya Dharmakīrti and *Nyāyabinduṭīkā* of Dharmottara Ācārya posits that the *Nyāya* inference to *Īśvara* is fallacious and fails the conditions of valid inference (*anumāna*), particularly the requirement of a *sapakṣa-dṛṣṭānta* — a positive instance of the probandum (thing to be proven) in a similar case. They also say that if *Īśvara* is said to be the uncaused cause of everything, and also eternal, what motivates creation? Motivation implies desire or deficiency, both incompatible with *Īśvara's* supposed perfection. And finally, if *Īśvara* is all-powerful and good, why is there suffering? *Nyāya* posits *karma* to explain this, but that again makes *Īśvara* redundant. Either *karma* controls the world or *Īśvara* does — both cannot be ultimate. All these are highly qualified and refined arguments that had arisen from Buddhist scholars. In *Nyāyakusumāñjali*, Udayanācārya responds to precisely these objections. For instance, he asserts that causal inference need not rely on positive examples alone — *arthāpatti* (postulation) justifies positing *Īśvara* as the only sufficient cause. Udayanācārya *accepts* that desire (*icchā*) in its ordinary sense is incompatible with *Īśvara's* perfection. But he reinterprets divine motivation not as personal need, but as the natural function (*svabhāva*) of *Īśvara's* omniscience and omnipotence. He posits that creation is a spontaneous expression (*svābhāvika-vyāpāra*) of *Īśvara's* knowledge and power, not an action driven by *lack*. Udayanācārya also accepts *karma* as the immediate cause (*nimitta-kāraṇa*) of individual fortunes, but insists that *karma* cannot operate autonomously— it needs a regulating intelligence. The text reflects this ongoing dialogue in its careful attention to Buddhist objections and its systematic responses to alternative explanations for apparent design and moral order. The relationship between *Nyāya* and *Sāṅkhya* also shaped the context for Udayanācārya's work. *Sāṅkhya* had developed an elaborate cosmological system that accounted for apparent design through the interaction of consciousness (*puruṣa*) and primordial matter (*prakṛti*) without requiring divine intervention. This position presented a particularly challenging alternative to theism, since it accepted many of the same metaphysical assumptions as *Nyāya* while reaching opposite theological conclusions.

Advaita Vedānta represented another significant challenge, though of a different sort. Sri Ādi Śaṅkarācārya accepted the existence of a supreme reality (*Brahman*) but argued that this reality transcends the distinction between binaries, such as non/existence and un/consciousness, employed in rational discourse. From this perspective, rational theology necessarily operates at the level of appearance (*vyāvahārika*) rather than ultimate truth (*pāramārthika*), limiting its significance for spiritual realization. The development of sophisticated logical techniques within various schools also influenced the context for rational theology. Buddhist logicians had developed precise methods for analysing inferential relationships, while *Nyāya* had created its own logical apparatus for evaluating arguments. For instance, Buddhist logicians like Ācārya Dharmakīrti would have inferred the presence of fire on a hill from smoke by applying the *trairūpya* criteria: the reason (smoke) must be present in the subject (hill), present in similar cases (for instance, kitchens with fire), and absent in dissimilar cases (for instance, lakes without fire), ensuring epistemic reliability through *vyāpti* (invariable concomitance). In contrast, *Nyāya* philosophers structured the same inference using a *pañcāvayava* or five-member syllogism — *"The hill has fire (pratijñā), because it has smoke (hetu); wherever there is smoke, there is fire, like a kitchen (udāharaṇa); the hill has smoke (upanaya); therefore, the hill has fire (nigamana)"* — emphasizing formal structure and public demonstrability in debate. These technical developments enabled more precise theological formulations while also raising the standards for acceptable arguments. The broader cultural context of medieval Indian philosophy emphasized the practical significance of philosophical positions for spiritual life. Unlike purely academic philosophy, Indian philosophical schools typically maintained that their positions had soteriological relevance—that correct philosophical understanding contributed to liberation from suffering and rebirth. This context explains the *Nyāyakusumāñjali's* attention to the practical implications of theistic belief and its concern with devotion (*bhakti*) as well as rational argument.

## The Modus Operandi

The *Nyāyakusumāñjali* exhibits several distinctive literary and methodological characteristics that reflect both its historical context and its philosophical intentions. As a work of systematic philosophy, it follows established conventions for presenting arguments while also innovating in significant ways. The text's organization reflects careful pedagogical planning. Udayanācārya begins with preliminary considerations about the nature and possibility of theological knowledge before proceeding to specific arguments for divine existence and attributes. Each major argument receives extensive development, including consideration of objections and alternative formulations. For instance, Udayanācārya begins by defending *anumāna* (inference) as a valid and reliable *pramāṇa* (means of knowledge) for establishing entities beyond direct perception, such as *Īśvara*. He argues that inference, grounded in observed *vyāpti* (invariable concomitance), can justifiably extend to unobservable causes—just as we infer fire from smoke or atoms from perceptible effects. He refutes Buddhist and *Sāṅkhyan* assumptions in *Nyāyakusumāñjali* verses 1.5-7,

> हेतुभूतिनिषेधो न स्वानुपाख्यविधिन च।
> स्वभाववर्णना नैवमवधेर्नियतत्वतः।।
>
> प्रवाहोऽनादिमानेष न विजात्येकशक्तिमान्।
> तत्त्वे यत्नवता भाव्यमन्वयव्यतिरेकयोः।।
>
> एकस्य न क्रमः क्वापि वैचित्र्यञ्च समस्य न।
> शक्तिभेदो न चाभिन्नः स्वभावो दुरतिक्रमः।।
>
> *Translation*: The denial of a cause cannot proceed by merely stating the absence of perceptual acquaintance, nor can one determine the nature of something in such a way, because determinacy requires necessity. This beginningless flow of the world, not being endowed with a single power capable of producing variety, must—by one who seeks the truth—be inferred through the methods of agreement and difference. A single, undifferentiated cause cannot exhibit sequence or variety; nor can what is uniform contain diverse powers—since intrinsic nature cannot be transgressed.

Through this, Udayanācārya establishes that inference is not only permissible but necessary in philosophical reasoning, especially in theology. This systematic approach contrasts with the more aphoristic style of earlier *Nyāya* texts and reflects the increased sophistication of medieval philosophical discourse. The argumentative method employed throughout the text exemplifies classical Indian philosophical reasoning at its most sophisticated. Udayanācārya typically presents each position in its strongest form before offering criticisms, creating a genuine dialogue rather than a mere refutation of straw men. This approach reflects both intellectual honesty and pedagogical effectiveness, since readers can appreciate the force of alternative positions before considering responses. The integration of logical analysis with broader philosophical considerations represents another distinctive feature of the text. While maintaining rigorous standards for valid inference, Udayanācārya also attends to metaphysical, epistemological, and practical implications of theological positions. This holistic approach prevents rational theology from becoming merely technical exercise while ensuring that broader conclusions rest on sound logical foundations.

The text's relationship to traditional sources reveals the complex balance characteristic of *Nyāya* rational theology. Udayanācārya frequently cites Vedic practices and earlier *Nyāya* authorities while maintaining that rational analysis provides the ultimate criterion for truth. He even comments on the decline of Vedic culture in *Nyāyakusumāñjali* verses 2.3,

> जन्मसंस्कारविद्यादेः शक्तेः स्वाध्यायकर्म्मणोः।
> हासदर्शनतो हासः सम्प्रदायस्य मीयताम्।।
>
> *Translation*: Since birth, initiation, study, and the power of recitation and ritual depend on human effort, and because we observe their decline, let the decline of the Vedic tradition itself be admitted.

Here, Udayanācārya seems to be highlighting that

the Vedic traditions cannot remain sacrosanct only with orthopraxy and that human effort is not secondary to any given ordained order of things. This nuanced position allows him to remain within traditional parameters while exercising considerable philosophical independence. The literary style of the *Nyāyakusumāñjali* combines technical precision with devotional warmth, reflecting Udayanācārya's conviction that rational theology serves religious as well as intellectual purposes. The text concludes with prayers and expressions of devotion that might seem incongruous in a work of systematic philosophy but actually reflect the integrated vision that motivates the entire enterprise. Udayanācārya's philosophical intentions in composing the *Nyāyakusumāñjali* extend beyond merely establishing divine existence to encompass several related goals that together define the project of rational theology within the *Nyāya* tradition. The primary intention involves demonstrating that theistic belief can be rationally grounded through valid philosophical argument. This goal responds to both skeptical challenges and alternative explanations by showing that divine existence follows from premises that reasonable people would accept. The demonstration requires not only positive arguments but also responses to objections and alternative theories, making the text as much a work of philosophical dialogue as systematic presentation.

A related intention involves clarifying the relationship between rational argument and religious authority. Unlike fideistic approaches that subordinate reason to revelation, or rationalistic approaches that reject religious authority entirely, Udayanācārya seeks to show that reason and revelation support each other when properly understood. In *Nyāyakusumāñjali* verse 1.12,

निमित्तभेदसंसर्गादुद्भवानुद्भवादयः।

देवताः सन्निधानेन प्रत्यभिज्ञानतोऽपि वा।।

*Translation*: Due to their connection with differing instrumental conditions, deities such as *Uddhava* and *Anuddhava* are recognized — either through their actual manifestation or through the process of recognition based on prior acquaintance

This synthetic intention reflects broader tendencies in Indian philosophy toward harmonization rather than exclusion of different sources of knowledge and modes of being. The text also aims to establish the practical relevance of theological knowledge for spiritual life. Udayanācārya maintains that correct understanding of divine existence and attributes contributes to liberation by generating appropriate attitudes and behaviors. This soteriological intention prevents rational theology from becoming merely academic exercise while ensuring that religious practice rests on sound intellectual foundations. Another significant intention involves responding to sophisticated philosophical opponents, particularly Buddhist schools that had developed detailed critiques of theistic assumptions. The *Nyāyakusumāñjali* represents one side of an ongoing philosophical dialogue, and its arguments must be evaluated partly in terms of their effectiveness against the strongest available alternatives, and in this book, we would be looking at contemporaneous challenges as well as possible responses to the same. The systematic intention underlying the entire work involves creating a comprehensive philosophical framework that integrates theological conclusions with broader metaphysical, epistemological, and ethical commitments. This systematic approach distinguishes classical Indian philosophy from more fragmentary approaches and creates the possibility for genuinely philosophical theology rather than merely apologetic argument.

## Contemporary Relevance

The contemporary relevance of the *Nyāyakusumāñjali* extends beyond historical interest to encompass several areas of ongoing philosophical concern. The text's sophisticated treatment of rational theology provides resources for current debates about the relationship between reason and religious belief, while its methodological innovations offer alternatives to approaches that have dominated Western philosophical theology. The epistemological framework developed in the text addresses perennial questions about the scope and limits of rational argument in religious matters. One such important question is that of the need for any metaphysical link between some action and its results, as highlighted (particularly in the context of ritual efficacy) in *Nyāyakusumāñjali* 4.1,

> अनव्याप्तेरधिकव्याप्तेरलक्षणमपूर्वदृक्।
> यथार्थानुभवो मानमनपेक्षतयेष्यते।।
>
> *Translation*: The definition of *apūrva* (an invisible force said to connect ritual actions to their unseen results) is flawed due to both under- and over-extension; instead, true experience is accepted as a valid means of knowledge, without dependence on such constructs.

In today's context, where we have seen extremes of fanatical piety and cynical atheism, this comes as a nuanced perspective. Udayanācārya's careful analysis of inferential reasoning and his attention to the conditions under which theological conclusions can be established provide insights relevant to contemporary discussions of natural theology and philosophical arguments for divine existence. The text's integration of logical analysis with broader philosophical considerations offers an alternative to approaches that artificially separate philosophical theology from metaphysics, epistemology, and ethics. This holistic approach may prove particularly relevant for contemporary philosophers seeking to develop comprehensive worldviews rather than merely technical solutions to isolated problems. The methodological commitments exhibited in the *Nyāyakusumāñjali* also speak to current debates about philosophical method and the relationship between systematic philosophy and critical analysis. Udayanācārya's combination of rigorous argumentation with synthetic ambition provides a model for philosophers seeking to move beyond purely negative criticism toward constructive philosophical work.

Perhaps most significantly, the text demonstrates the possibility of serious philosophical engagement with religious questions without sacrificing intellectual rigor or falling into dogmatism. This example may prove particularly valuable in contemporary contexts where discussions of religious topics often polarize between uncritical acceptance and dismissive rejection, leaving little room for the kind of sophisticated engagement that characterizes the best work in philosophical theology. In contemporary bioethics, debates on topics like abortion or end-of-life care often polarize: religious perspectives are dismissed as unscientific by secular institutions, while religious groups sometimes reject empirical data in favour of doctrine. Similarly, in public discourse on consciousness, materialist neuroscientific views dominate academic spaces, while spiritual interpretations are sidelined as irrational—despite ongoing unresolved questions that could benefit from rigorous cross-traditional dialogue, such as in the works of David Chalmers or cross-cultural philosophers engaging Advaita Vedānta or phenomenology. A particularly salient contribution of the *Nyāyakusumāñjali* to contemporary thought is its implicit challenge to epistemological reductionism—the privileging of empirical, sensory-based knowledge as the only valid form of cognition. In a philosophical climate increasingly shaped by scientism and data-driven reasoning, Udayanācārya's defense of *anumāna* (inference) as a means to access non-empirical entities—such as moral causality (*karma*), unobservable universals, and divine agency (*Īśvara*)—presents a sophisticated alternative model of rationality.

By systematically arguing that inference, when grounded in legitimate *pramāṇa* conditions, can yield warranted metaphysical conclusions, Udayanācārya expands the scope of rational inquiry beyond perceptual immediacy. This has direct relevance for current debates in the philosophy of mind and AI ethics, where questions surrounding consciousness, intentionality, and moral agency increasingly expose the limits of empiricism. His approach also aligns with emerging efforts in global philosophy to integrate logical analysis with metaphysical and ethical inquiry, challenging the compartmentalization of disciplines and illustrating how theological reasoning can operate within a framework of critical rationality. The *Nyāyakusumāñjali* thus models a form of inquiry that is both analytically precise and metaphysically substantive, offering a valuable precedent for expanding the contours of contemporary philosophical discourse. The text thus represents not merely a historical document but a living contribution to ongoing philosophical discussion. Its arguments require evaluation on their own merits, its methods deserve consideration as alternatives to more familiar approaches, and its synthetic vision provides inspiration for contemporary philosophers seeking to integrate rational analysis with broader human concerns. Understanding this text in its historical context enriches our appreciation of its achievements while preparing us to engage constructively with its continuing relevance for philosophical theology.

## A Way Forward

The development of rational theology within the *Nyāya* tradition represents one of the most sophisticated attempts in human history to ground religious belief in philosophical argument. From Ācārya Gautama's foundational epistemological work through Ācārya Vātsyāyana's initial theological elaborations to Udayanācārya's mature synthesis, the tradition demonstrates both the possibilities and the limitations of applying rational analysis to questions of ultimate reality. The distinction between rational and revealed theology, while useful for analytical purposes, proves less absolute in practice than it initially appears. The *Nyāya* tradition's commitment to rational demonstration never entirely separates itself from broader cultural and religious commitments, creating a complex relationship between reason and authority that generates both creative tension and occasional inconsistency. The historical development of *Nyāya* theology reflects the broader evolution of Indian philosophical culture from relatively unsystematic beginnings toward increasingly sophisticated and comprehensive systems. There is a rather interesting thought presented by Will Durant, in *Our Oriental Heritage*,

> *"Gautama's predecessors in Nyaya were apparently atheists; his successors became epistemologists. His achievement was to give India an organon of investigation and thought, and a rich vocabulary of philosophical terms."*

This development was driven both by internal logical pressures and by external challenges from competing schools, creating a genuine philosophical dialogue that advanced understanding on all sides. The *Nyāyakusumāñjali* represents the culmination of this development and one of the masterworks of classical Indian philosophy. Its systematic approach, technical sophistication, and synthetic vision create a comprehensive framework for rational theology that deserves sincere consideration from contemporary philosophers, regardless of their specific religious commitments.

The contemporary relevance of this tradition extends beyond historical interest to encompass methodological innovations, argumentative strategies, and synthetic visions that speak to ongoing philosophical concerns. As contemporary philosophy continues to grapple with questions about the relationship between reason and religious belief, the resources provided by the *Nyāya* tradition may prove increasingly valuable. The project of rational theology, as exemplified in the *Nyāya* tradition, remains both important and problematic. Important because questions about ultimate reality and divine existence continue to engage thoughtful people and deserve the most sophisticated treatment available. Problematic because the relationship between rational argument and religious commitment involves complexities that resist simple resolution. For instance, Udayanācārya initially does speak against the absolute potency of *Apūrva* before later accepting its relevance (albeit with the presence of *Īśvara*), in verse 5.12,

> अतिप्रसङ्गान्न फलं नापूर्वं तत्वहानितः।
> तदलाभान्न कार्यञ्च न क्रियाऽप्यप्रवृत्तितः।।
>
> *Translation*: Because of unwelcome consequences, the result is not rejected, nor is the unseen potency (*apūrva*), since that would undermine the reality of things. If that unseen potency were denied, then the effect (*kārya*) would not follow, nor would action (*kriyā*), due to the absence of initiation (*apravṛtti*).

This example illustrates how philosophical positions within the tradition evolved through nuanced reasoning and doctrinal negotiation. The *Nyāya* approach to these complexities—maintaining commitment to rational demonstration while acknowledging the practical and experiential dimensions of religious life—provides one model for navigating these difficulties. Whether this model ultimately succeeds depends partly on the evaluation of specific arguments and partly on broader judgments about the relationship between philosophical analysis and religious experience. What remains clear is that the *Nyāya* tradition's contribution to rational theology represents a remarkable intellectual achievement that continues to reward careful study and serious engagement. The sophistication of its arguments, the comprehensiveness of its vision, and the integration of theoretical and practical concerns create a legacy that enriches our understanding of both philosophical methodology and religious thought. The flowers of logic, as Udayanācārya termed his offering, continue to bloom in the philosophical garden, providing both beauty and nourishment for those seeking to understand the deepest questions of human existence through the careful application of rational analysis to matters of ultimate concern. In an age that often polarizes between uncritical faith and dismissive skepticism, the *Nyāya* tradition's middle path of rational theology offers a valuable alternative that deserves renewed attention and appreciation. We can extend this thrust of understanding in today's cynical world to talk of a rather paradoxical construct: the flowers of void. The concept of 'God' has often been seen as an onto-epistemology void, the *beyond*. One that defies articulation and characterization. But since there are immanent aspects to this reality, maybe, just maybe, we can find some flowers that arise from this void. Maybe, the Udayanācārya's flowers of logic can seed a bunch of flowers of this void that can adorn the mantles of modern life.

# Chapter Two
# The Shape of the Sacred

As time's river has flowed, skeptics have ascended the pulpit, wielding reason like a blade against the divine. But what if we could turn that very blade, and let it sing in defence of God? Udayanācārya, one of the most distinguished philosophers of the *Nyāya-Vaiśeṣika* tradition, stands as a towering figure in the history of Indian theistic philosophy. The *Nyāyakusumāñjali* represents perhaps the most sophisticated and systematic attempt in classical Indian philosophy to establish the existence of God (*Īśvara*) through rational argumentation. Writing at a time when Buddhism and other non-theistic systems had posed serious challenges to theistic beliefs, Udayanācārya crafted five intricate arguments that would influence theological discourse for centuries to come. The philosophical context of Udayanācārya's work cannot be understated. The *Nyāya-Vaiśeṣika* school had always maintained a theistic worldview, but earlier philosophers like Ācārya Gautama and Ācārya Kaṇāda had not provided detailed proofs for God's existence. The burden fell upon later thinkers to systematically defend this position against increasingly sophisticated critiques from Buddhist logicians like Ācārya Dharmakīrti and Ācārya Śāntarakṣita, who had developed powerful arguments against theistic doctrines. But this intellectual defence of theism did not stand apart from the broader Dhārmic understanding of *Īśvara's* transcendence.

Strikingly, Udayanācārya himself acknowledges the limitations of reason in fully apprehending the divine. In verse 3.23 of the *Nyāyakusumāñjali*, he concedes that even the sharpest tools of logic falter before the ultimate reality—suggesting that while reason can point toward God, it cannot fully contain *tat*,

> प्रत्यक्षादिभिरेभिरेवमधरो दूरे विरोधोदयः
> प्रायो यन्मुखवीक्षणैकविधुरैरात्मापि नासाद्यते।
> तं सर्वानुविधेयमेकमसमस्वच्छन्दलीलोत्सवं
> देवानामपि देवमुद्धवदतिश्रद्धाः प्रपद्यामहे।।
>
> *Translation*: That lower reality (or mundane truth) remains far even through means like direct perception and inference, due to arising contradictions. Generally, even the Self is not attained by those who are deprived even of a proper glimpse (of its face). To that One, unequaled and supreme, to whom all are subordinate, whose spontaneous play is a divine festival, the God of even the gods, we, with supreme faith—like Uddhava—take refuge.

Udayanācārya's contribution lies not merely in defending theism but in constructing positive arguments that deploy the very logical tools that had been turned against theistic belief. We will consider five arguments presented in the *Nyāyakusumāñjali*—*kāryāt* (from effect), *āyojanāt* (from combination), *dhṛtyādéḥ* (from sustenance), *padāt* (from functionality), and *saṁkhyāviśeṣāt* (from unique numbers)—represent different approaches to establishing divine existence. Each argument operates within the framework of *Nyāya* logic while drawing upon metaphysical principles from the *Vaiśeṣika* system. Together, they form a comprehensive case that addresses various aspects of divine causation, cosmic order, and scriptural authority.

We must examine each of these arguments, analysing their logical structure, metaphysical Before examining Udayanācārya's specific arguments, it is essential to understand the philosophical framework within which they operate. The *Nyāya*-Vaiśeṣika system represents a synthesis of rigorous logical methodology and atomistic metaphysics, offering the conceptual tools for systematic theistic argumentation. The *Nyāya* school, founded by Ācārya Gautama, developed sophisticated theories of inference (anumāna) that form the backbone of Udayanācārya's reasoning. Central to *Nyāya* logic is the concept of vyāpti (invariable concomitance), which establishes the necessary connection between a hetu (logical reason) and a sādhya (proposition to be proved). This connection is verified through careful observation of positive instances (*anvaya*), where both the reason and the conclusion are present, and negative instances (*vyatireka*), where the absence of the conclusion coincides with the absence of the reason. In *Nyāyakusumāñjali* verse 5.3, he says,

तर्काभासतया अन्येषां तर्कशुद्धिः अदुषणम्।
अनुकूलः तु तर्कः अत्र कार्यलोपः विभूषणम्।।

*Translation*: The clarification of others fallacious reasoning is not a fault; but here, the favourable reasoning is such that even the absence of an effect becomes an ornament (a supporting feature).

This is a rhetorical inversion: rather than seeing absence as a problem, he treats it as evidence of a deeper pattern, which aligns with *vyatireka* reasoning. Udayanācārya skillfully employs this *anvaya-vyatireka* methodology to ground his inferences about causation and cosmic order. In particular, his argument from *kāryatva* (effectness) asserts that wherever we observe complex, purposeful effects—such as those found in the natural world—they are invariably produced by intelligent agents, as in the case of man-made artifacts. Conversely, in the absence of such agents, such effects do not arise. By extending this logic to the universe as a whole, Udayanācārya argues for the existence of an ultimate intelligent cause: *Īśvara*. In doing so, he redefined the contours of theistic philosophy in India, offering a rational foundation that would shape debates across traditions for centuries.

The Vaiśeṣika metaphysical framework, established by Ācārya Kaṇāda, provides the ontological categories within which Udayanācārya's arguments operate. The system posits six fundamental categories (*padārthas*): substance (*dravya*), quality (*guṇa*), action (*karma*), universals (*sāmānya*), particularity (*viśeṣa*), and inherence (*samavāya*). Later *Vaiśeṣika* philosophers added a seventh category, non-existence (*abhāva*). This categorical system allows for a sophisticated analysis of causation, composition, and the relationship between parts and wholes. Particularly important for Udayanācārya's arguments is the *Vaiśeṣika* understanding of causation. The system distinguishes between different types of causes: the material cause (*upādāna kāraṇa*), the efficient cause (*nimitta kāraṇa*), and the inherent cause (*samavāyi kāraṇa*). In the *Vaiśeṣika Sūtra* 10.1.6, the subtlest—the inherent cause is spoken about,

> एकार्थसमवायि कारणान्तरेषु दृष्टत्वात्
>
> *Translation*: (Pleasure and Pain are not form of cognition), because they are observed, when there exist other causes co-inherent in one and the same object (the soul).

This sophisticated causal analysis enables Udayanācārya to argue that while the material elements of the universe may account for certain aspects of cosmic order, an intelligent efficient cause is necessary to explain the purposive arrangement and combination of these elements. The concept of dharma and adharma (merit and demerit) also plays a crucial role in the *Nyāya-Vaiśeṣika* system. These are understood as invisible qualities (*adṛṣṭa*) that adhere to individual souls as a result of their moral actions. However, as Udayanācārya argues, these qualities themselves require an intelligent overseer to ensure that they produce their appropriate results in the form of experiences of pleasure and pain.

## Kāryāt

In the grand theater of philosophical history, few arguments have displayed as much elegance and resilience as Udayanācārya's *kāryāt* proof for the existence of *Īśvara*—the intelligent agent behind the cosmos. At first glance, it appears deceptively simple, almost a variant of what Western thought labels the cosmological argument: *"Whatever is an effect has an intelligent cause; the world is an effect; therefore, the world has an intelligent cause."* But as one begins to trace the threads of Udayanācārya's reasoning in the *Nyāyakusumāñjali*, it becomes clear that what lies beneath this surface formulation is a tapestry of remarkable depth, woven with strands of logic, metaphysics, and a profound understanding of the natural world. To appreciate Udayanācārya's achievement is to step into a realm where reason itself is sculpted into a pathway toward the divine, and where every element of the cosmos—from the tiniest atom to the vast celestial spheres—becomes a testament to intelligent design. At the heart of this argument is the concept of *kāryatva*—'effectness'—a notion that Udayanācārya treats not as a trivial label but as a carefully honed philosophical tool. In *Nyāyakusumāñjali* verse 5.5, this is mentioned,

> कार्यत्वात् निरुपाधित्वम् एवं धृतिविनाशयोः।
> विच्छेदेन पदस्यापि प्रत्ययादेः च पूर्ववत्।।

*Translation*: Because of *kāryatva* (effect-ness), there is unconditionality (absence of conditions) similarly in persistence and destruction; Even in the separation of a word (*pada*), and of cognition (*pratyaya*), the same rule applies as before.

Unlike simplistic causation models that posit *"everything must have a cause"* and thereby invite the infamous problem of infinite regress, Udayanācārya meticulously defines the criteria that make something an effect. He highlights the importance of distinctness of effect in *Nyāyakusumāñjali* verse 1.16,

न वैजात्यं विना तत्स्यान्न तस्मिन्ननुमा भवेत्।
विना तेन न तत्सिद्धिर्नाध्यक्षं निश्चयं विना।।

*Translation*: That (object or property) would not exist without distinctness (*vaijātya*); without it, inference cannot proceed. Without inference, that (truth) cannot be established; and without certainty, perception does not yield conclusive knowledge

To validly infer a cause from an effect, the effect must be distinct from other objects that do not require such a cause — this distinctness is what Udayanācārya here calls *vaijātya*. For Udayanācārya, *kāryatva* primarily means production (*utpannatva*) and non-eternality (*anityatva*) of effects, with compositeness (*āvayavin*) being a general *Nyāya-Vaiśeṣika* view rather than an explicit focus in his definition. Anything possessing these features—anything made of parts, anything with a temporal beginning, anything whose existence involves a process of formation—bears the unmistakable hallmark of an effect. The earth itself, Udayanācārya argues, qualifies on all counts. It is an aggregate of atoms configured in precise ways, it is not eternal despite appearances to the contrary, and its features suggest purposeful arrangement. By establishing such a nuanced definition, Udayanācārya circumvents the need to ask whether *Īśvara* requires a cause, for God, by contrast, is defined precisely as that which lacks these markers: simple (*niravayava*), eternal (*nitya*), and unproduced (*svayaṁbhū*).

But how does one demonstrate that everything possessing *kāryatva* must be the result of intelligent causation? Here Udayanācārya deploys the powerful *Nyāya* methodology of *anvaya-vyatireka*—positive and negative concomitance. The *anvaya* can be established through countless examples from human experience: pots fashioned by potters, houses designed by architects, chariots crafted by artisans. In every case where we encounter complex, purposively arranged objects, an intelligent agent stands as their origin. The *vyatireka* reinforces this: wherever intelligence is absent, we do not observe such organized production. No chariot arises from a whirlwind, no house from a mere heap of bricks. Nature, left to randomness, does not yield artifacts imbued with purpose and coherence. Critics, both ancient and modern, have challenged this analogical leap from human craftsmanship to cosmic design. Buddhist philosophers like Ācārya Ratnakīrti argued that the analogy fails because the cosmos is fundamentally unlike a pot or a chariot; its scale and processes are vastly different. But Udayanācārya counters by pointing out that the magnitude of complexity only strengthens the need for intelligence. If a simple clay pot demands a potter, how much more must the infinitely intricate cosmos require a supremely intelligent creator? This is not a casual anthropomorphism; it is a scaling-up of the principle of purposive causation to the largest possible system. A subtler objection emerges from the problem of *asādhāraṇa*—non-generalizability. Skeptics note that we have never directly observed the creation of worlds, so how can we claim a universal principle about their causation? Udayanācārya's reply is sophisticated: he argues that universality in inference need not rely on enumeration of observed cases alone but can emerge from a deep grasp of essential natures. If the nature of compositeness and non-eternality entails dependence on external agency, then the inference holds regardless of our limited empirical scope.

Underlying this entire structure are metaphysical commitments that shape Udayanācārya's worldview. First, there is causal realism—the belief that causation reflects real relations in the world, not mere conceptual constructions or psychological habits as the Buddhists would have it. In fact, Udayanācārya speaks about the existence of stable perceptions, in *Nyāyakusumāñjali* 1.17,

> स्थैर्यदृष्टयोर्न सन्देहो न प्रामाण्ये विरोधतः।
> एकतानिश्चयो येन क्षणे तेन स्थिरे मतः।।
>
> *Translation*: There is no doubt between stable and momentary perceptions, nor is their validity as means of knowledge opposed. That moment which yields an uninterrupted certainty is thereby considered to affirm what is stable.

Then, there is the teleological principle—the intuition that systematic organization and purposiveness in natural phenomena are not brute facts but call for explanation. Finally, Udayanācārya assumes a form of the *Principle of Sufficient Reason*: contingent realities like earth and water cannot be their own explanation; they demand an external, necessary ground of being. When viewed from a modern vantage point, the *kāryāt* argument resonates with surprising relevance. It parallels contemporary discussions of fine-tuning and intelligent design, which highlight the astonishing complexity and apparent purposiveness in the structure of the universe. Yet there is a crucial difference. Whereas modern arguments often appeal to gaps in scientific knowledge, Udayanācārya's reasoning is fundamentally metaphysical, not empirical. He does not hinge his case on unknown mechanisms or improbabilities but on the ontological status of effects as dependent entities. Critics today might invoke Darwinian evolution and complex systems theory, suggesting that apparent purposiveness can emerge from blind, natural processes. But Udayanācārya might respond, with characteristic precision, that these processes themselves presuppose laws and regularities—features of the cosmos that exhibit an even deeper level of order requiring explanation. Natural selection operates within a framework of physical laws; self-organizing systems emerge in contexts defined by mathematical regularities. From where do these structures arise if not from a mind of surpassing intelligence?

Here lies the quiet brilliance of Udayanācārya's *kāryāt* argument. It does not rest upon gaps in scientific explanation but upon the very possibility of explanation itself. To speak of a law-governed cosmos, of atoms obeying any kind of regularities, of forces maintaining some form of balance, is already to presuppose an intelligible structure whose source lies beyond the contingent interplay of matter. For Udayanācārya, the cosmos is not merely a fact to be accepted but a sign to be interpreted—an effect pointing unerringly to its cause. In the end, Udayanācārya's vision invites us into a world alive with meaning. Every stone and star, every breath of wind and flicker of flame, becomes a thread in a grand tapestry, woven by a mind whose intelligence surpasses our own. Reason, in his hands, is no enemy of faith but its most loyal ally, leading us step by step from the seen to the unseen, from the composite to the simple, from the transient to the eternal. In an age where skeptics have often wielded reason as a weapon against the divine, Udayanācārya shows how the same blade can be turned—reforged in the fires of philosophical rigor—to defend the presence of a cosmic intelligence. It is a testament not only to his genius but to the enduring power of rational theology: that in seeking to understand the world, we may yet come to glimpse its ultimate source.

## Āyojanāt

In the quiet before creation, Udayanācārya invites us to imagine a universe in its most elemental form—a vast emptiness filled only with countless infinitesimal atoms of earth, water, fire, and air. These *aṇu*, the indivisible seeds of matter, exist in perfect isolation, each resting silently in its own place, with no movement, no combination, no world. According to the ancient Vaiśeṣika atomists, this was the primordial condition of reality: an endless sea of potential, waiting for something—or someone—to stir it into the dynamic dance that gives rise to stars, planets, life, and consciousness. And so a profound question emerges: what initiates the grand orchestration of the cosmos? What invisible hand reaches into this timeless stillness and awakens it into the splendor of existence? This is the mystery Udayanācārya tackles with his *āyojanāt* argument—the argument from combination. At first sight, the logic appears simple, even deceptively so: every combination of previously separate elements requires an intelligent combiner; the atoms were once separate but are now arranged in breathtakingly complex forms; therefore, an intelligent agent must have combined them. But simplicity here is the surface of a deep and intricate philosophical system, where Udayanācārya probes questions about causation, time, and purpose that remain alive in contemporary cosmology. He is not content to accept the world as a brute fact. For him, the world's very order cries out for explanation. In *Nyāyakusumāñjali* verse 2.4, we have

कारं कारमलौकिकाद्भुतमयं मायावशात् संहरन्।
हारं हारमपीन्द्रजालमिव यः कुर्वन् जगत् क्रीडति।।

तं देवं निरवग्रहस्फुरदभिध्यानानुभावं भवं।
विश्वासैकभुवं शिवं प्रति नमन् भूयासमन्तेष्वपि।।

*Translation*: Tat which, by the power of Māyā, dissolves one world-form into another, shaking off even miraculous forms as if they were nothing but illusion — Tat who, stringing garland after garland (of universes), plays with the cosmos like a conjurer with his magic — to that *Īśvara*, who shines forth in unobstructed meditative awareness, Who is the source of becoming, the sole ground of trust and existence, the auspicious One (Śiva) — May I continue to bow, even at all ends.

To understand the force of Udayanācārya's reasoning, we must first appreciate the ancient Indian view of matter's architecture. Atoms, he explains, are naturally inert. Left to themselves, they neither move nor combine. In their default state, they rest in perfect separation—eternally individual, devoid of any internal impulse toward complexity. When they do combine, it happens step by step: two atoms (*dvyaṇuka*) unite to form a dyad, three dyads (*tryaṇuka*) join to create a triad, and from these humble beginnings emerge the gross objects we see around us—mountains, rivers, trees, and even our own bodies. This process, called *saṁyoga*, is a cornerstone of *Vaiśeṣika* physics. Yet here lies the crux: what triggers this process? Why should these atoms, so content in their solitude, suddenly begin to link arms and build a cosmos? Udayanācārya's insight is as elegant as it is provocative. Atoms do not combine on their own; combination is not an automatic feature of their nature. Instead, it requires direction—intelligent, purposive direction. He invites us to consider a simple analogy: a heap of bricks lying scattered in a field. No one would seriously suggest that these bricks could, by some spontaneous accident, arrange themselves into a house with doors, windows, and a roof that keeps out the rain. To achieve such systematic arrangement demands an architect—someone who possesses not just knowledge of construction but also the intention to create a dwelling. Likewise, Udayanācārya's line of argument would posit that the atoms of the cosmos do not organize themselves into the intricate machinery of galaxies, ecosystems, and human minds unless guided by a supreme intelligence.

But Udayanācārya's argument does not stop at this straightforward analogy; he delves into a subtler and more profound problem—the problem of timing. If atoms are naturally at rest, what causes them to begin combining at a particular moment rather than another? Why this cosmic cycle, here and now, instead of an endless inertia? This `timing problem' is not merely a technicality; it cuts to the heart of any cosmological theory. Udayanācārya argues that the initiation of change requires a deciding agent—an intelligence that chooses when to awaken the slumbering atoms and set the wheels of creation in motion. Without such an agent, the birth of the cosmos remains inexplicable, suspended in an eternal *"why not yet?"* Here, Udayanācārya's reasoning anticipates a principle that would resurface centuries later in Western thought—the *Principle of Sufficient Reason*. Every change demands an adequate explanation. The shift from a state of atomic separation to one of combination cannot be accounted for by the atoms themselves, since their nature, by definition, is to remain static unless acted upon. He even talks of the cause of non-existence in *Nyāyakusumāñjali* 1.10,

भावो यथा तथाऽभाव: कारणं कार्यवन्मत:।
प्रतिबन्धो विसामग्री तद्धेतु: प्रतिबन्धक:।।

*Translation*: Just as positive existence has a cause, so too does non-existence — like an effect, it is considered to arise from a cause. The absence of necessary conditions constitutes an obstruction, and this obstruction itself is the cause of non-arising.

These insights show Udayanācārya's remarkable grasp of the logic of causation, long before it became a centerpiece of modern philosophy. Predictably, critics of his era sought to escape the need for a divine combiner by appealing to *adṛṣṭa*—the unseen force of *karma* accumulated from prior cycles of existence. Could this karmic residue not provide the impetus for atomic combination? Udayanācārya's response is incisive. He does discuss the influence of unseen factos, in *Nyāyakusumāñjali* verse 3.6,

दृष्ट्यदृष्ट्योः क्व सन्देहो भावाभावविनिश्चयात्।
अदृष्टिबाधिते हेतौ प्रत्यक्षमपि दुर्लभम्।।

*Translation*: Where is the room for doubt between the seen and the unseen, when their presence or absence can be definitively established? Even direct perception becomes unreliable when the basis is obstructed by an unseen defect

However, *Adṛṣṭa*, it is explained, is a passive quality (*guṇa*) adhering to individual souls; it is inert, lacking agency. In *Nyāyakusumāñjali* verse 5.4

स्वातन्त्र्ये जडताहानिर्नादृष्टं दृष्टघातकम्।
हेत्वभावे फलाभावो विशेषस्तु विशेषवान्।।

*Translation*: If (*Adṛṣṭa*) were independent (*svatantra*), it would lose its inert nature (*jaḍatā-hāni*); It is not unseen (*adṛṣṭa*) that causes seen to be destroyed. The absence of the cause leads to the absence of the effect—but specific (effects) arise only from specific (causes).

Just as heat cannot spontaneously light a fire without a spark to bring it into contact with fuel, adṛṣṭa cannot independently organize atoms into functioning worlds. It requires activation by an intelligent being who understands the blueprint of cosmic order. Moreover, even if adṛṣṭa could somehow trigger combination, it would still fail to explain the astonishing regularity and purposiveness of creation. The cosmos does not emerge as a random jumble of atoms; it unfolds with a meticulous logic, ensuring that beings are born into worlds precisely suited for the working out of their karmic destinies. This, Udayanācārya insists, reveals the hand of an architect, not the blind force of past deeds.

Strikingly, Udayanācārya's *āyojanāt* argument finds unexpected resonance in contemporary cosmology. Today, physicists ask why the fundamental constants of nature—gravitational strength, electromagnetic force, the mass of elementary particles—have the precise values necessary for the formation of stable atoms, molecules, stars, and ultimately life. This "fine-tuning" problem mirrors Udayanācārya's ancient question about atomic combination. Why do the building blocks of reality assemble in just the right way to produce a cosmos capable of sustaining observers like us? Some scientists invoke the anthropic principle or posit an infinite multiverse to explain away the mystery. Yet others argue, as Udayanācārya might have, that such intricate balance points to a designer who not only initiates creation but calibrates it with exquisite care. And so, across a thousand years and cultures, Udayanācārya's voice seems to echo in our modern debates, urging us to look deeper. He challenges us to see the universe not as a random assembly of parts but as a symphony—one that requires not just instruments but also a composer. His āyojanāt argument is more than an intellectual exercise; it is an invitation to wonder. It reminds us that behind every star that burns, every atom that bonds, every breath we take, there may lie an intelligence vast enough to bind the first particles of matter together and wise enough to weave them into the tapestry of life.

## Dhṛtyādéḥ

Among the foundational arguments advanced by Udayanācārya in the *Nyāyakusumāñjali* to establish the existence of *Īśvara*, the third—*Dhṛtyādéḥ*, or the argument from sustenance—offers a deeply compelling vision of divine agency not merely as creator, but as ongoing regulator of the cosmos. In *Nyāyakusumāñjali* verse 5.1,

> कार्यायोजनधृत्यादेः पदात् प्रत्ययतः श्रुतेः
> वाक्यात् संख्याविशेषाच्च साध्यो विश्वविदव्ययः।।
>
> *Translation*: From the arrangement and maintenance of effects, from linguistic usage (words), from perceptual awareness, from scriptural testimony, and from specific numerical order—the eternal, all-conquering Lord (*Īśvara*) is to be inferred as the conclusion.

This line of reasoning is grounded in the observation that the universe is not only produced but preserved in a state of astonishing order and regularity. The sustained cycles of days and nights, the rhythmic alternation of seasons, the recurrence of cosmic ages, and the law-like functioning of natural phenomena all speak to a system governed by stability and coherence. Udayanācārya asks: how is this possible in a world composed of inert, unconscious matter? What sustains the delicate balance of the elements, or the continual progression of time-bound events? His answer is unambiguous: an intelligent, conscious sustainer—*Īśvara*—is required not just to initiate the universe but to uphold it moment by moment. Unlike the earlier argument from effect (*kāryāt*), which establishes God as the cause of the world's origination, the

*Dhṛtyādéḥ* reasoning pivots on the idea that continuity and coherence themselves demand explanation. In classical *Nyāya* thought, causation is not a momentary event but a continuous relation; a pot does not merely require a potter to come into being—it requires conditions to persist in its form. Similarly, the world, in all its intricate functionality, must be supported by an ongoing cause. Udayanācārya draws an analogy from everyday life: a kingdom does not run merely because it was founded; it endures only under sustained governance. In like manner, the cosmos, with its astronomical precision and moral intelligibility, demands a governor who possesses both knowledge and will.

Crucially, this argument undermines the position of rival schools such as *Sāṅkhya*, which attributes cosmic activity to the empirical principle *prakṛti*. Udayanācārya points out that while prakṛti may explain material transformations, it lacks awareness and cannot explain the purposive, intelligent adaptation observed in nature. He insists that mere conjunction of atoms or unconscious tendencies cannot yield the degree of harmony we observe—only a being endowed with cognition and volition could organize and maintain such order. Furthermore, Udayanācārya anticipates and rebuts the idea that so-called natural laws might suffice to explain cosmic regularity. Laws, he notes, do not execute themselves; they are descriptive, not generative. They require a substrate in which to operate and an agency that ensures their applicability across time. Epistemologically, Udayanācārya's argument from sustenance draws upon the *Nyāya* method of inference, particularly the *anvaya-vyatireka* model—establishing invariable concomitance through the presence and absence of effects in relation to their causes. Wherever we find sustained, law-governed systems (*anvaya*), we find the presence of intelligence. Wherever such intelligence is absent (*vyatireka*), disorder and decay follow. Therefore, the consistent order of the world, as an effect, necessarily points to an intelligent sustainer. It is not enough that the world exists; the fact that it functions intelligibly and reliably is what demands *Īśvara's* presence. Moreover, the *Dhṛtyādéḥ* argument transcends mere cosmology and moves into the ethical and spiritual dimensions of Indian philosophy. If the universe is under constant divine regulation, then so too are the moral laws that govern human life. The fruits of *karma*, the rhythms of rebirth, and the possibility of *mokṣa* are all situated within a universe that is not merely mechanistic, but moral and conscious. The same order that governs stars and seasons also governs the ethical order of human existence. Thus, belief in a sustaining deity is not only rationally necessary—it is spiritually indispensable. In the broader intellectual history of India, Udayanācārya's argument from sustenance represents one of the earliest and most refined articulations of what in later Western philosophy would be called the teleological or design argument. But unlike many modern versions that rely on probabilistic inference or statistical fine-tuning, Udayanācārya's *Dhṛtyādéḥ* argument is rooted in a robust metaphysical framework that sees the entire cosmos as permeated with intelligibility. This intelligibility cannot be a brute fact; it must itself be grounded in a conscious, purposive principle.

What makes *Dhṛtyādéḥ* especially relevant in our own time is that it addresses the question of meaningful continuity in a seemingly disenchanted universe. This is highlighted in the context of linguistic continuity and persistence, in *Nyāyakusumāñjali* verse 5.5,

कार्यत्वान्निरूपाधित्वमेवं धृतिविनाशयोः।
विच्छेदेन पदस्यापि प्रत्ययादेश्च पूर्ववत्।।

*Translation*: Because of being an effect, the absence of qualifiers similarly applies to both persistence and destruction. Due to separation, even in the case of a word, the substitution of affixes takes place as before.

In an age where physical theories often reduce the cosmos to blind forces and impersonal laws, Udayanācārya offers a vision in which intelligence is not an accidental byproduct of matter, but its very condition of coherence. The world does not merely happen to be intelligible—it is intelligible because it is sustained by intelligence. *Īśvara*, in this view, is not an unnecessary hypothesis, but the very ground of order, meaning, and persistence in the universe. In presenting this argument, Udayanācārya not only defends theism against contemporary non-theistic systems like Buddhism and *Sāṅkhya*, but also affirms a deeply integrated vision of reality in which logic, cosmology, and spirituality converge. The *Dhṛtyādéḥ* argument is thus not merely a proof of God's existence; it is a profound meditation on the nature of continuity, coherence, and the unseen hand that holds the world together.

## Padāt

Among his many arguments, one of the most insightful and foundational is the *Padāt* argument, which essentially asserts that functionality (*kāryatva*) arises from the reality and structure of a word (pada). Though this argument originates in the domain of language and grammar, Udayanācārya expands it into a wider metaphysical principle—namely, that real, enduring entities are necessary to explain the functional nature of both words and things. The term *Padāt* is derived from *pada* meaning 'word' and *āt* meaning 'from'—so the phrase means *"functionality arises from the word."* The starting point for Udayanācārya's *Padāt* argument is an observation from linguistic experience: words have the power to generate meaning, trigger recognition, guide memory, and even produce action. For instance, when a speaker commands "Bring the cows," the hearer responds accordingly—identifying cows, locating them, and acting in line with the instruction. This behavioural response demonstrates that the word has not merely produced a fleeting mental image but has conveyed a functionally effective meaning. Udayanācārya argues that this capacity to produce effects—what can be called *arthakriyākāritva*, or 'efficacy in fulfilling a purpose'—can only be explained if the word (*pada*) is a real, structured, and enduring entity, not a mere sequence of fleeting sounds or mental constructs. This position is directly opposed to the Buddhist theory of *apoha*, or exclusion, proposed by thinkers like Ācārya Dignāga and Ācārya Dharmakīrti. According to apoha theory, words do not refer to real universals or entities but instead function by excluding other concepts. The word 'cow', for example, does not refer to a universal 'cow-ness' but merely indicates 'not non-cow'. This exclusion-based semantics denies the existence of real referents and sees language as a system of mental constructions. Udayanācārya critiques this by emphasizing that the actual use of words in cognition and behaviour cannot be adequately explained through mere exclusions. He argues that if words function by merely excluding other concepts, there would be no reason for them to produce specific, consistent effects, such as directing one to fetch a cow rather than a horse.

Central to Udayanācārya's *Padāt* argument is the idea that a pada, or a grammatically complete word, is not just a sound but a complex structured unit composed of elements like roots (*dhātu*), suffixes (*pratyaya*), and sometimes prefixes (*upasarga*). For example, the Sanskrit word '*gām*' (accusative singular of 'cow') is not a random sound but a morphologically defined term. Its structure and grammatical form give it the capacity to convey meaning. This structured unity is what allows the word to persist, be identified, and exert causal influence. Thus, functionality arises from structure, and structure implies persistence. A momentary flash or isolated sound has no capacity to sustain function, produce recognition, or guide action. Therefore, the functionality of a word (its ability to mean something and do something) is grounded in its real existence and enduring nature—this is the heart of Udayanācārya's claim: *padāt kāryatvam*. Moreover, Udayanācārya notes that *pada* is not destroyed even when it is split for grammatical analysis. In technical linguistic discussions, he observes that when a word is broken into its root and affix (as in Pāṇinian grammar), the process of affix-substitution (*pratyayādeśa*) still operates 'as before' (*pūrvavat*). That is, the functionality of the grammatical system continues, which suggests that the pada's structural identity and causal power are preserved even when it undergoes formal transformation. This reinforces the point that pada is not a passive or illusory construct but a real unit with operative power, anchored in rules and capable of producing effects. Udayanācārya then extends this linguistic realism to a metaphysical framework. Just as a word must be real and structured to produce meaning, so must objects in the world be real and enduring to perform their functions. A sword cuts because it possesses sharpness—a quality that inheres in it—and because it is a persistent, structured object. A pot holds water because it has a cavity and integrity. A fire cooks because it endures long enough to transfer heat. In each case, kāryatva—functional ability—is not possible without structure, persistence, and internal coherence. These qualities, Udayanācārya claims, cannot belong to something that is momentary, as Buddhist nominalists argue. Momentariness would dissolve all functional continuity. Therefore, just as a word must be real for language to work, objects must be real for the world to function.

This principle is then further applied to epistemology and the self. Memory, recognition, and identity all presuppose continuity. When I remember something I experienced yesterday, there must be a persistent self (*ātman*) that connects the two moments. Without such a self, memory is unintelligible, and so is moral responsibility or intentional action. Udayanācārya argues that the self, too, has *kāryatva*—it performs the function of cognition, agency, and memory—and hence must be real and enduring, not a transient mental stream. Once again, functionality reveals reality. Finally, Udayanācārya applies the same logic to the existence of God (*Īśvara*). The world exhibits order, teleology, and structure. These qualities are functional in nature, and their presence points to an intelligent designer. The functionality of the cosmos—regularity of seasons, predictability of causation, harmony of elements—suggests the existence of a cosmic agent, just as the functionality of a pot suggests a potter. Hence, by the *Padāt* logic, the world's function implies the existence of a real, intelligent cause, namely God. In summary, Udayanācārya's *Padāt* argument begins with a linguistic insight—that words function because they are structured, real, and enduring entities—and expands into a universal metaphysical principle: anything that produces consistent, directed effects must be real. Functionality implies structure, structure implies persistence, and all three imply reality. This argument not only critiques Buddhist nominalism and momentariness but also defends a robust realist worldview in which language, cognition, agency, and the cosmos all depend on real, enduring entities capable of functionality. In Udayanācārya's hands, the simple fact that a word conveys meaning becomes a profound proof of metaphysical realism: *"If it functions, it is real."*

## Saṁkhyāviśeṣāt

The problem of numerical specification, as developed in Udayanācārya's *Nyāyakusumāñjali*, draws the reader into one of the most mesmerizing and least intuitive questions in cosmological philosophy: why does the universe exhibit precisely the quantitative features it does, rather than an infinite spectrum of alternative numerical arrangements? It is a question that at once feels deceptively simple—after all, numbers are everywhere, in the orbits of planets, in the ratios of chemical elements, in the cycles of time described by ancient cosmologies—but also bewilderingly profound, for it asks us to contemplate whether these numbers are merely brute facts of existence or evidence of a deeper intelligence orchestrating reality. In *Nyāyakusumāñjali* verse 5.11,

> आक्षेपलभ्ये सङ्ख्येये नाभिधानस्य कल्पना।
> सङ्ख्येयमात्रलाभेऽपि साकाङ्क्षेण व्यवस्थितिः॥
>
> *Translation*: When the number is obtained through implication, the assumption of an explicit expression is not justified. Even when only the numerical object is obtained, its meaningful placement requires syntactic expectancy.

The very aspect of numerals and numerics is not always overt but also implied. The synactic, and even semantic, implication of this is profound. It highlights how even numbers follow intent. In the context of Vaiśeṣika atomism, where atoms combine in fixed ratios—dyads, triads, and beyond—to form all matter, the issue becomes acute: what determines these ratios and not others? Could it be sheer chance, an impersonal physical necessity, or must there be a chooser—an intelligent being—who selected these specific numerical relationships out of an infinite possibility space? Udayanācārya's *saṁkhyāviśeṣāt* argument answers unflinchingly: every instance of specific numerical determination, every moment when the universe could have taken one path but takes another, cries out for an intelligent determiner capable of choosing among alternatives. In *Nyāyakusumāñjali* verse 5.17, there is another rather interesting application of this argument,

> स्यामभूवं भविष्यामीत्यादिसङ्ख्या च वक्तृगा।
> समाख्याऽपि न शाखानामाद्यप्रवचनादृते।।
>
> *Translation*: The use of expressions like *"syām"(may I be), "abhūvam" (I was), "bhaviṣyāmi" (I will be)*—that is, the numerical or person-based reference in such expressions—belongs to the speaker (is speaker-dependent). Similarly, the designation (*samākhyā*) of the Vedic branches (*śākhās*) does not exist independently; it depends solely on the original utterance or first speaker.

This verse illustrates how even linguistic structures—rooted in notions of time, self, and identity—are unintelligible without a conscious agent. Words like *"syām"* (may I be) presuppose a speaker who projects themselves across time, embedding numerical identity (first person, singular) into verbal forms. Such usage is not merely grammatical; it reflects an underlying intentionality. Likewise, the naming of Vedic branches (*śākhās*) cannot arise spontaneously or emerge from inert matter—it necessitates a first speaker who initiates designation. Just as a tree doesn't name its own limbs, the Veda does not name its own parts; naming is a cognitive act, not a material one. Thus, Udayanācārya's appeal to saṅkhyāviśeṣa (specific numerical differentiation) is not limited to atoms and their configurations; it extends into language, identity, time, and tradition, reinforcing his central claim: a conscious, intelligent agent (*Īśvara*) must be posited as the original source and determiner of order—whether in the cosmos or in cognition.

Matter alone, Udanayachara reasons, is indeterminate—it offers no intrinsic reason why atoms should form triads instead of tetrads, why planetary orbits should complete in particular intervals instead of different ones, or why cosmic cycles should run for specific durations rather than longer or shorter spans. To illustrate, Udayanācārya offers an analogy that still resonates in the age of quantum mechanics: imagine a pile of lumber lying untouched. In theory, it could become a house, a bridge, or a ship; yet unless a carpenter or architect intervenes, no particular structure will emerge. The wood is inert to purpose. So too with atoms: left to themselves, they harbor infinite potential configurations, yet exhibit none of the specificity we see unless something beyond matter—the cosmic Architect—imposes determination. Nowhere is this more evident than in the temporal rhythms of the cosmos described by Hindu cosmology, with its majestic cycles of creation, sustenance, and dissolution measured in eons. Why, Udayanācārya asks, should these cycles last for such precise periods? Why should a kalpa endure for 4.32 billion years and not 10 billion or 100 million? The atoms themselves are indifferent; time itself, as a dimension, offers no preference. To posit that these durations are mere accidents, unchosen and purposeless, is to ignore their startling regularity and functional elegance. To posit that natural laws dictate them is to beg the question, for why should natural laws exhibit the precise mathematical form they do rather than alternatives? Even if physical constants and equations impose certain constraints, they still leave open a staggering range of possible numerical values. Why does the gravitational constant have its value and not a slightly different one, a change that would render stars unstable and life impossible? Why is the speed of light exactly as it is, allowing for complex chemistry, rather than faster or slower, with catastrophic consequences for cosmic structure? Udayanācārya's argument, though crafted over a millennium ago, anticipates with uncanny prescience the fine-tuning debates of modern physics, where the apparent "luck" of our universe's constants has led some to postulate a multiverse—an infinite ensemble of universes, each with different parameters, of which we inhabit the rare life-permitting one. Yet Udayanācārya would likely retort that the multiverse hypothesis merely displaces the question: who or what determines the distribution of constants across universes? Why should a mechanism capable of producing such a range of realities exist at all, and why should it favour life-bearing configurations in any measure?

The specification problem persists, now metastasized to a higher level. Critics of Udayanācārya's view have historically raised the 'alternative possibilities' objection, claiming that perhaps no alternatives actually exist; perhaps the universe's numerical structure is the only one logically or physically possible. But Udayanācārya dismisses this as an illusion born of familiarity. The very existence of numerical determinations implies choice because matter alone cannot account for them. Natural laws themselves—those elegant equations with their precisely calibrated coefficients—are not brute necessities but expressions of imposed order. Without intelligence to fix values, the universe would dissolve into an entropic haze of unrealized potentials. The metaphysics of such divine choice is subtle and fascinating. Are God's selections arbitrary whims, or do they reflect profound principles? Udayanācārya leans toward the latter. Divine choices, he argues, flow from perfect wisdom (*jñāna*) and boundless compassion (*karuṇā*). God does not pick numbers at random, nor is He constrained by anything external. Instead, He chooses numerical specifications that best serve the moral and spiritual evolution of sentient beings, creating a cosmos finely balanced to permit karmic causation, free will, and ultimate liberation (*mokṣa*). This view situates God as neither a capricious tinkerer nor a cosmic machine bound by impersonal necessity, but as a wise and benevolent craftsman whose design optimizes the conditions for life and enlightenment. The saṁkhyāviśeṣāt argument integrates seamlessly with Udayanācārya's broader suite of theistic proofs, reinforcing the cumulative case for a divine intelligence. While the kāryāt argument posits that composite entities necessitate a creator due to their contingent nature, *saṁkhyāviśeṣāt* deepens this by explaining why these composites exhibit specific quantitative configurations—precise ratios, counts, and measures—rather than arbitrary arrangements. The *āyojanāt* argument shows that elements require an intelligent agent to bring about meaningful combinations; *saṁkhyāviśeṣāt* complements this by highlighting how intelligence guides the exact proportions and structural regularities that emerge. Similarly, the *dhṛtyādeḥ* argument, which appeals to the continuity, stability, and sustenance observed in nature, points to an underlying oversight or governance; *saṁkhyāviśeṣāt* reveals how such governance is expressed in calibrated cycles of time, cosmic rhythms, and moral laws—such as *karmic justice*—that require a rational and purposive order.

Even the *padāt* argument, which draws upon the intelligibility and functionality of linguistic and conceptual categories, aligns with *saṁkhyāviśeṣāt*, since functional order itself presupposes quantitative precision. Together, these arguments form a tightly woven philosophical tapestry, with *saṁkhyāviśeṣāt* contributing the crucial insight that order is not just structured but measured—and thus points not merely to a cause, but to a wise and discerning cause. What emerges from Udayanācārya's analysis is a vision of the cosmos not as a mechanical inevitability but as a work of sublime artistry, its numerical parameters as deliberate as the brushstrokes in a master painting or the notes in a symphony. Each proportion, duration, and ratio is not simply there; it was chosen for reasons that reflect the purposes of a conscious, purposive mind. In the modern era, where physics continues to uncover deeper layers of mathematical structure in nature, Udayanācārya's insight feels newly resonant. As we peer into the fine-tuned universe and puzzle over its improbable hospitality to life, we are drawn into the very same mystery that confronted him centuries ago: why this universe and not another? His answer, bold and unapologetic, still challenges us: because Someone chose it to be so.

## The Method of *Anvaya-Vyatireka*

Across all five of Udayanācārya's arguments for God's existence, there runs a subtle but powerful thread: the masterful use of *anvaya-vyatireka*, the twin pillars of *Nyāya* logic. To the casual reader, these Sanskrit terms might sound arcane, but their meaning is surprisingly elegant. *Anvaya* means 'positive concomitance'—the observation of cases where a reason (*hetu*) and what it proves (*sādhya*) are both present. *Vyatireka* is 'negative concomitance'—the analysis of cases where both are absent. Together they create a rigorous method for establishing universal relationships (*vyāpti*), the kind that undergirds sound reasoning about the world. Udayanācārya does not simply assume that God exists; he builds his case step by step, drawing on this methodology to show how effects, combinations, moral orders, testimonies, and numerical specifications point inexorably toward an intelligent cause. Take the *kāryāt* argument—the first and perhaps most intuitive of his five. Here, Udayanācārya looks at positive instances of effects produced by intelligent agents: pots made by potters, houses designed by architects, machines constructed by engineers. In every case, wherever we see a complex, purposive arrangement arising from simpler elements, we also see the hand of intelligence behind it. Then we can examines the negative:

where no intelligence is present, such systematic effects do not spontaneously emerge. Nature unaided produces no palaces, no poems, no purposeful machines. From these observations, we can establish a universal principle: "Whatever is an effect must have an intelligent cause." This is not mere analogy; it is an inductive generalization built on *anvaya-vyatireka*.

The *āyojanāt* argument follows the same pattern but focuses on the act of combination itself. Positive instances include all human activities where separate elements are brought together—bricks arranged into walls, letters into words, ingredients into a recipe. Negative instances reveal that random collisions of elements do not yield systematic wholes with coherent function. From these, Udayanācārya reasons that even the invisible atoms posited by *Vaiśeṣika* philosophy must have been intelligently combined to produce the ordered world we inhabit. In the *dhṛtyādéḥ* (from sustenance) argument, Udayanācārya applies this method to the ongoing stability and order of the universe. Positive instances show that where systems persist through ordered sustenance—like a maintained household, a flourishing garden, or a balanced ecosystem—there is always some form of intelligent regulation ensuring continuity. Negative instances show that without such oversight, structures decay, systems collapse, and no sustained harmony arises. The universal concomitance here is clear: sustained order, especially on a cosmic scale, requires a sustaining intelligence. The world does not merely emerge—it endures, and that endurance demands a conscious cause. Even the *padāt* (from functionality) argument employs *anvaya-vyatireka* with clarity and rigor. Udayanācārya focuses here not on tools, but on verbal cognition (*śābdabodha*)—how meaningful understanding arises from language. He observes that a sentence (*vākya*) produces cognition only when its parts (words) are properly configured in accordance with expectancy (*ākāṅkṣā*), proximity (*sannidhi*), and syntactic fitness (*yogyatā*). When these are in place, comprehension follows (*anvaya*); when they are absent—if the words are jumbled or lack mutual expectation—no understanding results (*vyatireka*). This, he argues, mirrors the principle behind all functional wholes: whether in language or the world at large, mere aggregation does not yield function unless the elements are deliberately arranged.

Thus, Udayanācārya concludes that functionality—in language, cognition, and nature—presupposes intentional arrangement, which in turn implies an intelligent agent. Just as a grammatically functional sentence points to a speaker, the functional structures of the world point to a divine arranger (*Īśvara*). The *anvaya-vyatireka* pattern here is not abstract but observable in every act of communication and understanding: where parts are assembled with purpose, function arises; where they are not, it does not. From this, Udayanācārya infers that purpose-driven structures—like bodies, minds, and linguistic systems—must be the result of intelligent configuration, not random assembly. The very presence of function in the world points to a functional cause—a conscious designer. Finally, in the *saṁkhyāviśeṣāt* argument, Udayanācārya extends *anvaya-vyatireka* to the mystery of numerical specification. Positive instances show that whenever specific choices are made from among many alternatives—a sculptor selecting proportions, a composer choosing time signatures—it is the result of intelligent deliberation. Negative instances reveal that without such choice, material processes tend toward randomness and indeterminacy, not the precise ratios and durations that structure our cosmos. Thus, the particular numerical features of the universe also imply a conscious chooser. What makes Udayanācārya's reasoning so compelling is its disciplined consistency. Each argument is not an isolated assertion but part of a cumulative case, each brick laid carefully atop another. His *anvaya-vyatireka* method keeps him from falling into dogma; it requires him to test his claims against both presence and absence, to search for universal principles in the patterns of reality itself. The result is not just an argument for God's existence but a breathtaking vision of a universe suffused with intelligence, where every effect, every combination, every moral law, every spoken truth, and even every number whispers of a cosmic mind.

## The Problem of *Asādhāraṇa*

One of the most sophisticated and subtle challenges ever leveled against Udayanācārya's reasoning comes in the form of the *asādhāraṇa* objection—an accusation of over-exclusiveness, or, in modern terms, non-generalizability. Critics, particularly sharp *Nyāya* opponents and later Buddhist logicians, argue that several of Udayanācārya's logical reasons (*hetu*) suffer from this flaw because they appear to apply only to the unique case under dispute and therefore fail to establish a universal principle (*vyāpti*). The concern strikes at the heart of his enterprise: if his reasoning is *asādhāraṇa*, then his grand arguments for the existence of a supreme being rest on a fragile logical foundation. As Viśvanātha Nyāyapañcānana Bhaṭṭācārya explains in *Bhāṣāpariccheda* (verse 72), this type of defect belongs to a broader class of *anaikāntika hetus*—fallacious reasons that fail to demonstrate a necessary connection:

> आद्यः साधारणस्तु स्यात् स्यदसाधारणपरः।
> तथैवानुपसंहारी त्रिधा अनैकान्तिको भवेत्।।
>
> *Translation*: The first is the *sādhāraṇa* (common) type, The second is *asādhāraṇa* (uncommon), And similarly, the third is *anupasaṁhārī* (non-generalizing); In these

three ways, the reason (*hetu*) may be fallacious.

This framework provides a precise lens through which to assess Udayanācārya's reasoning. Take, for instance, the *kāryāt* argument—perhaps the most foundational of his theistic proofs. Consider the *kāryāt* argument. Here Udayanācārya's reasoning pivots on the claim that 'being an effect' (*kāryatva*) entails having an intelligent cause. His opponents push back: they argue that this reason applies only to particular worldly artifacts—pots, houses, machines—whose creation we have actually witnessed. But in the case of the earth, the stars, and the wider cosmos, we have no direct experience of their origination. How then can we generalize from observed artifacts to an entire universe? Without multiple instances of cosmic creation to examine, they say, Udayanācārya's inference lacks the evidential scope needed to be universal. It is a devastatingly clever challenge, but Udayanācārya's response is even more ingenious. Instead of retreating into mere analogy, he moves to a deeper, more abstract plane of reasoning—one rooted in the *Nyāya* analysis of essential natures (*svabhāva*). He argues that universal principles need not be established by brute enumeration of multiple observed cases. Rather, they can be discerned through careful examination of what it means for something to possess a certain characteristic. Once we understand the essential nature of 'being an effect'—that it involves composition from parts, non-eternality, and production from antecedent conditions—we realize that these features, by their very essence, entail a cause. More than that: they entail an intelligent cause, because purposive organization cannot arise from blind matter alone.

This is where Udayanācārya draws on another brilliant *Nyāya* distinction—the types of inference known as *kevalavyatireka* (purely negative) and *kevalaanvaya* (purely positive). In cases where we lack multiple positive instances of a phenomenon (as with the creation of worlds), we can still establish valid inferences by observing negative instances: where intelligence is absent, systematic effects do not arise. Every disorganized heap of matter, every random aggregation in nature, reinforces the point. Conversely, in cases where all observed instances exhibit a certain concomitance (as with artifacts and intelligent makers), a purely positive inference suffices. In this way, Udayanācārya transforms what looks like a crippling limitation into a triumph of logical subtlety. His arguments do not depend on endless empirical sampling of universes; they rest on grasping the necessary relationship between certain attributes and their causes. For Udayanācārya, logic reaches beyond the contingent to the necessary. It is this extraordinary ability to weave essentialist metaphysics into inductive reasoning that makes his work feel startlingly modern, even in its ancient Sanskrit dress.

## The Theistic Hypothesis

Udayanācārya's five arguments for God's existence are not discrete weapons fired one after another; they are more like overlapping waves, each reinforcing the other, creating a rising tide that seeks to sweep away the doubts of skeptics and the objections of rival schools. To understand their force, one must step into the world of 11th-century India, a world alive with fierce philosophical debate, where *Nyāya* logicians like Udayanācārya were engaged in an intellectual duel with Buddhist thinkers like Ācārya Nāgārjuna and Ācārya Dharmakīrti, who questioned the very fabric of causality and existence. At the foundation of Udayanācārya's cumulative case stand the *kāryāt* and *āyojanāt* arguments, which lay the groundwork for intelligent causation of the cosmos. The *kāryāt* argument begins with an intuition as old as human reason itself: that effects require causes, and that complex, composite entities—whether they be pots crafted by potters or houses raised by architects—do not spring into being uncaused. Udayanācārya invites us to look at the universe not as an undifferentiated whole but as a vast, intricate system composed of countless parts, each interdependent, each finely tuned. Is it reasonable, he asks, to suppose that this vast cosmic artifact, far more complex than any man-made structure, arose without an artisan? The *āyojanāt* argument reinforces this by moving from existence to arrangement. Even if the universe's raw material somehow existed, how were its particles assembled, its laws fine-tuned, its conditions coordinated to support life and consciousness? Here Udayanācārya anticipates modern arguments about the 'fine-tuning' of the cosmos, raising a question as urgent today as it was a thousand years ago: why do the constants of physics possess precisely the values required for stars, planets, and life, rather than others that would lead to chaos or emptiness?

Randomness, he insists, does not produce purpose; only intelligence can. From this foundation, Udayanācārya pivots to governance with the *dhṛtyādeḥ* and *saṁkhyāviśeṣāt* arguments, addressing not merely how the universe came to be but how it continues to operate with astonishing regularity and moral order. The *dhṛtyādeḥ* argument observes the deep coherence of the persisting phenomena and realities. How is karmic causation—so vast, so subtle—coordinated? Only an omniscient overseer, Udayanācārya argues, could manage the intricate web of cause and effect across lifetimes, ensuring justice in the moral economy of the cosmos. The *saṁkhyāviśeṣāt* argument draws attention to numerical specificity. Why this number of planetary systems? Why these particular species, these precise ratios, these elegant symmetries? He argues that the selection of specific configurations from infinite possibilities implies a chooser, an intelligence capable of weighing alternatives and actualizing the optimal set. Finally, Udayanācārya's *padāt* argument appeals to functionality arising coherently. The brilliance of Udayanācārya's cumulative structure lies in its resilience. Should one dismiss the *śruteḥ* argument, which we have not discussed in our formulation and which relies on textual testimony, for relying on culturally contingent texts, the rational arguments remain unscathed. Should one raise doubts about teleological reasoning, the moral and testimonial arguments stand as independent pillars. Together they form a web of mutually reinforcing lines of thought, like a spider's silk: delicate in appearance, yet impossible to break without destroying the whole. Beneath these arguments lies a deeper metaphysical commitment to causal realism and the principle of sufficient reason. Udayanācārya flatly rejects the Buddhist contention that causation is a conceptual fiction, a mere projection of human habits of thought. Ācārya Nāgārjuna, in his *Mūlamadhyamakakārikā*, had argued that cause and effect cannot coexist, nor can they exist separately, nor can they be produced by themselves or others, leading him to the radical conclusion of emptiness (*śūnyatā*). Ācārya Dharmakīrti, with his momentarism, denied enduring causal continuity, reducing existence to a flicker of momentary phenomena. Udayanācārya's response is uncompromising: without genuine causal relations, the universe collapses into an inexplicable chaos, its order and purposiveness rendered unintelligible. He invokes the principle of sufficient reason—that every contingent fact must have an adequate explanation, and that this chain of explanations must terminate in a necessary being whose existence is self-explanatory. This necessary being, Udayanācārya argues, is God.

Central to this vision is a teleological understanding of nature. Unlike mechanistic worldviews, which explain phenomena as the blind play of efficient causes, Udayanācārya sees the cosmos as a theatre of meaning, where ends are achieved through deliberate orchestration. Seeds grow into trees; organs perform specific functions; ecosystems flourish in delicate balance. Such purposiveness, he insists, is not illusory but real, and requires explanation. Mechanistic accounts may describe how processes unfold but cannot tell us why these processes exist, why they produce life and consciousness, why there is something rather than nothing. Even natural laws, those bedrocks of scientific explanation, are for Udayanācārya not ultimate but derivative—features of a rationally ordered cosmos that itself demands an ordering intelligence. His arguments prefigure today's debates about fine-tuning and intelligent design, where some scientists marvel at the razor's edge on which life depends, while others insist that multiverses or anthropic principles suffice to dissolve the mystery. Udayanācārya's response would be pointed: even infinite universes governed by lawlike regularities beg the same question—why these laws, these structures, this order? The cumulative effect of Udayanācārya's arguments is not only to establish divine existence but also to sketch a rich portrait of divine attributes. From his reasoning emerges a God who is omniscient, capable of overseeing the moral order and selecting optimal configurations of reality; omnipotent, able to create and arrange the cosmos; benevolent, as seen in the moral structure that rewards virtue and punishes vice; eternal, as required to avoid infinite regress in causal explanation; and singular, for the unity and coherence of cosmic order point to a single coordinating intelligence rather than a chaotic committee of deities. Yet these very attributes invite profound questions: if God is omniscient and benevolent, why does evil persist? If God is eternal and perfect, how can such a being engage in temporal acts like creation and governance? Udayanācārya acknowledges these puzzles, offering hints of resolution in the karmic law and in the distinction between God's timeless nature and temporal manifestations, but he also leaves space for further philosophical reflection. What makes Udayanācārya's reasoning so compelling, even a millennium later, is its holistic vision. He does not rely on a single 'silver bullet' argument; he constructs a multidimensional case, where metaphysics, ethics, and theology intertwine like the strands of a rope. His method resembles a seasoned advocate presenting multiple lines of evidence in court: each witness may be imperfect, but together their testimonies form an overwhelming case. For Udayanācārya, the universe is not a meaningless machine grinding out existence through blind necessity; it is a meaningful whole, luminous with purpose, woven together by a divine intelligence whose existence is as necessary as it is profound.

## The Relationship Between Reason and Faith

Udayanācārya's inclusion of the *śruteḥ* argument—his appeal to sacred testimony—alongside a rigorous battery of rational proofs raises a fascinating and still-relevant question: what, exactly, is the relationship between reason and revelation in his philosophical system? Is scripture merely a supplement to reason, filling in where logic cannot reach? Or do rational arguments act as scaffolding to support the lofty claims of revelation? And what happens if the two ever pull in opposite directions? For Udayanācārya, there is no contest. Reason and revelation are not rivals vying for authority, nor are they separate streams flowing toward different oceans. Rather, they are two tributaries of a single river, converging and strengthening one another as they move toward the same theistic truth. In *Nyāyakusumāñjali* verse 1.3,

न्यायचर्चेयमीशस्य मननव्यपदेशभाक्।
उपासनैव क्रियते श्रवणानन्तरागता।।

*Translation*: This deliberation on *Īśvara* through *Nyāya*

is part of *manana* (rational reflection) as prescribed by scriptural instruction. What follows after *śravaṇa* (listening to revealed texts) is indeed *upāsanā* (meditative worship), which is thereby carried out.

Rational inquiry, through careful observation and logical analysis, can establish *Īśvara's* existence and sketch a rough outline of divine attributes: omniscience, omnipotence, benevolence, eternality, unity. But it is scripture—*śruti*—that completes the picture, offering details of *Īśvara's* nature, intentions, and the moral architecture of the cosmos that lie beyond unaided human reason. For Udayanācārya, then, *śruti* is not invoked to do the work reason cannot; it is invoked as an independent witness whose testimony confirms and enriches what reason already uncovers. This vision of harmony is striking because it avoids two extremes that have plagued religious and philosophical thought for centuries. On one side lies the rationalist rejection of revelation, the belief that reason alone suffices to penetrate ultimate reality. On the other side looms fideism, the rejection of reason in favour of blind faith. This reinforces the root-intent of the broader Dharmic activities, which is the attainment of *Īśvara*, as highlighted in *Nyāyakusumāñjali* verse 5.16,

कृत्स्न एव हि वेदोऽयं परमेश्वरगोचरः।
स्वार्थद्वारैव तात्पर्यं तस्य स्वर्गादिवद्विधौ।।

*Translation*: Indeed, the entire Veda is concerned with *Parameśvara* (the Supreme Lord). Its purport (*tātparya*) is directed toward *tat*, even when it speaks of other goals such as heaven (*svarga*), because those are meaningful only through their relation to Him.

Udayanācārya navigates between these cliffs with

remarkable dexterity. He insists that reason has an indispensable role in theology: without it, we risk mistaking superstition for truth or failing to recognize contradictions in our own beliefs. But he also sees the limits of unaided reason. The divine is not merely an object of philosophical curiosity; it is a living reality whose depths can be fully plumbed only through the insights of seers and sages, recorded in sacred texts. Yet this harmonious model raises a harder question: what if reason and revelation seem to conflict? What if careful logical analysis suggests a conclusion that sacred texts deny—or vice versa? Udayanācārya's system is not blind to this possibility. He provides criteria for authentic scripture—texts that are consistent, self-validating, and free from error in their transmission. Apparent conflicts, he suggests, are more likely to result from misinterpretations: either a failure in our reasoning or a misunderstanding of the true meaning of the scripture. A conflict is, in this view, a red flag that invites deeper inquiry, not a signal of irreconcilable difference. And yet Udayanācārya's openness to this tension gives his system a rare intellectual honesty. He acknowledges—however faintly—that the possibility of genuine conflict cannot be entirely ruled out. It is here that his philosophy gestures toward a larger truth: ultimate reality may demand from us both the rigor of reason and the humility of faith.

## Modern Resonances

When we read Udayanācārya today, it is impossible not to sense a striking familiarity in his arguments—as though the ancient *Nyāya* philosopher were quietly conversing across centuries with the likes of William Lane Craig, Richard Swinburne, and C.S. Lewis. Far from being a relic of a distant intellectual past, Udayanācārya's reasoning anticipates many of the most pressing debates in contemporary philosophy of religion and natural theology. His case for the existence of God—specifically the *kāryāt*, *āyojanāt*, *dhṛtyādéḥ*, *saṁkhyāviśeṣāt*, and *padāt* arguments—maps surprisingly well onto modern philosophical strategies, raising questions that are as alive in the twenty-first century as they were in the eleventh. Let us consider the *kāryāt* argument, for instance. Udayanācārya argues that because the universe is an effect—a composite, contingent whole—it must have a cause, and not just any cause, but an intelligent one capable of organizing its intricate parts. This reasoning parallels modern cosmological arguments like those advanced by William Lane Craig and Alexander Pruss, who focus on the contingency of the physical cosmos and insist that its existence requires a necessary being as ultimate explanation. Both Udayanācārya and his contemporary counterparts see the impossibility of an infinite regress of contingent causes and posit God as the necessary foundation of all being. The *āyojanāt* argument, which zeroes in on the precise arrangements and combinations of cosmic elements, resonates even more strongly with today's fine-tuning arguments. Modern physicists and philosophers marvel at the narrow range of physical constants—like the gravitational constant, the cosmological constant, the ratio of electromagnetic to gravitational forces—that make life possible in our universe. Udayanācārya's ancient insight that specific configurations of matter require an intelligent arranger prefigures this contemporary wonder at 'the Goldilocks universe', where everything is 'just right' for complexity and life. To Udayanācārya, as to modern fine-tuning theorists, chance alone seems an insufficient explanation for so delicate a balance.

Then there is the *dhṛtyādéḥ* argument. Udayanācārya's insight—that the sustained order and stability of the universe implies a sustaining intelligence—parallels modern arguments in philosophy of science and cosmology that emphasize the fine-tuning and coherence of the cosmos. Thinkers like Paul Davies and Roger Penrose have pointed out that the delicate balance of physical constants and the persistence of natural laws seem improbably ordered in the absence of an intelligent ground. Likewise, in theology, scholars such as Richard Swinburne argue that the very fact of a law-governed, intelligible universe is best explained by the existence of a rational divine sustainer. Udayanācārya, with characteristic *Nyāya* precision, observes that sustained functionality—whether in the rotation of planets, the recurrence of seasons, or the reliable structure of cognition—cannot emerge from brute matter alone. Just as maintained systems in human contexts (like a city or an ecosystem) require intentional regulation, so too the cosmic order requires an enduring intelligent sustainer (*Īśvara*). Mere mechanical laws may describe how things operate, but they cannot account for why they endure in such a fine-tuned, cohesive manner. The *saṁkhyāviśeṣāt* argument, which reflects on the specific numerical determinations and structured regularities of the cosmos, finds echoes in contemporary reflections on the 'unreasonable effectiveness' of mathematics in describing the natural world. Eugene Wigner's famous essay on this topic continues to haunt philosophers: why should the universe, at its deepest levels, be so astonishingly receptive to elegant mathematical formulation? Udayanācārya would likely have nodded knowingly, seeing in this mathematical resonance yet another sign of a rational mind behind the universe's architecture. Udayanācārya argues that functional wholes, such as meaningful language or complex biological systems, cannot arise from mere aggregation; they require intentional arrangement. This mirrors contemporary arguments in the philosophy of mind and design, where thinkers like Alvin Plantinga and Thomas Nagel explore how the emergence of consciousness, language, and rational faculties defies explanation through blind physical processes alone. In linguistics and cognitive science, the systematicity and coherence of language point toward purposeful structuring, not random assembly.

Udayanācārya's insight is grounded in the *Nyāya* theory of sentence cognition: comprehension arises only when words are arranged with expectancy (*ākāṅkṣā*), proximity (*sannidhi*), and semantic fitness (*yogyatā*). Absent that, there is no meaning—only noise. This principle generalizes: functionality presupposes a functional cause. Just as language implies a speaker, the intricate order of the cosmos—teeming with function at every level—implies a conscious arranger. For Udayanācārya as for modern thinkers, function is not an illusion—it is a clue. It demands an explanation that matter alone cannot supply, pointing instead toward *Īśvara*, the intelligent cause behind order and meaning. What makes Udayanācārya's contribution especially enduring, however, is not simply the content of his arguments but their form and method. His careful use of the method of concomitance demonstrates a level of methodological sophistication that rivals modern discussions of inductive reasoning and causal inference. By analyzing where certain effects occur alongside certain causes (*anvaya*) and where their absence coincides (*vyatireka*), he builds a case for universal principles without resorting to dogmatic leaps. This technique resonates with contemporary philosophical concerns about how to justify universal generalizations from finite data. Udayanācārya also anticipates the now popular strategy of cumulative argumentation. Rather than relying on a single knock-down proof, he layers multiple arguments, each addressing different aspects of the theistic hypothesis. This strategy recognizes that individual arguments may face objections or limitations but together form a robust, mutually reinforcing case. Contemporary philosophers like Richard Swinburne and Alvin Plantinga similarly argue that a cumulative case—where the convergence of many lines of evidence increases the probability of theism—is stronger than any single argument standing alone. Udayanācārya's philosophical architecture already models this strategy with remarkable clarity. His integration of logical technique with substantive metaphysical analysis also feels strikingly modern. Udayanācārya does not merely play with formal logic; he deploys it to engage deep questions about causation, composition, moral order, and the ultimate ground of reality. His system represents a fusion of analytic rigor and metaphysical vision that provides a template for contemporary natural theology, which strives to combine logical precision with existential relevance.

And yet, despite these enduring insights, Udayanācārya's arguments are not immune to modern critique. Today's scientific worldview has furnished naturalistic explanations for many phenomena that Udayanācārya once attributed to divine agency. Evolutionary theory explains the appearance of design in biological systems without invoking an intelligent designer. Astrophysics and cosmology describe how galaxies and planetary systems emerge from primordial matter under the influence of impersonal physical laws. Neuroscience investigates the origins of moral intuitions as adaptive traits in the evolutionary history of social primates. While these scientific narratives may not answer every metaphysical question, they shrink the explanatory gaps into which God was once placed. Moreover, Udayanācārya's metaphysical framework—the *Nyāya-Vaiśeṣika* system—faces competition from alternative worldviews. Process philosophy, for instance, envisions the cosmos as a self-organizing flow of events marked by inherent tendencies toward complexity and order, obviating the need for an external intelligent agent to impose structure on passive matter. On such views, the universe is internally dynamic, rather than governed by a transcendent sustainer. This directly challenges the *dhṛtyādéḥ* argument, which posits that the persistence and reliability of cosmic order point to a conscious sustaining intelligence. Udayanācārya holds that the continued existence and function of systems—be it the solar system, the cycles of nature, or the operations of cognition—demand more than just initial causation. He argues that mere laws or matter cannot explain why these systems remain stable. Yet critics may counter that natural laws are not arbitrary but arise from mathematical symmetries and probabilistic necessity, requiring no agent to uphold them. The notion of a personal sustainer may thus appear superfluous within a scientific paradigm that sees stability as emergent rather than imposed. Similarly, the *padāt* argument, which ties meaningful functionality to purposeful configuration, encounters challenges in light of contemporary explanations. Modern theories in complex systems, computation, and artificial intelligence demonstrate how apparent functionality can emerge from self-organizing processes or stochastic optimization. For example, neural networks develop meaningful outputs through training, not by the hand of a conscious designer. Udayanācārya's claim—that functional wholes require intelligent assembly, as words must be syntactically arranged to convey meaning—now faces reinterpretation. Could functionality arise from selection, feedback, and adaptation rather than divine orchestration?

Still, such critiques may not fully undermine the argument's force. Even in systems like AI or natural evolution, the processes that yield function seem themselves finely tuned and guided by intelligible principles—raising questions about why such a fertile structure exists at all. Udayanācārya's point may thus persist beneath modern formulations: function does not emerge from randomness alone; it presupposes intelligibility and coherence, which demand philosophical explanation. Contemporary thinkers have also sharpened classical objections such as the problem of evil. If Udayanācārya's *Īśvara* is omnipotent, omniscient, and benevolent, why does such a world contain so much gratuitous suffering? The *dhṛtyādéḥ* argument emphasizes divine sustenance, but critics might ask: what does it mean for a benevolent God to sustain a world that includes earthquakes, pandemics, and famine? While Udayanācārya defends cosmic justice through karmic law, modern critics are likely to press the problem of natural evil, where suffering appears unlinked to moral agency or desert. The padāt argument, too, confronts new pressures in an age of pluralism and technological development. In a world filled with diverse systems of meaning—religious, cultural, computational—the claim that meaningful structure implies a singular divine origin must contend with alternative accounts of function. Competing linguistic philosophies, for instance, may view language not as a divinely grounded tool, but as a socially evolved system shaped by pragmatic needs. Similarly, some strands of postmodern thought challenge the very notion of objective function, treating it as a human-imposed frame rather than a metaphysical reality. And yet, despite these critiques, Udayanācārya's thought retains a profound philosophical significance. The foundational questions he raises—why is there persistence rather than chaos? why does meaningful function pervade the universe? —remain alive. His arguments invite us to reflect not just on specific mechanisms, but on the preconditions for intelligibility, order, and sustained coherence. More importantly, his dialectical method—layering logic, metaphysics, and epistemology—offers a cumulative case approach to theism that remains intellectually rich. He reminds us that the deepest questions are not confined to any one culture or era. In an age of global philosophy, Udayanācārya calls us to engage Indian traditions as serious partners in the inquiry into ultimate reality. His voice does not merely echo from a distant past—it speaks across boundaries of time and culture, urging a shared pursuit of truth, meaning, and reason.

## Sustained Rationality

Udayanācārya's arguments for the existence of *Īśvara* stand as one of the most sustained and sophisticated philosophical projects in human history. Composed nearly a thousand years ago within the intellectual world of *Nyāya* logic and *Vaiśeṣika* metaphysics, these arguments tackle an audacious question: can reason alone lead us to the divine? For Udayanācārya, the answer was an emphatic yes! And his case remains one of the boldest attempts ever to build a rational bridge between human thought and ultimate reality. What makes Udayanācārya remarkable is not simply that he believed in God—millions have. It's that he insisted belief must be earned through rigorous argumentation. His *Nyāyakusumāñjali* is a masterwork of precision and ambition. Here, he sets out five lines of reasoning—*kāryāt* (from effects), *āyojanāt* (from arrangement), *dhṛtyādéḥ* (from coherence and continuation), *padāt* (from functionality), and *saṁkhyāviśeṣāt* (from numerical specification)—each aimed at revealing aspects of a theistic worldview. Together, they form a cumulative case that addresses creation, governance, moral law, revelation, and the uncanny regularities of the cosmos. But the enduring significance of Udayanācārya's work lies in more than historical curiosity. His philosophical sophistication speaks directly to questions that still vex contemporary thinkers. Why is there something rather than nothing? Why does the universe exhibit such elegant order? Is there an ultimate ground for moral values? Are revelation and reason enemies, or allies in the pursuit of truth?

Udayanācārya's genius lay in his methodological clarity. He applied *anvaya-vyatireka*, a method of positive and negative concomitance, to establish universal principles from finite observations. Long before Western philosophers like Hume wrestled with induction, Udayanācārya explored how we can infer causes from effects and how apparent regularities might point beyond themselves. His arguments were not naïve appeals to gaps in knowledge; they were sophisticated analyses of causality, composition, and intelligibility. To be sure, modern developments in science, logic, and comparative religion pose challenges to parts of Udayanācārya's system. Evolutionary theory, cosmology, and neuroscience now offer naturalistic accounts for phenomena he attributed to divine agency. Religious pluralism complicates his appeal to *śruti* (revealed scripture). And yet, these critiques do not erase the value of his project. If anything, they make it more relevant, forcing us to confront the question of how—and whether—reason and faith can converge in an age of competing worldviews. Perhaps most inspiring is Udayanācārya's vision of philosophy as more than technical puzzles. For him, rigorous logic was not an end in itself but a means to explore ultimate questions of existence, meaning, and value. In a world increasingly fragmented between analytic precision and existential longing, Udayanācārya models a way of thinking that unites both. The *Nyāyakusumāñjali* remains a monument to humanity's audacity to ask—and to attempt answering—the biggest questions. Whether we agree with Udayanācārya or not, his arguments remind us that the search for ultimate truth is one of philosophy's most ambitious and noble enterprises, worthy of our admiration and our critical engagement.

## *Chapter*
## *Three*
# The Architecture of Faith

The oriental is never quite the reflection of the occidental (or the other way around), and rightly so. Imagine a world of evenness and metaphysical monotony! The encounter between Indian philosophical traditions and Western rational theology is one of the most fascinating and fertile dialogues in the entire history of human thought. At the heart of this dialogue stands an enigmatic figure from medieval India: Udayanācārya, a philosopher whose bold, rigorous arguments for the existence of God—*Īśvara*—continue to intrigue scholars and believers alike. Working within the framework of *Nyāya* logic and *Vaiśeṣika* metaphysics, Udayanācārya's writings in the *Nyāyakusumāñjali* present one of the most sophisticated attempts anywhere in the world to establish theistic conclusions through pure reason. What is striking is how his proofs, developed in an Indian context nearly a millennium ago, echo and even anticipate arguments later made in the West by thinkers like Thomas Aquinas, Gottfried Wilhelm Leibniz, and Immanuel Kant. This intellectual convergence is no accident. Both traditions—Indian and Western—arose from deeply philosophical cultures where the existence and nature of the divine were not merely matters of faith but urgent philosophical questions. For centuries, Indian thinkers from *Nyāya*, *Vedānta*, Buddhism, and Jainism engaged in fierce debates about the origins of the universe, the foundations of morality, and the possibility of liberation. Similarly, in medieval Europe, scholastic philosophers developed intricate systems of thought in which reason and faith were seen as allies in the search for ultimate truth. Talking of *Nyāya-Vaiśeṣika*, Karl Potter once said,

> "*Nyaya-Vaisheshika offers one of the most vigorous efforts at the construction of a substantialist, realist ontology that the world has ever seen. It provides an extended critique of event-ontologies and idealist metaphysics. (...) This ontology is Platonistic, realistic, but neither exclusively physicalistic nor phenomenalistic.*"

Udayanācārya's *Nyāyakusumāñjali* belongs to this same grand tradition of rational theology. Composed during a period when Buddhism's sophisticated critiques of theism dominated Indian intellectual life, the text is not a mere repetition of inherited dogma. Instead, it is a daring attempt to meet the skeptics on their own ground, deploying the full arsenal of *Nyāya* logic to demonstrate that belief in *Īśvara* is not only rationally defensible but philosophically necessary. Unlike earlier *Nyāya* thinkers, who often assumed God's existence as given, Udayanācārya recognized that in the face of powerful Buddhist arguments, a fresh, systematic defence was urgently needed. What emerges from his work is a set of five interlocking arguments, each addressing different dimensions of the theistic question. Together, they form a cumulative case for the existence of a divine creator, sustainer, and moral governor. The first, the *Argument from Effect* (*Kāryāt*), begins with a simple yet profound observation: every effect we encounter in the world implies a cause. Houses are built by architects, tools are crafted by artisans, and even a humble clay pot requires a potter. Why then, Udayanācārya asks, should the universe—an infinitely more intricate and vast effect—be any different? He argues that the universe, being a composite and contingent whole, cannot exist without a cause capable of bringing it into being. Unconscious atoms, no matter how eternal, cannot themselves account for the astonishing organization we observe in nature. Just as a heap of bricks does not spontaneously arrange itself into a palace, the universe's carefully structured order points beyond itself to a conscious, intelligent cause—*Īśvara*. The logic is elegantly simple: all effects require a cause; the universe is an effect; therefore, the universe requires a cause—an omniscient and omnipotent agent.

The second, the *Argument from Combination* (*Āyojanāt*), focuses on the nature of combinatorics, particularly in the context of atoms themselves. According to the Vaiśeṣika system, atoms (*paramāṇus*) are eternal and inert—they lack consciousness and the ability to self-organize. For these atoms to combine into dyads, triads, and ultimately the vast structures of the cosmos, there must exist a conscious agent who initiates and directs their combination. Udayanācārya compares this to grains of rice or beads of gold: they do not organize themselves into a meal or a necklace without a cook or a goldsmith. In the same way, the precise combination of unconscious atoms into functional wholes requires an intelligent arranger—*Īśvara*. The third, the *Argument from Sustenance* (*Dhṛtyā*), extends beyond creation to the continued order of the cosmos. Udayanācārya observes the regularity of natural laws, the cycles of seasons, and the delicate balance of forces that allow life to flourish. These phenomena are not one-time events but ongoing processes requiring constant regulation. Left to itself, the universe could lapse into chaos or cease functioning altogether. Therefore, there must be a sustaining principle—an intelligent overseer—who preserves cosmic harmony and ensures the continued operation of natural law. The fourth, the *Argument from Functionality* (*Padāt*), focuses on the purposeful structure of tools, systems, and articulate speech. Udayanācārya's reasoning is all about functional wholes—whether an axe, a chariot, or a grammatically ordered sentence. These arise only when their components are arranged with intent and precision toward a goal. Such arrangement is not explained by the mere presence of parts or chance conjunction. The *anvaya* (positive concomitance) shows that function consistently follows from intelligently assembled structure; the *vyatireka* (negative concomitance) confirms that in the absence of such arrangement, functionality does not arise. Extending this to the cosmos, it can be argued that the intricate coherence and purposiveness evident in the natural world similarly indicate intelligent organization. Therefore, just as a functioning tool implies a craftsman, the world's order implies an intelligent cause—*Īśvara*—whose agency accounts for its operability and meaning.

The fifth, the *Argument from Numerical Specification* (*Saṅkhyāviśeṣāt*), highlights the universe's astonishing quantitative precision. From the specific number of atoms required to form distinct substances, to the exact proportions and constants that govern cosmic structures, this numerical order cannot be the result of blind chance. Just as the perfect tuning of a musical instrument points to a skilled musician, the precise numerical specifications of the cosmos point to an intelligent designer. Together, these five arguments form a cumulative case for the existence of *Īśvara*. Udayanācārya's approach does not rely on a single proof but builds a robust theistic framework where metaphysics, epistemology, and ethics converge. His reasoning remains strikingly relevant, resonating with contemporary discussions about the fine-tuning of the universe, the problem of sustaining laws of nature, and the origin of moral and spiritual knowledge. These arguments rest on key metaphysical assumptions drawn from

*Nyāya-Vaiśeṣika* philosophy: atomic pluralism (reality consists of eternal, inert atoms), dualistic ontology (a fundamental distinction exists between unconscious matter and conscious self), causal realism (every effect requires a sufficient cause), and moral realism (ethical properties have objective reality and require divine administration for their fruition). Together, these assumptions support a vision of the universe as a morally ordered, intelligently designed system requiring a conscious, omniscient, and omnipotent *Īśvara*. What makes Udayanācārya's project especially fascinating in a global philosophical context is how closely his reasoning parallels that of Western thinkers, despite their radically different cultural settings. His *Argument from Composition* anticipates Thomas Aquinas's Fifth Way—the argument from design. His *Initial Motion* argument parallels the cosmological reasoning of Aristotle and Aquinas. The moral argument resonates with later claims by Immanuel Kant, who held that practical reason compels us to postulate God as the guarantor of moral law. Even his appeal to scripture echoes debates in Western theology about the role of revelation in supplementing reason.

Yet there are also telling contrasts. Where Aquinas and Leibniz worked within a monotheistic framework inherited from Abrahamic traditions, Udayanācārya operated in a pluralistic intellectual landscape marked by intense debates with Buddhists, Jains, and other Hindu schools. Where Kant famously critiqued the possibility of speculative metaphysics, Udayanācārya maintained that careful inference—if properly structured—could reveal truths about ultimate reality. In many ways, Udayanācārya represents a model of what rational theology can aspire to be: rigorous, cumulative, and open to dialectical challenge. He recognizes that no single argument is unassailable, yet together they form a robust network of reasoning. He is keenly aware of objections and addresses them with meticulous care, showing how apparent difficulties often dissolve upon closer logical examination. The *Nyāyakusumāñjali* is thus not a museum piece. It is a living testament to the human urge to seek ultimate answers through the disciplined use of reason. In an age where philosophy is increasingly specialized and fragmented, Udayanācārya's work reminds us of a time when logic and metaphysics were directly connected to questions of existence, meaning, and moral order. Whether or not we accept his conclusions, Udayanācārya challenges us to think more deeply about the big questions: Why is there something rather than nothing? Why does the universe exhibit such intricate order? Are moral truths real, and if so, what grounds them? His genius lies in showing that these are not merely theological questions—they are philosophical ones, demanding our most careful reasoning.

## Aquinas and the Five Ways

The towering figure of Thomas Aquinas (1225–1274) stands at the intersection of faith and reason, a philosopher-theologian whose synthesis of Aristotelian thought with Christian doctrine remains one of the great achievements of Western intellectual history. Writing in the vibrant context of medieval scholasticism, where universities were flourishing and Aristotelian texts had been newly rediscovered and translated into Latin, Aquinas faced a daunting challenge: to offer rational demonstrations of God's existence that would satisfy the demands of philosophy without undermining the revealed truths of theology. His answer came in the form of the celebrated *Five Ways* (*Quinque Viae*), outlined in his *Summa Theologica*, which have shaped centuries of debate about the relationship between reason, science, and the divine. Aquinas did not invent these arguments out of thin air. They arose from a deep engagement with Aristotelian metaphysics, particularly

Aristotle's notions of actuality and potentiality, efficient and final causation, and the hierarchy of being. But Aquinas, ever the synthesizer, adapted these concepts to a Christian framework that emphasized God's radical transcendence, his role as the Creator ex nihilo, and the intimate distinction between Creator and creation. For Aquinas, the enterprise was not merely academic; it was an attempt to show that the human mind, unaided by revelation, could rise to a certain, though limited, knowledge of God as the necessary foundation of all reality. The first of the *Five Ways*, the *Argument from Motion* (*Ex Motu*), begins with an observation as ancient as philosophy itself: the world is full of motion. Leaves flutter in the wind, rivers flow to the sea, stars wheel across the night sky. But Aquinas probes deeper, asking what it means for something to move. He famously said, in Opuscule II in *De Regno,*

*"Reason in man is rather like God in the world."*

Drawing from Aristotle, he sees motion not merely as change of place but as the actualization of potentiality—the process by which something moves from being potentially in a certain state to actually being so. But whatever is in motion must be set in motion by something already actual, since nothing can actualize its own potential. This chain of movers cannot regress infinitely, for then there would be no first mover to give motion to the rest. Therefore, Aquinas concludes, there must be a first unmoved mover, itself pure act, and this we call God. The second way, the *Argument from Efficient Causation* (*Ex Causa Efficiente*), closely parallels the first but focuses on causation in the realm of existence rather than motion. In *Summa contra Gentiles* (III, 69, 15), he says

*"The perfection of the effect demonstrates the perfection of the cause, for a greater power brings about a more perfect effect. But God is the most perfect agent. Therefore, things*

*created by Him obtain perfection from Him. So, to detract from the perfection of creatures is to detract from the perfection of divine power."*

Everything in the world is an effect of a cause; a tree grows because of a seed, the seed because of another tree, and so on. But this sequence of causes, too, cannot extend backward infinitely in what Aquinas calls an essentially ordered series—where each cause depends on the prior cause for its very power to cause. Without a first cause, there would be no subsequent causes, and nothing would exist at all. Thus, reason demands a first efficient cause, itself uncaused, which Aquinas identifies with God. The third way, the *Argument from Contingency and Necessity* (*Ex Contingentia*), adds a subtle twist. Aquinas notes that all the beings we encounter—plants, animals, people, even planets—are contingent; they come into existence and pass away. But if everything were contingent, then at some point in the infinite past nothing would have existed, and nothing can come from nothing. There must therefore exist at least one necessary being, one that contains within itself the reason for its existence and is not dependent on anything else. This necessary being, the ground of all contingent existence, is God.

The fourth way, the *Argument from Degrees of Perfection* (*Ex Gradibus*), turns to the qualitative aspects of reality. We notice degrees of goodness, truth, nobility, and other perfections in the world: one act is more virtuous than another; one truth is clearer than another; one beauty more sublime than another. But such gradations presuppose an ultimate standard, a maximum in that genus, by which all others are measured. As fire is the hottest thing and the source of all heat, so too must there be a most perfect being, the cause of all perfections in other beings. This source of all goodness and truth is God. This is beautifully said in *On the Apostles' Creed* (Art. 1),

> *"Suppose a person entering a house were to feel heat on the porch, and going further, were to feel the heat increasing, the more they penetrated within. Doubtless, such a person would believe there was a fire in the house, even though they did not see the fire that must be causing all this heat. A similar thing will happen to anyone who considers this world in detail: one will observe that all things are arranged according to their degrees of beauty and excellence, and that the nearer they are to God, the more beautiful and better they are."*

Finally, the fifth way, the *Argument from Governance* (*Ex Gubernatione*), brings a teleological perspective. Aquinas observes that natural things lacking intelligence—like plants or celestial bodies—nonetheless act toward ends in a consistent, orderly way. The acorn becomes an oak; the planets trace elegant orbits. This purposiveness, Aquinas argues, cannot be self-explained. Just as an arrow reaches its target only because it is directed by an archer, so too natural objects act toward their ends because they are directed by an intelligent being. This universal director is God. Underlying all five arguments is Aquinas's metaphysical vision. He presupposes the principle of causality: every effect must have an adequate cause. He rejects infinite regress in essentially ordered series, insisting that without a first cause or mover, no dependent series could exist at all. His doctrine of act and potency provides a framework for understanding change and existence itself. And his conviction that natural things tend toward specific ends—teleology—grounds his argument for governance. The *Five Ways* have inspired admiration and critique alike. Modern science has challenged their Aristotelian physics, while philosophers like David Hume and Immanuel Kant have questioned their metaphysical assumptions. Yet they endure, not because they provide a knockdown proof in the modern sense, but because they offer a profound vision of a cosmos infused with order, purpose, and intelligibility. For Aquinas, reason leads us to the threshold of the divine, and there theology takes over to complete the journey. In the grand intellectual cathedral of the Middle Ages, the *Five Ways* remain among its most elegant arches, pointing upward toward the transcendent mystery that Aquinas called God.

## Leibniz and the *Principle of Sufficient Reason*

Gottfried Wilhelm Leibniz was not content to merely ponder why the universe exists; he wanted to know why this universe exists rather than some other—or none at all. It was a question that haunted him, a riddle he approached with the tools of logic, mathematics, and metaphysics. Unlike Thomas Aquinas, who worked within the sturdy categories of Aristotle, Leibniz constructed a metaphysical edifice of his own design, a dazzling system in which every corner of reality would ultimately reveal the imprint of a rational Creator. At the heart of his philosophy lay two guiding principles: the *Principle of Sufficient Reason*—that nothing happens without an adequate reason—and the *Principle of Non-Contradiction*—that whatever is self-contradictory cannot possibly exist. There is a rather interesting argument using geometry for the construction of metaphysics in the *Dissertatio Exoterica De Statu Praesenti et Incrementis Novissimis Deque Usu Geometriae*,

> *Nam filum labyrintho de compositione continui deque maximo et minimo ac indesignabili at que infinito non nisi geometria praebere potest, ad metaphysicam vero solidam nemo veniet, nisi qui illac transiverit.*
>
> *Translation*: Only geometry can hand us the thread [which will lead us through] the labyrinth of the continuum's composition, the maximum and the minimum, the infinitesimal and the infinite; and no one will arrive at a

> truly solid metaphysic except he who has passed through this [labyrinth].

From these seemingly simple axioms, Leibniz unfolded a vision of God's existence that was as rigorous as it was breathtaking. Leibniz's first and perhaps most famous argument, the *Cosmological Argument from Sufficient Reason*, begins with a deceptively straightforward observation: everything that exists must have a reason why it exists rather than not. We can trace chains of explanation—a tree because of a seed, the seed because of another tree, and so on—but Leibniz asks what grounds the whole chain. It cannot rest in the series of contingent beings itself, for contingent things—things that might not have existed—cannot account for their own existence. Instead, the ultimate reason must lie in a necessary being, one whose existence is self-explanatory and who holds within itself the reason for all that is. This necessary being, Leibniz argues, is God. His version of the cosmological argument departs from earlier forms by emphasizing not causation but explanation. The question is not "*Who pushed the first domino?*" but "*Why is there any domino at all?*" For Leibniz, existence itself demands a sufficient reason—and only a necessary being can provide it.

Leibniz also took up the ontological argument, refining it to meet the objections raised against St. Anselm's earlier formulation. He defined God as 'the most perfect being', a being containing every possible perfection. Existence, Leibniz reasoned, must be counted among these perfections, for a being lacking existence would be less than perfectly perfect. But could such a being exist only possibly, as a mere idea? Here Leibniz's logic sharpens to a point: if God's existence is possible—if the concept of a most perfect being involves no contradiction—then God must necessarily exist. After all, a necessary being cannot exist contingently. Leibniz argued that the concept of God is indeed free of contradiction and therefore reality must include such a being. This was no theological sleight of hand but an exercise in the power of pure reason to grasp the foundations of existence. Yet Leibniz's metaphysical theology did not stop there. In his *Argument from Eternal Truths*, he considered the timeless verities of logic and mathematics—the laws of identity, the truths of geometry, the principles of arithmetic. Where are these truths grounded? They cannot depend on the shifting, contingent world; their necessity requires a necessary mind. For Leibniz, eternal truths reside in the intellect of God, who is not only the source of the world's being but also of its rational structure. Every theorem, every law of nature, every equation, in some sense reflects the divine understanding. He also speaks about the universality of knowledge in *Discours touchant la méthode de la certitude et de l'art d'inventer pour finir les disputes et pour faire en peu de temps de grands progrès*,

> *Pour ce qui est des connaissances non-écrites qui se trouvent dispersées parmi les hommes de différents professions, je suis persuadé qu'ils passent de beaucoup tant à l'égard de la multitude que de l'importance, tout ce qui se trouve marqué dans les livres, et que la meilleure partie de notre trésor n'est pas encore enregistrée.*
>
> *Translation*: I am convinced that the unwritten knowledge scattered among men of different callings surpasses in quantity and in importance anything we find in books, and that the greater part of our wealth has yet to be recorded.

Perhaps most distinctive of all is Leibniz's *Argument from Pre-established Harmony*. Here he turned to the curious coordination between mind and body, between mental acts and physical movements. How do these two distinct realms interact so seamlessly? Leibniz's answer was radical: they do not interact at all. Instead, God has synchronized them from the beginning, like two perfectly wound clocks keeping identical time. This pre-established harmony extends beyond mind and body to the entire universe, where every '*monad'*—Leibniz's term for the fundamental units of reality—unfolds its own internal program in perfect correspondence with all others. Only an infinite intelligence could orchestrate such a symphony of being.

Underlying these arguments is Leibniz's most provocative doctrine: *this is the best of all possible worlds*. To modern ears, often cynical and bruised by history, the phrase sounds almost naive. But for Leibniz it followed inexorably from his metaphysical principles. God, being omniscient, surveyed all possible worlds; being omnibenevolent, he willed the greatest good; being omnipotent, he actualized the one world that balances perfection and freedom in the fullest possible way. Evil exists, but only insofar as it is the necessary shadow cast by a greater good. Every detail of the cosmos—every joy and sorrow, every triumph and tragedy—forms part of a larger rational plan whose coherence lies beyond human comprehension but within divine reason. This vision emerges from Leibniz's intricate metaphysics. Reality, he argued, consists of simple substances or 'monads', each a unique center of perception and appetite, reflecting the universe from its own perspective. No two monads are alike; no monad interacts causally with another; yet all unfold harmoniously according to God's design. The principles of sufficient reason, non-contradiction, and the identity of indiscernibles weave together in a tapestry of logical necessity. Even God's choice itself, Leibniz contends, conforms to reason: he created this world not arbitrarily but because it is the most rationally excellent of all possible options. Leibniz's arguments do not rest on appeals to faith or revelation. They arise from an audacious confidence in the intelligibility of reality. For him, to think rationally about the world is already to glimpse its divine ground. The universe, in all its complexity, beauty, and strangeness, testifies not merely to the existence of God but to the perfection of his wisdom and will. In Leibniz's metaphysical cathedral, reason and faith are not rivals but allies, their combined light illuminating the deepest questions of existence.

## Kant's Critical Philosophy

Immanuel Kant stands like a colossus astride the landscape of Western philosophy, a figure whose thought marks a decisive turning point in the centuries-long effort to ground belief in God on the firm foundations of reason. Before Kant, rational theology—the proud tradition of arguing for God's existence through pure intellect—was considered the pinnacle of philosophical inquiry. After Kant, it would never be the same. With his critical philosophy, Kant delivered a stunning series of blows to traditional theistic proofs, yet paradoxically he did so not to annihilate religious belief, but to preserve a space for faith within the moral life. He famously declared that he had to *"limit knowledge in order to make room for faith,"* a line that captures his extraordinary balancing act: demolishing centuries of rational theology while simultaneously giving religion a new foundation in practical reason. He famously said, in *What is Enlightenment?* (1784),

> *Aufklärung ist der Ausgang des Menschen aus seiner selbst verschuldeten Unmündigkeit. Unmündigkeit ist das Unvermögen, sich seines Verstandes ohne Leitung eines anderen zu bedienen. Selbstverschuldet ist diese Unmündigkeit, wenn die Ursache derselben nicht am Mangel des Verstandes, sondern der Entschließung und des Mutes liegt, sich seiner ohne Leitung eines anderen*

> *zu bedienen. Sapere aude! Habe Mut dich deines eigenen Verstandes zu bedienen! ist also der Wahlspruch der Aufklärung.*
>
> *Translation*: Enlightenment is man's leaving his self-caused immaturity. Immaturity is the incapacity to use one's intelligence without the guidance of another. Such immaturity is self-caused if it is not caused by lack of intelligence, but by lack of determination and courage to use one's intelligence without being guided by another. *Sapere Aude!* Have the courage to use your own intelligence! is therefore the motto of the enlightenment.

At the heart of Kant's project lies what he called his "*Copernican revolution*" in philosophy. Just as Copernicus upended the medieval worldview by placing the sun, not the earth, at the center of the cosmos, Kant proposed a revolution in epistemology. He argued that human reason does not passively receive knowledge about the world; rather, it actively structures all experience. We do not know things as they are '*in themselves*' (*noumena*); we know only things as they appear to us (*phenomena*), filtered through the innate categories of our understanding and the forms of space and time. This seemingly abstract shift had breathtaking consequences. If we are forever barred from knowing reality in itself, what becomes of our attempts to deduce the existence of a transcendent God, a being defined precisely as beyond all experience?

In the *Critique of Pure Reason*, Kant confronted the venerable arguments for God's existence head-on. He divided them into three major types: the ontological, cosmological, and physico-theological (or teleological) proofs. One by one, he dismantled them with surgical precision, exposing the flaws that had lain hidden beneath their logical grandeur. The ontological argument, most famously advanced by Anselm of Canterbury and later refined by Descartes, begins with the concept of God as a supremely perfect being. From this, it reasons that existence must be included among God's perfections—because a God who exists is greater than a God who does not. But Kant saw through this elegant move. Existence, he argued, is not a "real predicate" that adds something to a concept. To say that a hundred real dollars are more perfect than a hundred imagined ones is a category mistake. Existence does not enrich a concept; it merely posits that such a concept is instantiated in reality. The ontological argument, Kant concluded, tries to smuggle existence into a concept as though it were a property like wisdom or power, but in doing so it leaps illicitly from thought to reality. Next came the cosmological argument, which traces its lineage back to Plato and Aristotle, and reached its classic form in the work of Thomas Aquinas. This argument begins from the undeniable existence of contingent beings—things that might not have existed—and reasons toward the necessity of a non-contingent, necessary being as the ultimate ground of existence. But here too Kant lowered the axe. The principle of causation, he argued, is one of the categories of human understanding. It applies only within the realm of possible experience—the phenomenal world. To extend it beyond experience, to the noumenal realm of God or a necessary being, is to misuse it entirely. Worse yet, Kant showed that the cosmological argument ultimately collapses back into the ontological one. For when we inquire into the nature of this necessary being, we find ourselves once again defining it as a being whose nonexistence is impossible—thus resurrecting the flawed ontological proof under another guise.

The teleological argument—often called the *argument from design*—fared slightly better in Kant's estimation. He admitted it was the "oldest, clearest, and most accordant with the common reason of mankind." Its appeal lies in the evident order, beauty, and purposefulness of the natural world, which seem to point to an intelligent designer. Yet even here, Kant found fatal weaknesses. The argument may suggest an architect of the world but gives no warrant for identifying this architect with the infinite, omnipotent God of theology. It offers no proof that there is only one designer rather than many. And once again, it cannot escape dependence on the cosmological argument, which—as Kant had already shown—secretly relies on the ontological one. At this point, the prospects for rational theology might seem grim. But Kant's critique was not born of hostility toward religion. On the contrary, he recognized the profound importance of the idea of God for human life. Though theoretical reason—our capacity to know—cannot prove God's existence, Kant observed that reason naturally and inevitably produces the idea of God as the 'transcendental ideal'. This idea functions not as a proof, but as a guiding principle, a regulative ideal that shapes our pursuit of knowledge and moral order. It reflects reason's insatiable demand for systematic unity: the longing to trace all conditioned things back to an unconditioned ground. But it was in his moral philosophy, particularly the *Critique of Practical Reason*, that Kant sought to secure a more robust footing for faith. Here, he advanced his so-called moral argument for God's existence. Unlike the discarded theoretical proofs, this argument does not claim to demonstrate God's existence as an objective fact. Rather, it appeals to the practical necessity of belief in God for the moral life to make sense.

At the center of Kant's ethics stands the 'moral law'—a fact of reason that imposes categorical obligations on us as rational agents. He once famously said, as quoted in *German Thought, From The Seven Years' War To Goethe's Death : Six Lectures* (1880) by Karl Hillebrand,

> *"[Religion should be] .... successively freed from all statutes based on history, and one purely moral religion rule over all, in order that God might be all in all. The veil must fall. The leading-string of sacred tradition with all its appendices becomes by degrees useless, and at last a fetter ... The humiliating difference between laymen and clergymen must disappear, and equality spring from true liberty. All this, however, must not be expected from an exterior revolution, which acts violently, and depends upon fortune In the principle of pure moral religion, which is a sort of divine revelation constantly taking place in the soul of man, must be sought the ground for a passage to the new order of things, which will be accomplished by slow and successive reforms."*

This 'moral law' directs us toward the highest good (*summum bonum*), an ideal state where perfect virtue is united with perfect happiness. Yet in the empirical world, such a state seems unattainable: virtue and happiness often diverge rather than converge. This disjunction leads Kant to postulate the existence of God as a necessary condition for the possibility of the highest good. Only a moral ruler of the universe could ensure the ultimate harmony of virtue and happiness, thus giving meaning and coherence to our moral striving. Belief in God, for Kant, is not an act of theoretical knowledge but a moral necessity. This distinction between knowledge and faith lies at the heart of Kant's critical philosophy. Human cognition, he insists, is confined to the realm of phenomena. Things-in-themselves—including God—lie forever beyond our epistemic reach. Yet this very limitation opens the door to a different kind of certainty. By denying reason the power to grasp the divine directly, Kant made room for a faith grounded not in speculative metaphysics but in the lived reality of moral obligation. In the end, Kant's critical turn was not the end of theology but its transformation. He shifted the focus from proving God's existence as a theoretical object to understanding God's role in the moral life of rational agents. Theoretical reason, he taught, must accept its boundaries. Practical reason, however, gives us a glimpse of the supersensible—not as knowledge, but as a postulate necessary for living rightly. Thus, human reason remains unified in its quest for the unconditioned, even as it recognizes that some truths are beyond knowing and must instead be trusted. Kant's legacy is therefore paradoxical: he both dismantled the traditional edifice of rational theology and offered a profound new vision of faith's place within reason. By limiting what we can know, he liberated what we can believe—not as speculative guesswork but as the moral confidence of finite beings striving toward the highest good.

## Where the Rivers Meet (and Not)

Imagine standing at the crossroads of three worlds: ancient India's vibrant philosophical debates, medieval Europe's scholastic cathedrals of thought, and the dazzling rationalism of early modern Europe. For the purposes of this triadic *Sangam*, let us visualise: At each turn, a towering figure greets us—Udayanācārya, Thomas Aquinas, and Gottfried Wilhelm Leibniz—each offering a vision of reality stitched together by reason's careful hand. Separated by centuries and civilizations, these thinkers nonetheless share an audacious goal: to show that the universe, in all its complexity and motion, cries out for an ultimate explanation, a necessary being to ground it. Yet, when we step closer, we see that their arguments, while converging on the divine, chart strikingly divergent paths shaped by distinct metaphysical landscapes and epistemological commitments. At first glance, Udayanācārya's reasoning in the *Nyāyakusumāñjali* appears remarkably parallel to Aquinas's famed Five Ways. Both thinkers confront a world teeming with motion, change, structure, and intelligibility—and conclude that such a world cannot ground itself. For Udayanācārya, inert atoms—the basic building blocks of matter—do not spontaneously form orderly compounds or complex systems; their consistent combination, disintegration, and recombination require a conscious overseer. *Īśvara* is not a passive creator but an ongoing sustainer, ensuring the functional continuity and purposive orientation of the cosmos. While the *Nyāya* tradition frames these arguments primarily in epistemological and causal terms, the implications are unmistakably ontological: without *Īśvara*, there is no final grounding for the coherence or directedness of reality. Aquinas, drawing from Aristotelian metaphysics, approaches the same problem from the language of being: all motion implies a transition from potentiality to actuality, which cannot proceed infinitely. Thus, he posits a First Mover—pure act, without potentiality—as the ontological wellspring of all existence. Though differing in terminology and method, both philosophers converge on a powerful insight: the world, in its order and function, points to a necessary, intelligent, and sustaining reality beyond itself.

At first glance, Udayanācārya's reasoning in the *Nyāyakusumāñjali* seems uncannily aligned with Aquinas's Five Ways, especially in their cosmological thrust. Both look out at a world teeming with motion, change, and composite entities and assert: these phenomena cannot explain themselves. For Udayanācārya, the inert atoms of *Nyāya*-Vaiśeṣika metaphysics—eternally existent, indivisible, and lifeless—cannot, by themselves, assemble into complex, purposeful structures. An intelligent agent, *Īśvara*, is required not only to initiate but to continuously orchestrate their combinations and separations in accordance with karmic order. His God is not a remote architect but an ever-present supervisor, sustaining order in a pluralistic reality populated by many co-eternal entities—atoms, selves, time, space, and mind. Aquinas, drawing from Aristotle, similarly posits that motion and change require explanation, but he frames this within a more unified metaphysics. For him, every change is a movement from potentiality to actuality, and no being can actualize itself. This necessitates a first mover—God—who is pure actuality (*actus purus*), entirely free from potentiality. Unlike Udayanācārya's *Īśvara*, Aquinas's God sustains all being at every moment not through ongoing intervention, but as the ontological source of all that exists. God, for Aquinas, is the necessary being in whom essence and existence are identical—the metaphysical wellspring from which all contingent beings flow. Then enters Leibniz, who shifts the focus from causation to reason. Rather than emphasizing motion or composition, he builds his cosmological argument on the *Principle of Sufficient Reason*: that nothing exists without a rational explanation for why it is so and not otherwise. His answer is that God, being rational and good, freely chose to create the best of all possible worlds—one marked by maximal harmony and order. In Leibniz's system, God's perfection is expressed not through continuous governance, but through a front-loaded creation where every monad unfolds its internal program without real interaction. His doctrine of pre-established harmony eliminates the need for constant divine supervision, standing in contrast to Udayanācārya's hands-on governor and Aquinas's sustaining presence.

When the discussion turns to design and purpose, resonances reappear. Udayanācārya's argument from functional organization (*Padāt*)—the inference from the appropriateness of effects to an intelligent agent—bears structural similarity to Aquinas's Fifth Way. Both argue that non-conscious matter cannot account for the apparent purposiveness in natural processes. For Udayanācārya, the orderly formation of macro-structures from insentient atoms and the moral administration of *karma* point to a guiding intelligence. Aquinas similarly contends that non-rational beings act toward ends as though guided by knowledge, and thus there must be an intelligent director. While their metaphysical backdrops differ—pluralistic realism for Udayanācārya, participatory being for Aquinas, and rationalist optimism for Leibniz—all three converge on the idea that the structure and intelligibility of the cosmos point beyond itself to a rational ground, which they each name as God. Leibniz's response is subtle. Instead of continuous divine governance, his pre-established harmony ensures that all things behave as if orchestrated, though they act solely from their internal principles. The monads, like actors in a perfectly rehearsed play, move in sync without causal interaction. God's intelligence is visible not in constant intervention but in His ability to conceive and actualize such a self-regulating cosmos. Where the ontological argument is concerned, the three part ways. Udayanācārya avoids this line of reasoning entirely, reflecting the *Nyāya* school's commitment to empirical inference. In *Nyāyakusumāñjali* verse 2.2, he says

> वर्षादिवद् भवोपाधिः वृत्तिरोधः सुषुप्तिवत्।
> उद्भिद्वृश्चिकवद्वर्णाः मायावत्समयादयः।।
>
> *Translation*: The conditions of worldly existence are like the rain (seasonal and cyclic); the cessation of mental activity is like deep sleep; variegated beings (such as plants and scorpions) arise like sprouts or from dung; and diversity (like caste or colour) is as illusory as magic—so too are time and such constructs.

This verse critiques explanations of the world that rely on chance, illusion, or convention, rather than grounded inference to a conscious cause. Similarly, Aquinas also distances himself from purely conceptual arguments for God's existence. He rejects Anselm's ontological argument, insisting that existence cannot be derived from mere ideas alone, without empirical grounding. Leibniz, ever the rationalist, takes the opposite route. He refines Anselm's logic, suggesting that if the idea of a perfect being is possible, it must exist; existence itself, being a perfection, is entailed in such a being's essence. This divergence is rooted in their metaphysical architectures. Udayanācārya's pluralistic realism recognizes many eternal substances—atoms, minds, souls, and time—all coordinated by God. Aquinas's Aristotelian-inspired metaphysics posits a great chain of being, with God as ipsum esse subsistens—subsistent being itself—on which all else depends. Leibniz's monadic idealism envisions a universe of metaphysical points reflecting the whole in miniature. Each system frames God's relation to the cosmos in radically different ways: administrator, sustainer, planner. Their treatments of evil likewise reveal deep differences. Udayanācārya invokes *karma*: suffering and joy are fruits of past actions, ensuring cosmic justice. Aquinas distinguishes physical evil (the limitations of creatures) from moral evil (the misuse of free will), arguing that God permits evil to bring about greater goods—virtue, free will, and the unfolding drama of redemption. Leibniz, confronted by the horrors of his era, proposes that this is indeed the best of all possible worlds. Evils exist only because their removal would diminish goods greater still.

Their epistemologies further highlight these contrasts. Udayanācārya works within the *Nyāya* framework of *pramāṇas*—perception, inference, comparison, and testimony—anchoring his arguments in empirical observation Aquinas, while recognizing revealed truths in theology, bases his Five Ways squarely on natural reason. Leibniz, in his rationalist optimism, prioritizes logical analysis over sensory data, trusting the mind's capacity to uncover necessary truths. And then, like a seismic shift, Immanuel Kant enters the scene. His critical philosophy calls into question the entire enterprise of metaphysical theology. According to Kant, human knowledge is confined to phenomena—the world as shaped by our cognitive faculties. We can never access the noumenal realm, the reality beyond appearances. God, freedom, and immortality are not objects of theoretical knowledge but postulates of practical reason, necessary for moral life. Kant's critique strikes at the heart of Udayanācārya's causal reasoning, undermines Aquinas's *Five Ways*, and even challenges Leibniz's *Principle of Sufficient Reason*. All assume a metaphysical reach Kant denies to human reason. Yet Kant does not banish God entirely. Instead, he relocates Him: no longer an object of speculative knowledge, God becomes a postulate of ethics, the guarantor of the highest good where virtue and happiness converge. For Udayanācārya, Aquinas, and Leibniz, this would seem a retreat, a concession to skepticism. For Kant, it is a liberation, freeing faith from the pretensions of reason. Thus, we witness a dramatic turn in the history of ideas: from confident rational theology to a chastened philosophy acknowledging its limits.

Yet what unites Udayanācārya, Aquinas, and Leibniz across their differences is their shared conviction that the universe is not a brute fact but a rational order. Each, in his own idiom, affirms that reason can trace the threads of existence back to their source. Udayanācārya's detective-like reasoning, Aquinas's metaphysical architecture, and Leibniz's logical elegance all embody a faith in the intelligibility of reality. In our postmodern age, where truth is often deemed a construct and meaning a mirage, their voices ring out with striking clarity. They remind us that the quest for ultimate explanation is not naïve but noble, not an outdated relic but an enduring human endeavour. Their disagreements enrich rather than diminish this legacy, offering diverse models of how God might relate to the world: as an ever-active overseer, a sustaining source of being, or a perfect planner of harmonious monads. In the end, we are left with a choice. Do we, like Kant, step back from the ambition of metaphysical theology, content to let faith stand alone? Or do we press on, inspired by Udayanācārya's inference, Aquinas's hierarchy, and Leibniz's harmony, believing that reason's light, though finite, can illuminate even the deepest mysteries? Perhaps this is the true gift of their conversation. It is not a set of settled answers but a living dialogue—a testament to the human spirit's refusal to accept chaos and its relentless search for meaning in the vast, enigmatic cosmos.

## A Unified Vision?

As we stand on the far shore of centuries of metaphysical exploration, the question looms with ever greater urgency: is it possible to weave the divergent threads of Udayanācārya's *Nyāya*, Aquinas's Thomism, and Leibniz's rationalism into a single tapestry? Or must their differences—rooted as they are in cultural, metaphysical, and epistemological commitments—forever resist synthesis? The temptation to unify these visions is strong. After all, they share a strikingly similar impulse: to move beyond the brute fact of existence and discern an ultimate ground, a perfect being whose nature explains and sustains the cosmos. And yet, the closer we approach their inner workings, the more their differences assert themselves—not as minor variations on a theme but as deeply entrenched worldviews. The first and perhaps most insurmountable divergence lies in their metaphysical commitments. Udayanācārya's pluralistic ontology populates the cosmos with eternal atoms, souls, and minds, coordinated by a divine overseer. Aquinas's vision, elegant and hierarchical, sees being itself cascading in degrees from the pure actuality of God to the fragile contingency of creatures. Leibniz, ever the metaphysical innovator, replaces material substance entirely with monads—windowless centres of perception whose synchronicity is orchestrated by divine pre-establishment. Yet Kant's intervention renders these grand metaphysical architectures newly precarious. He does not so much demolish them as he relativizes them, recasting each as a heuristic framework—a culturally and historically situated attempt to map the noumenal onto the phenomenal. For Kant, the limits of human cognition mean that none of these systems can claim objective, demonstrable metaphysical truth. They are not failures, but noble fictions: scaffolds for thought rather than foundations of reality.

Equally profound is their disagreement over the role of reason. Pre-Kantian thinkers—from Udayanācārya's analytic inferences to Aquinas's Aristotelian Five Ways to Leibniz's Principle of Sufficient Reason—trusted in reason's power to scale the heights of metaphysics. Kant, however, draws an unbreachable boundary. Rational demonstration, he insists, reaches only as far as phenomena, the world as it appears to us. Beyond that horizon lies the noumenal realm, which may be postulated for moral reasons but never known with certainty. Theology, in his vision, must shift from speculative reason to practical reason—from metaphysical proof to ethical necessity. Yet Kant's radical critique does not leave these systems in ruins. Instead, it forces them into a new and surprising kind of dialogue. From the vantage point of the 21st century, we can discern a subtle convergence emerging from the wreckage of their metaphysical ambitions. All three traditions, in their own ways, come to recognize the limits of reason. Udayanācārya's *Nyāya* philosophers acknowledged that certain ultimate truths are only partially accessible to inference, supplementing reason with scriptural testimony. Aquinas drew a sharp distinction between philosophical theology (the domain of reason) and revealed theology (the domain of faith). Even Leibniz, for all his rationalist optimism, conceded the mystery of divine freedom in choosing this world over others. Kant's critical philosophy crystallizes these intuitions into a rigorous epistemological boundary: what lies beyond experience is not to be known, but to be hoped for.

There is also a shared appreciation for the moral dimension of theology. Udayanācārya's doctrine of *karma-phala* binds divine justice to the moral arc of countless lives, where ethical action is rewarded and vice punished across cosmic cycles. Aquinas embeds morality within a teleological framework, where human flourishing consists in aligning one's will with divine order. Kant reframes this entirely: God's existence becomes a practical postulate, a necessary hypothesis to preserve the meaningfulness of moral striving. In fact, there is a rather interesting way in which criticism becomes a point of focus for understanding the true nature of reality, as mentioned by Walter Benjamin,

> *"Through Kant's philosophical works, the concept of criticism took on an almost magical meaning for the younger generation [of Germans in the Romantic movement]. To be critical meant to raise thought so far above all constraint that, through the perception of the falseness of constraints, knowledge of the truth takes flight as if by magic."*

Across traditions, the divine is not only an object of contemplation but a guarantor of moral coherence in the human story. Finally, there is a remarkable convergence on the ideal of a perfect being. Though their metaphysical scaffolding differs—pluralistic in Udayanācārya, hierarchical in Aquinas, monadic in Leibniz—all posit a principle of ultimate perfection, intelligence, and goodness. Even Kant, despite his epistemological austerity, acknowledges the necessity of such an ideal as a regulative principle of thought and action. What, then, does this centuries-spanning dialogue offer us in our own time—a time often skeptical of grand metaphysical systems, yet restless for meaning? First, it underscores the universality of philosophy's great questions. Whether in the dense logic of *Nyāya* syllogisms, the Aristotelian categories of Thomism, or the baroque metaphysics of monads, we find humanity wrestling with the same enigmas: Why is there something rather than nothing? What sustains the order of the cosmos? What is the source of moral obligation? This universality is a call to humility and curiosity in the face of diverse intellectual traditions.

It highlights the value of comparative study. Placing Indian and Western rational theologies side by side does more than illuminate their differences; it reveals hidden affinities and shared aspirations. The cross-pollination of these traditions might yet yield fresh insights, perhaps pointing toward a global metaphysics for a global age. It also insists on the continuing relevance of these questions. Today's debates about science and religion, free will and determinism, ethics and the possibility of God, are deeply indebted to the trajectories set by Udayanācārya, Aquinas, Leibniz, and Kant. Their struggles remain ours. The dream of a unified metaphysics—one that reconciles reason's ambitions with its limits, and integrates the insights of East and West—remains tantalizingly out of reach. Yet perhaps this is as it should be. As Kant reminds us, the human longing for ultimate explanation may never be fully satisfied within the confines of finite reason. But the quest itself is far from futile. It sharpens our thinking, deepens our ethical commitments, and continually reorients us toward the horizon of the unknown. In this light, Udayanācārya, Aquinas, and Leibniz are not so much rival architects of competing systems as fellow pilgrims on a shared journey—each offering tools, insights, and warnings to those who follow. Their legacy is not a final answer but an invitation: to keep pressing forward, to keep reasoning, hoping, and believing in the face of mystery. And perhaps this is the most profound convergence of all. For across their divergences, they share a defiant conviction: that reality is intelligible, that meaning is not an illusion, and that reason—even if bounded—is not bereft of power. In an age where skepticism and relativism often seem triumphant, their voices remind us that the adventure of thought is not over. It is only beginning.

# *Chapter*
# *Four*
# The Edge of Unbelief

It begins with silence—not the reverent hush of a cathedral, but the cold, infinite silence of space. Once, humanity heard a voice in that silence, or thought it did. The voice of gods whispering through thunder, the voice of a singular God speaking in sacred books and moral law. But in the modern age, as telescopes pierced the heavens and microscopes the cell, that voice seemed to recede. And where it once echoed with authority, there now yawns a *void*. Now is this the onto-epistemological void of *Īśvara* or more/less than that? This void is the terrain on which modern atheism and agnosticism stand—not in defiance of God as the ancients imagined God, but in quiet suspicion that God was never there at all. For centuries, western philosophers built cathedrals of argument in *His* name. In the last chapter, we saw how everything from Udayanācārya in India crafting proofs of a supreme being to Aquinas weaving Aristotle and scripture into seamless theology illuminated a strand of rational theology that stood for the idea that thought alone could help us ascend to God or *Īśvara*. Even Maimonides and Feuerbach, though worlds apart, wrestled with the divine—the former defending a God of necessary existence and negative attributes, the latter exposing the idea of God as a psychological projection of human ideals. Feuerbach famously said,

> *"What man calls Absolute Being, his God, is his own being. The power of the object over him is therefore the power of his own being. Thus, the power of the object of feeling is the power of feeling itself; the power of the object of reason is the power of reason itself; and the power of the object of will is the power of will itself."*

Even Avicenna and David Hume, though separated by time and temperament, confronted the divine question—the one affirming the necessity of a self-subsisting cause, the other questioning whether such a cause is anything more than the mind's tendency to imagine necessity where there is only custom. But in our age of particle accelerators and neural networks, something has shifted. The old arguments feel like relics—elegant, intricate, but belonging to a time when stars were thought to be pinholes in a firmament. Modern atheism does not always roar. Sometimes it whispers. It does not need to thunder *"God is dead"* like Nietzsche, though his proclamation still reverberates like a struck bell. Instead, it simply asks: why? Why posit a cosmic architect when nature, through blind processes, can carve out stars, galaxies, life itself? Why presume design where randomness and selection suffice? Isaac Asimov once famously admitted,

> *"I am an atheist, out and out. It took me a long time to say it. I've been an atheist for years and years, but somehow I felt it was intellectually unrespectable to say one was an atheist, because it assumed knowledge that one didn't have. Somehow, it was better to say one was a humanist or an agnostic. I finally decided that I'm a creature of emotion as well as of reason. Emotionally, I am an atheist. I don't have the evidence to prove that God doesn't exist, but I so strongly suspect he doesn't that I don't want to waste my time."*

This quiet certainty, grounded more in skeptical intuition than militant denial, echoes a much older voice. David Hume, writing in the age of candles and carriages, already saw through the teleological argument, asking why an imperfect world would point to a perfect designer. Today, Richard Dawkins, in a world of gene sequencing and artificial intelligence, sharpens that critique: the watchmaker is blind, and evolution is enough.

But even more profound than the scientific rebuttals are the existential ones. Albert Camus speaks of the absurd: we live in a universe indifferent to our yearnings, and yet we act as though meaning burns in every gesture. Jean-Paul Sartre declares us condemned to be free, cast into existence without an essence, left to author ourselves in the void. To Dostoevsky, the death of God meant moral chaos; to Nietzsche, it meant moral possibility—the chance to forge values untethered from divine command. Agnosticism, too, emerges—not as cowardice, as some atheists accuse, but as a fierce intellectual humility. Bertrand Russell famously quipped he was agnostic about God as he was agnostic about a celestial teapot orbiting the sun. The analogy was cutting, but beneath it lies a deeper unease: can we ever know? The agnostic stands at the threshold, unwilling to leap into faith but also unwilling to declare the mystery resolved. Perhaps reality, in its vastness, exceeds the categories of reason. Perhaps the divine, if it exists, is not what rational theology envisioned—a being among beings—but something altogether stranger, less graspable. This modern critique does not merely reject God; it destabilizes the very project of knowing Him. Kant warned that metaphysics has a tendency to collapse under its own ambition, mistaking the scaffolding of human thought for the architecture of ultimate reality. The cosmological argument? Undermined if causality itself is only a framework for phenomena. The ontological proof? A semantic sleight of hand. The moral argument? At best, a longing clothed as logic. Rational theology becomes, in this light, a kind of beautiful poetry—illuminating, yes, but no more compulsory than Homer's hymns to Olympus. And yet. Even here, in the heart of doubt, the questions will not go away. Why is there something rather than nothing? Why does the universe hum with mathematical elegance? Why do we feel the pull of moral law, the "ought" that resists reduction to neurons firing? Atheism answers with contingency and accident. Agnosticism answers with suspended judgment. But the itch remains. Science tells us how, but not why. It explains mechanisms but is silent on meanings. As cosmologist Martin Rees notes, the universe could have been different in countless ways; it could have collapsed in on itself or never produced life at all. Why does it permit conscious observers at all—us, standing here, staring out into the dark?

Perhaps this is why rational theology, though bruised, is not dead. It mutates. It becomes more cautious, less triumphalist. No longer does it strut with syllogisms claiming to capture God; it speaks with tentative language of horizons and mysteries. God becomes less the object of proof than the ground of being, the 'why' behind the 'how'. It is no longer about constructing an edifice of logic reaching heavenward but about recognizing that reason, at its furthest reach, arrives at a door it cannot unlock. In this new light, faith is not opposed to reason but grows in the soil of reason's limits. It is not certitude but courage: the courage to hope in the absence of guarantees, to orient oneself toward meaning even when the cosmos gives none. This is no longer the faith of medieval certainty. It is faith after the death of God, faith in a silent universe, faith that maybe silence itself conceals a hidden music. We live now in an age where atheism and agnosticism are not revolts—they are default settings. To believe is the stranger act. But the perennial questions still haunt us, unexorcised. Whether one finds solace in equations, in existential freedom, or in some transcendent presence glimpsed only in longing, the search continues. It may be that God, as rational theology once imagined Him, never existed. Or it may be that our proofs were too small for the reality they sought. Either way, the flowers of the void continue to bloom. We pluck them carefully, each petal a question: What is ultimate? What is real? And, perhaps most urgently: how shall we live in the shadow of what we cannot know?

## The Humean Interlude

When David Hume strode onto the stage of 18th-century thought, the air was already thick with arguments for God. Priests, philosophers, and naturalists alike spoke with confidence of design in the world, of first causes, of a moral law written in the human heart. But Hume's mind, restless and razor-sharp, refused to bow to inherited certainties. He stood as a kind of philosophical iconoclast, dismantling metaphysical claims with the cool precision of a surgeon. In his hands, even the most time-honoured proofs for God's existence began to look less like eternal truths and more like comforting illusions. Hume was, above all, an empiricist—a thinker convinced that all knowledge must ultimately flow from sensory experience. Anything beyond that—anything abstract, a priori, metaphysical—he regarded with deep suspicion. *"Commit it then to the flames,"* he famously said of books trafficking in metaphysics and theology, *"for it can contain nothing but sophistry and illusion."* In this single line, centuries of rational theology seemed to tremble. How can we speak of an ultimate, extra-mental reality like *Īśvara* of *Nyāya* if we cannot verify it through perception? For Hume, such talk was at best speculation, at worst a dangerous distraction from the modest task of understanding the world as it appears to us. His *Dialogues Concerning Natural Religion* strikes at the heart of the classical design argument. He says, in Philo to Cleanthes, Part XII,

> *"If the whole of natural theology, as some people seem to maintain, resolves itself into one simple, though somewhat ambiguous, at least undefined proposition, that the cause or causes of order in the universe probably bear some remote analogy to human intelligence: If this proposition be not capable of extension, variation, or more particular explication: If it affords no inference that affects human life, or can be the source of any action or forbearance: And if the analogy, imperfect as it is, can be carried no farther than to the human intelligence, and cannot be transferred, with any appearance of probability, to the other qualities of the mind; if this really be the case, what can the most inquisitive, contemplative, and religious man do more than give a plain, philosophical assent to the proposition, as often as it occurs, and believe that the arguments on which it is established exceed the objections which lie against it?"*

For millennia, theologians had pointed to the apparent order and complexity of the universe as evidence of a divine designer. A watch implies a watchmaker; so too, the intricate mechanisms of life and the cosmos must imply God. But Hume's skeptical characters are unrelenting: Why should the analogy hold? A watch is a product of human intention, true, but the universe? Might not its order arise from some wholly natural principle? And even if we were to concede a designer, what follows? Must this designer be infinite, omnipotent, omnibenevolent? Why not, as Hume mischievously suggests, a finite craftsman—or a committee of gods, squabbling and imperfect? Worse yet, if the world demands a designer, does not the designer demand one too? Who designed the designer? The regress threatens to spiral endlessly.

Then comes the problem of evil. The world, Hume observes, is filled with suffering—earthquakes swallow cities, disease ravages innocents, and moral evils abound in every human society. If the cosmos is indeed the handiwork of a perfect, benevolent deity, why is it so shot through with pain? Why does order not entail goodness? Perhaps, he suggests with chilling detachment, the world is the product of a morally indifferent force—or a deity lacking either the power or the will to eliminate suffering. The old equilibrium between order and moral perfection cracks under the weight of Hume's relentless questioning. And yet, while Hume's critique has become a cornerstone of modern skepticism, it is not unanswerable. Across continents and centuries, Indian philosophers had already grappled with these very doubts, though in a different register. Udayanācārya offers a strikingly different epistemic framework in his Nyāyakusumāñjali. Unlike Hume, who distrusted abstraction, Udayanācārya affirmed that human reason, when properly disciplined, could ascend beyond the immediately perceptible. He anchored his arguments in the *aṇvīkṣikī* method—a science of critical inquiry demanding rigorous *pramāṇas*: perception (*pratyakṣa*), inference (*anumāna*), analogy (*upamāna*), and reliable testimony (*śabda*). These tools, far from being mere abstractions, constituted a calibrated epistemology designed to sift truth from illusion. Where Hume's empiricism recoiled from metaphysics, *Nyāya*'s *pramāṇika* inference embraced it cautiously but confidently. The existence of *Īśvara*, Udayanācārya argued, was not a gratuitous hypothesis but a necessary conclusion from observed effects. Just as smoke implies fire by the universal concomitance (*vyāpti*) between the two, so too does the order of the world imply an intelligent cause. Hume's analogy critique—his suggestion that universe-to-artifact comparisons are arbitrary—finds a counter in *Nyāya's* careful distinction between universal inference and accidental resemblance. The watch-to-watchmaker analogy is, for *Nyāya*, not the heart of the argument but an illustration; the real force lies in the *vyāpti* grounding of causation itself.

On the problem of evil, Indian thought moves in directions Hume scarcely imagined. Where Hume saw suffering as evidence against God, Sri Ādi Śaṅkarācārya viewed it through the lens of *avidyā*—ignorance of the true, non-dual reality. For him, the apparent world, with its pains and pleasures, is *māyā*: a provisional reality superimposed upon Brahman, the infinite consciousness that alone is real. In this framework, ultimate blame cannot be placed on a deity because suffering, like joy, belongs to a world of appearances. *Nyāya* and *Mīmāṃsā* thinkers such as Ācārya Kumārila Bhaṭṭa offered a more theistic response. They appealed to the doctrines of *karma* and *līlā*. *Karma*, the moral law of cause and effect, explains suffering not as divine injustice but as the natural result of past actions. *Līlā*, *Īśvara's* play, frames creation not as utilitarian engineering but as a cosmic drama where beings journey through joy and sorrow toward *mokṣa*—liberation. Udayanācārya, synthesizing these currents, defended a morally coherent cosmos: God permits suffering not out of indifference but as a condition for moral growth and ultimate freedom. In this view, evil is not a flaw in design but a feature of a world where free agents must learn, act, and transcend. Hume, of course, would remain unconvinced. *Karma* might seem to him a rationalization, and *mokṣa* an unverifiable hope. But what emerges from this East-West encounter is not so much a clear victor as a profound dialogue. Hume reminds us of reason's limits; Udayanācārya reminds us that those limits are not necessarily impassable. Hume feared that metaphysical speculation leads to illusion; Indian rational theologians believed that disciplined speculation leads to liberation. In the modern world, Hume's questions remain alive. Science and secularism have carried his skepticism into every corner of culture. Yet, the *Nyāya*-Vedānta responses also remain provocatively relevant. If reason is not to be trusted in metaphysics, how do we trust it even in science? If the universe appears indifferent, must we too be indifferent—or is there room to posit an underlying order, not as dogma but as a postulate of moral and existential coherence? Perhaps what is needed today is not the silencing of one tradition by another, but their convergence in humility. Hume teaches us to doubt; *Nyāya* teaches us to inquire. Between doubt and inquiry lies the restless human spirit, still seeking, still asking. Is there more than what we see? Must the flowers of the void bloom for no reason—or might they still point, subtly, to a gardener unseen?

## Russell's Suspicion

Bertrand Russell, one of the most influential philosophers of the twentieth century, was a central figure in the development of analytic philosophy and a vocal critic of religion. A mathematician, logician, and Nobel laureate in literature, Russell's intellectual legacy is marked by a commitment to clarity, empiricism, and rational analysis. His philosophical work—particularly in logic and the foundations of mathematics, as seen in *Principia Mathematica* (co-authored with Alfred North Whitehead)—sought to ground knowledge in rigorously defined symbolic systems. Yet his public writings on religion, such as *Why I Am Not a Christian* (1927) and *Religion and Science* (1935), represent an equally significant contribution to modern secular thought. In these works, Russell mounted a sustained critique of traditional religious doctrines, arguing that they are not only unsupported by evidence but actively obstruct human intellectual and moral progress. Nowhere is this more powerfully expressed than in his celebrated essay *A Free Man's Worship*, where Russell confronts the full existential weight of a godless universe without retreating into illusion:

> *"Such... but even more purposeless, more void of meaning, is the world which Science presents for our belief. Amid such*

*a world, if anywhere, our ideals henceforward must find a home. That Man is the product of causes which had no prevision of the end they were achieving; that his origin, his growth, his hopes and fears, his loves and his beliefs, are but the outcome of accidental collocations of atoms; that no fire, no heroism, no intensity of thought and feeling, can preserve an individual life beyond the grave; that all the labours of the ages, all the devotion, all the inspiration, all the noonday brightness of human genius, are destined to extinction in the vast death of the solar system, and that the whole temple of Man's achievement must inevitably be buried beneath the débris of a universe in ruins—all these things, if not quite beyond dispute, are yet so nearly certain, that no philosophy which rejects them can hope to stand. Only within the scaffolding of these truths, only on the firm foundation of unyielding despair, can the soul's habitation henceforth be safely built."*

This passage captures the austere courage at the heart of Russell's worldview: a refusal to deny the bleak implications of scientific materialism, coupled with a defiant call to construct meaning despite them. Russell's critique of religion draws heavily on the epistemological ethos of logical positivism, particularly the verification principle advanced by the Vienna Circle. According to this principle, a statement is cognitively meaningful only if it can be empirically verified or is analytically true (meaning, true by definition). On this basis, metaphysical claims—especially theological assertions about a transcendent deity—are deemed literally meaningless, since they cannot be subjected to empirical confirmation or falsification. In Russell's own writings, while not always adhering strictly to positivist doctrine, the influence is evident. He frequently characterized God-talk as speculative at best and irrational at worst, holding that belief in God arises not from reasoned inference but from psychological and sociological motives—fear, tradition, or wishful thinking. In *Religion and Science*, he argues that theological propositions lack explanatory power when compared to scientific theories, and that moral guidance traditionally supplied by religion can be better grounded in secular humanism.

It is important to note that Russell's atheism is not merely a denial of the God of Abrahamic faiths but a broader rejection of metaphysical realism as it pertains to the divine. He does not simply contend that there is no empirical evidence for God; he suggests that the very language of divinity is epistemologically suspect. Statements such as 'God exists' are, in this view, not false in the sense of being disproven, but nonsensical in the sense of lacking the conditions for meaning. This position places Russell within a philosophical lineage that sees metaphysics, particularly in its theological form, as a holdover from a less enlightened past—intellectually indefensible and destined for obsolescence in the face of scientific progress. Yet this perspective, while internally consistent within the framework of analytic philosophy, is not universally applicable. When juxtaposed with the epistemological structures of Indian philosophical systems, it reveals certain limitations and cultural assumptions. Classical Indian philosophy does not operate under the same constraints of sensory empiricism that characterize modern Western thought. Instead, it recognizes a multi-faceted theory of knowledge (*pramāṇa-śāstra*), wherein empirical perception (*pratyakṣa*) is only one among several legitimate means of acquiring valid cognition. In addition to perception, Indian epistemology embraces inference (*anumāna*), postulation (*arthāpatti*), comparison (*upamāna*), non-cognition (*anupalabdhi*), and verbal testimony (*śabda*), especially as preserved in the Vedic tradition. Within this expansive framework, metaphysical claims are not discarded for being non-empirical; rather, they are subjected to careful logical analysis and tested against criteria such as coherence, explanatory scope, and pragmatic utility.

The concept of *Īśvara*—the supreme governing principle or Lord—is a case in point. In the *Nyāya* school, which exemplifies Indian rationalism, *Īśvara* is not accepted on the basis of scriptural fiat or emotional appeal, but through inference grounded in observation. The world, with its complex order, causal regularities, and ethical intelligibility, is seen as requiring an explanatory ground. Using the method of concomitances, *Nyāya* philosophers argue that just as the presence of intelligent design in artifacts implies a designer, so too does the regularity and teleology of the cosmos imply an intelligent agent. *Īśvara* is posited not as a supernatural being beyond reason, but as a logically necessary postulate to explain phenomena such as moral causation (*karma-phala*), the reliability of cognition, and the coordination of means and ends across the natural world. In this philosophical context, metaphysical discourse about divine principles is not epistemically void but methodologically robust. The existence of *Īśvara* is neither dogmatically asserted nor uncritically believed; it is inferred in a manner structurally similar to how modern science infers unobservable entities like electrons or dark matter—through their explanatory power and predictive success. The Indian tradition thereby maintains a form of metaphysical realism that remains rationally defensible even as it transcends empirical verifiability. Far from being an obsolete relic, *Īśvara* is construed as an ontological and ethical necessity, a postulate that renders the universe intelligible both causally and morally. Thus, Russell's blanket dismissal of religious or metaphysical language as meaningless appears, from this comparative perspective, as an artifact of a particular intellectual milieu—one shaped by disillusionment with dogmatic Western theism, but ill-equipped to engage with more sophisticated traditions of metaphysical reasoning. Indian philosophical systems do not conflate the non-empirical with the irrational. They present a layered ontology and a pluralistic epistemology that allow reasoned engagement with questions beyond the reach of the senses. In this light, Russell's critique, though incisive in its own domain, lacks the universality it often claims. It underestimates the philosophical depth of traditions that have long navigated the terrain of the non-empirical with intellectual rigor and methodological precision.

## The God Collusion

Richard Dawkins's 'Ultimate Boeing 747' argument posits that invoking God as an explanation for cosmic complexity is self-defeating: a deity capable of designing the universe would, by necessity, be more complex than the universe itself, thereby increasing explanatory burden rather than alleviating it. This objection, grounded in a probabilistic interpretation of explanatory parsimony, assumes that God must be a complex, contingent entity whose existence is less probable than the natural phenomena he is posited to explain. Coupled with evolutionary theory's capacity to account for biological complexity via non-teleological mechanisms, Dawkins concludes that theism is both explanatorily redundant and statistically implausible. In his speech at the Edinburgh International Science Festival in 1992,

> *"Faith is the great cop-out, the great excuse to evade the need to think and evaluate evidence. Faith is belief in spite of, even perhaps because of, the lack of evidence."*

Yet what Dawkins dismisses as blind belief is, within the *Nyāya* tradition, a carefully reasoned metaphysical conclusion grounded in systematic logic and empirical observation. In *Nyāya* metaphysics, *Īśvara* is not an artifact-like being composed of parts or emergent properties, but a non-composite, eternal, and omniscient conscious agent. Complexity, as understood in the *Nyāya* ontology, is a predicate of *kārya* (effect)—entities that are spatially or temporally divisible. *Īśvara*, as *akārya* (uncaused cause), is not contingent on constituents and therefore not subject to compositional complexity. The inference to *Īśvara* proceeds from the observed regularities of nature—causal uniformity, purposive arrangement, and the intelligibility of moral causation—which, according to *Nyāya* logic, entail a conscious regulator (*niyāmaka*). The structure of this inference is formalized as a warranted metaphysical generalization from empirical invariance. The probabilistic model of complexity Dawkins applies presumes a naturalistic ontology and conflates explanatory simplicity with physical reducibility. For *Nyāya*, explanatory simplicity lies in causal sufficiency and non-redundancy, not in empirical tractability. The appeal to *Īśvara* is justified not because complexity is difficult to explain, but because certain forms of regularity—for instance, the coordination of moral outcomes via *karma-phala*—require intentional agency.

The critique that evolution renders God obsolete is also inapplicable here. *Nyāya* does not require fixed species or special creation. Evolutionary mechanisms can be accepted as secondary causes (*upādāna-kāraṇa*) operating under the purview of *Īśvara's* general governance. Biological complexity, including speciation and adaptation, does not preclude the existence of a primary cause who initiates and sustains natural laws. Moreover, karmic causation—which governs moral and experiential outcomes—does not conflict with evolutionary biology, as it functions on a different causal axis. Dawkins's epistemological assumptions are also narrower than those sanctioned by *Nyāya*. Restricting valid cognition (*pramā*) to empirical perception and scientific modeling excludes reliable verbal testimony (*śabda*) and postulation (*arthāpatti*), both of which are accepted in *Nyāya* as legitimate *pramāṇas* under conditions of non-contradiction and necessity. *Nyāya* admits exceptional cases of *alaukika-pratyakṣa* (non-ordinary perception), such as yogic cognition, under strict criteria of mental discipline and testimonial convergence—not as fideistic commitments but as qualified forms of direct knowledge. Theism as articulated in *Nyāya* is therefore immune to Dawkins's critique on multiple fronts: *Īśvara* is not complex in the way the critique presumes; the inference to *Īśvara* does not violate parsimony given the explanatory role played in both causal and ethical domains; and the epistemological foundations of theism in this context are broader and more formally articulated than allowed by Dawkins's empiricist framework. As such, the 'Ultimate Boeing 747' gambit misfires when directed against a metaphysically simple, logically inferred, and epistemologically integrated conception of divinity such as that advanced in the *Nyāya* tradition.

## The Staccato Silences of Science

Contemporary science, while often construed as an empirically grounded and methodologically self-contained enterprise, is undergirded by a series of philosophical presuppositions that are not themselves scientifically demonstrable. Its epistemic framework is rooted in methodological naturalism—the commitment to explaining phenomena through natural causes without recourse to supernatural agency—and an operationalist stance that privileges testability, replicability, and predictive power. Yet this ostensibly neutral methodology tacitly relies on metaphysical assumptions regarding the structure of reality, the reliability of human cognition, and the ontological status of causal regularities. A foundational presupposition of the scientific enterprise is the intelligibility and law-governed nature of the cosmos. That the universe operates according to consistent principles—often expressed as mathematical laws—is not a conclusion derived from scientific data but a precondition for the possibility of empirical inquiry. This assumption of uniformity across time and space, known in philosophy of science as the *"principle of the uniformity of nature,"* cannot be empirically verified without presupposing it in advance. Thus, the very practice of induction—inferring general laws from finite observations—rests on a metaphysical commitment that science itself cannot justify without circularity, as famously noted in Hume's critique of induction. Moreover, scientific realism—the view that theoretical entities posited by scientific theories (for instance, electrons, fields, genes) refer to actual constituents of the world—entails a commitment to a correspondence theory of truth and to a mind-independent reality. While anti-realist or instrumentalist accounts (for instance, Bas van Fraassen's constructive empiricism) challenge this view, much of scientific practice operates under the realist assumption that theories aim to describe the way the world is, not merely to organize observations. Yet the ontological status of theoretical constructs remains a live issue in the philosophy of science.

The methodological preference for causal explanation further reflects metaphysical commitments. Scientific explanations typically seek to identify regular, lawlike relations among variables, often modeled mathematically. However, the nature of causation—whether it is deterministic, probabilistic, or merely correlational—is not settled by empirical data alone. Indeed, various interpretations of causality (for instance, Humean regularity theory, counterfactual accounts, and mechanistic models) reflect differing metaphysical stances. Science also excludes final causes or teleological explanation in favour of efficient causality, a move traceable to the mechanistic revolution of the seventeenth century. While successful in domains such as physics and biology, this restriction arguably limits the explanatory scope of science with respect to phenomena like consciousness, normativity, and intentionality. Finally, science presupposes the epistemic reliability of human cognitive faculties—perception, memory, reason—without being able to justify them through scientific methods alone. Evolutionary arguments for cognitive reliability face their own limitations, particularly when applied to abstract reasoning or theoretical physics, which are far removed from survival-oriented cognition. In sum, modern science proceeds with methodological rigor but rests upon a metaphysical substratum that includes presuppositions about order, intelligibility, causality, and cognitive access to truth. A comprehensive understanding of science thus requires philosophical reflection on these foundational commitments that structure the very possibility of scientific inquiry. Richard Feynman once famously said, in the 15$^{th}$ annual meeting of the National Science Teachers Association in New York City in 1966,

> *"Science is the belief in the ignorance of experts. ... Science doesn't teach anything; experience teaches it."*

Yet for all its explanatory success, science is marked by what might be called *staccato silences*: abrupt epistemic gaps where inquiry ceases not because the question is incoherent, but because the tools of science are methodologically unequipped to engage it. These silences are not merely temporary lacunae in empirical knowledge, waiting to be filled by future research. Rather, they signal structural boundaries within scientific rationality itself. Questions concerning the intrinsic nature of consciousness, the first-person perspective, the grounding of normativity, or the ontological status of mathematical entities do not admit of empirical resolution in any straightforward sense. While functional correlates of consciousness can be mapped, the *qualia*—the irreducibly subjective dimension of experience—resist third-person description. Similarly, while neuroscience can track neural substrates of moral judgment, it cannot derive or adjudicate the normative force of moral obligations. In such cases, science provides correlates, but not explanations in the full philosophical sense. These domains fall outside the purview of scientific method not because they are illusory, but because they involve modes of knowing or being that science does not—and cannot—methodologically accommodate. These silences are not failings but indicators of discipline-specific scope. The scientific method, by design, abstracts from subjective experience, final causes, or existential meaning to focus on patterns of regularity and causal interaction. But the very act of abstraction entails exclusion. Thus, when science is treated as a totalizing epistemology, these exclusions are misrepresented as non-existence. The metaphysical, the aesthetic, the ethical, and the contemplative are not eliminated but muted. A silence becomes mistaken for a negation. The staccato rhythm of scientific advance—punctuated by moments of discovery and long plateaus of interpretive suspension—reveals this paradox: the more precisely science speaks, the more sharply we perceive what it does not say. In this light, philosophy, particularly metaphysics and phenomenology, remains not an archaic precursor to science, but a necessary partner—concerned with the very questions science leaves unanswered or systematically excludes. To recognize the staccato silences of science is not to undermine its authority, but to clarify its boundaries, and thereby preserve space for forms of inquiry that exceed the reach of empirical method without abandoning rigor or intelligibility.

## Bang Went the Cosmos

The modern scientific narrative of cosmic origins, dominated by the Big Bang model, posits that the universe as we know it—space, time, matter, and energy—emerged approximately 13.8 billion years ago from a state of extreme density and temperature. This model, supported by cosmic microwave background radiation, redshift data, and large-scale structure formation, suggests not only that the universe had a temporal beginning, but that time itself began with this event. Unlike earlier Newtonian conceptions of an infinite, eternal cosmos, contemporary cosmology now speaks in terms of a *singularity*—a boundary to physical laws beyond which conventional descriptions break down. For many philosophers and theologians, this dramatic convergence of time and matter at a single origin point lends renewed weight to classical metaphysical arguments for creation. If the universe had a beginning, they argue, it demands a cause. And since the cause cannot be part of space-time, it must be transcendent—uncaused, changeless, and immaterial. Such reasoning echoes the cosmological argument in various traditions, asserting that the finitude of the cosmos implies a First Cause beyond it. This line of thinking finds intriguing resonance in Indian philosophy, particularly in the *Nyāya* school, which advances a sophisticated cosmological argument grounded in causal inference and epistemological rigor. *Nyāya* holds that every event or composite entity must have a cause, and that causes are of three kinds: material (*upādāna*), instrumental (*nimitta*), and efficient or final (*prayojana*). Crucially, it argues that the existence of contingent, mutable, and composite entities in the world points to a permanent, non-composite, and causally sufficient ground. This is the *Īśvara* of *Nyāya*—a supreme conscious agent who, unlike the created world, is not made of parts, does not change, and exists necessarily. The existence of change and multiplicity in the universe, which science reveals in extraordinary detail—from particle decay to galactic motion—only reinforces *Nyāya*'s conclusion: that what changes must be grounded in that which does not. From this perspective, the Big Bang does not displace God but draws attention to the finitude and contingency of the cosmos—features that, for *Nyāya* thinkers, strengthen the case for *Īśvara's* existence.

Moreover, Indian thought is uniquely equipped to integrate metaphysical causality with scientific models without collapsing one into the other. In classical Advaita Vedānta, the Supreme Reality—*Brahman*—is absolute, beyond all limitations of time, space, and causality. Although Brahman itself remains unchanged and without attributes, it appears as the manifest universe through *māyā*, an inscrutable cosmic principle. *Māyā* is not merely "illusion" in the sense of simple falsehood, but rather the power by which Brahman, though unmanifest, is experienced as the world of multiplicity. However, this manifestation is only apparent and does not involve any real change in Brahman; from the standpoint of ultimate reality, only Brahman truly exists, while the perceived universe arises and persists within the realm of *māyā*. *Nyāya* philosophy, being a theistic and realist system, does not accept *māyā* as a cosmic veiling or illusory power. Instead, it affirms the real existence of both an unchanging, omniscient *Īśvara* (Supreme God) and the changing, pluralistic empirical world. In *Nyāya*, *Īśvara* is the efficient cause of the world, but the world's reality and distinctness from *Īśvara* are fully acknowledged. Unlike Advaita Vedānta, *Nyāya* does not posit *māyā* as a principle that obscures or projects the world; rather, the world is genuinely real, and *Īśvara* and the world maintain a clear ontological distinction. Thus, *Nyāya* maintains a strict realist and theistic dualism without reliance on *māyā* as a veiling or manifesting power.

The Big Bang theory characterizes time as emergent—coming into being with the universe rather than existing beforehand. This notion aligns conceptually with the classical Advaita Vedānta view that the ultimate reality (Brahman) transcends time, which arises only as part of the manifested empirical universe through *māyā*. However, this differs from *Nyāya* philosophy, which tends to treat time as a real, independent entity and affirms a theistic realism where an unchanging *Īśvara* and the changing world co-exist objectively, without time being seen as emergent or illusory. In *Nyāya-Vaiśeṣika* philosophy, *kāla* (time) is accepted as the sixth *dravya*—a real, eternal, and omnipresent substance, though beyond direct perception. It is the silent framework on which all events unfold. Annaṃbhaṭṭa defines *kāla* as the special cause behind our use of terms like *past*, *present*, and *future*. What has happened is the past, what is happening is the present, and what is yet to happen is the future. *Kāla* thus enables not only the flow of action but also our understanding of it. Ācārya Viśvanātha Nyāyapañcānana mentions in his work *Bhāṣāpariccheda* the definition of *kāla* as

> जन्यानां जनकः कालो जगतामाश्रयो मतः।
> परापरत्वधिहेतुः क्षणादिः स्यादुपाधितः।।
>
> *Translation*: Time is the cause of things that are produced and is considered to be the substratum of the universe. It is the cause of the notion of priority and posteriority. It appears as measurable elements like moments owing to its limiting adjuncts.

There is a similar definition in the *Vaiśeṣikasūtropaskāra* (7.1.25) by Śaṅkaramiśra,

> परापरव्यतिकरयौगपद्यायौगपद्यचिरक्षिप्रप्रत्ययकारणं द्रव्यं कालः
>
> *Translation*: Time (*kāla*) is the substance (*dravya*) that causes the notions of succession and simultaneity, of long and short duration, and of the sequence between prior and posterior events.

*Īśvara*, being causally prior to time, is not temporally "before" the universe in the way one event precedes another. Rather, *Īśvara* is *ontologically* prior: that from which time emerges, but who is not subject to temporal succession himself. This idea is further enriched by integrating certain Buddhist insights, such as Ācārya Nāgārjuna's doctrine of emptiness (*śūnyatā*), with the metaphysical implications of cosmogenesis. While Ācārya Nāgārjuna famously deconstructs all fixed ontologies, he does so not to deny causal order, but to reveal the interdependent, contingent, and non-substantial nature of all phenomena. The Big Bang as a physical theory does not describe a thing in itself but marks the limit of current models. That the universe emerged from a state of "nothing"—not nothing in an absolute sense, but rather a state beyond spacetime and physical description—resonates with Ācārya Nāgārjuna's idea that ultimate reality is empty of intrinsic nature yet still functionally real. When *Nyāya*'s causal *Īśvara* is read in dialogue with Ācārya Nāgārjuna's emptiness, what emerges is not a contradiction but a complementarity: a view in which the ground of being is neither brute material nor nihilistic void, but a non-composite source from which both form and temporality emerge. This synergy finds echoes in the idea of *sūkṣma-vastu*—subtle reality—as discussed in various Indian cosmological schemata, suggesting that what precedes the gross universe is a subtle substratum, imperceptible yet ontologically rich.

At the same time, a note of philosophical caution is warranted. As George Coyne, former director of the Vatican Observatory, wisely noted, theology must remain open to the evolving discoveries of science. To treat any current model—whether the Big Bang or quantum loop cosmology—as the final metaphysical statement is premature. The Big Bang model, though dominant, has itself undergone refinements and faces open questions: what caused the inflationary period, what lies beyond the Planck epoch, and whether the initial singularity is even a physical entity or a mathematical artifact. The integration of metaphysics with cosmology should therefore remain dialectical, not dogmatic—rooted in principled reasoning but responsive to empirical developments. Indian traditions, especially Hindu cosmology, have historically embodied this flexibility. The idea of cyclical time—*kalpas*, *manvantaras*, and Lord Brahmā's day and night—posits that the universe goes through infinite cycles of creation, dissolution, and rebirth, and that there are various scales of temporality. In such a view, the Big Bang could be interpreted as the beginning of the current cycle, not of time per se. This allows for a congruence with observational data without collapsing into literalism or denying the metaphysical scope of these ancient narratives. What distinguishes the Indic approach, then, is its capacity to hold scientific temporality within a larger metaphysical framework. The beginning of this particular cosmic expansion—the current *sṛṣṭi*—need not conflict with the deeper idea of a cyclical or infinite cosmos. As Sri Ādi Śaṅkarācārya remarks in his commentaries, beginning and end are relational constructs within the field of *vyāvahārika* (conventional reality), while from the standpoint of *pāramārthika* (ultimate reality), time itself is a manifestation. Similarly, *Nyāya* does not insist on a linear or infinite timeline as a theological requirement; its concern is with the causal ground of temporal processes, not their specific durations or configurations. For instance, in the *Saptapadārthī* of Śivāditya – the first syncretic work of *Nyāya* and *Vaiśeṣika*, we have

> आदित्यपरिवर्तनोत्पद्यपरत्वापरत्वासमवायिकारणाधारः परत्वापरत्वानधिकरणं कालः

*Translation*: Time (*kāla*) is the substratum of the non-inherent cause of priority and posteriority, which arise from the movement of the sun. It is the locus of these temporal relations.

This elegant formulation does not merely define time as an abstract continuum, but grounds it in experience — as a relational category born of motion, perception, and causality. Time, for *Nyāya-Vaiśeṣika*, is not a passive backdrop but an active ontological principle: the unseen foundation upon which the rhythm of succession and simultaneity plays out. Thus, the Big Bang, rather than displacing Indic metaphysics, invites renewed philosophical engagement. It encourages a reconsideration of ancient arguments—not as relics to be defended or dismissed, but as living frameworks capable of dialoguing with cosmology, theoretical physics, and contemporary metaphysics. *Īśvara* as the non-composite initiator of time and space, when viewed in light of a temporally bounded universe, emerges not as an optional addendum but as a concept with renewed philosophical necessity. The Big Bang may mark the beginning of observable time, but it also reopens the oldest of questions: what stands beyond time, what gives rise to order, and how can something arise at all? In this inquiry, science and metaphysics are not opponents but interlocutors—and Indian philosophy, with its rich tools of inference, epistemology, and metaphysical nuance, remains uniquely poised to contribute to that dialogue.

## Fine-Tuning the Universe

Among the most provocative arguments in contemporary philosophy of science is the *fine-tuning argument*, which observes that the fundamental constants of nature—the values of gravitational force, the cosmological constant, the strengths of the electromagnetic and nuclear interactions, the ratio of proton to electron mass, and others—fall within extraordinarily narrow ranges that permit the existence of life. Were these constants even slightly different, the universe would either have expanded too quickly for matter to form, collapsed back into a singularity, or never produced the chemical diversity required for biological systems. Sir Fred Hoyle, once said, in his article titled *The Universe: Past and Present Reflections*, published in the Annual Review of Astronomy and Astrophysics in 1982,

> *"Would you not say to yourself, in whatever language supercalculating intellects use, 'Some supercalculating intellect must have designed the properties of the carbon atom, otherwise the chance of my finding such an atom through the blind forces of nature would be less than 1 part in $10^{40000}$'. Of course you would. ... I have always been intrigued by the remarkable relation of the 7.65 Mev energy level in the nucleus of $^{12}C$ to the 7.12 Mev level in $^{16}O$. If you wanted to produce carbon and oxygen in roughly equal quantities by stellar nucleosynthesis, these are the two levels you would have to fix ... A common sense interpretation of the facts suggests that a super-intellect has monkeyed with physics, as well as with chemistry and biology, and that there are no blind forces worth speaking about in nature."*

The number and specificity of such conditions fine-tuned to permit life have led many, including Hoyle, to reconsider whether the universe is an accident at all. His musings do not confirm a doctrine of creation, but they reopen the ancient question: Is cosmos merely a dance of particles and forces, or is there an underlying intelligence — a *ṛta*— that guides its emergence? For instance, the cosmological constant is fine-tuned to an accuracy of 1 part in $10^{120}$—an adjustment so delicate that it defies intuitive comprehension. From this, proponents of the design inference argue that the most plausible explanation is the existence of a conscious, intentional agent—a cosmic architect who tuned the dials of reality to permit life, complexity, and consciousness. Yet the fine-tuning argument has not gone unchallenged. One common response appeals to the multiverse hypothesis: that our universe is but one among an immense, possibly infinite, ensemble of universes, each with its own set of parameters. In such a framework, it is no surprise that some universe—ours—has the right conditions for life; we simply find ourselves in the one where observation is possible. This is often combined with the anthropic principle, which states that any valid explanation for the universe must account for the existence of conscious observers. Just as no one is surprised to find they were born on a planet where oxygen exists, we should not be surprised to find ourselves in a universe where life is possible. Critics of fine-tuning further point out that many parameters cannot yet be mathematically normalized, making probability assignments speculative at best. In this view, the design inference is premature—a leap to metaphysics based on a snapshot of incomplete physics.

However, from the standpoint of classical Indian philosophy, particularly the *Nyāya* school, the design argument is neither speculative nor anthropocentric. Rather, it is a natural extension of inference from order (*vyavasthā*) to a conscious lawgiver. *Nyāya's* epistemology recognizes *anumāna*, or inference, as a legitimate source of knowledge when there is consistent concomitance (*vyāpti*) between phenomena. When we observe order—systematic relationships, predictability, coordination—especially in domains that are not the product of human activity, we infer a non-human, intelligent cause. The sheer intelligibility of natural law, the precision of cosmological parameters, and the logical structure of the physical world collectively suggest not randomness but order. For the *Naiyāyika*, this grasping order is indicative of a supreme regulating intelligence: *Īśvara*. In *Nyāya* metaphysics, *Īśvara* is not merely an artisan fashioning the world from pre-existing materials, but is the supremely intelligent and omniscient efficient cause (*nimitta-kāraṇa*) of the universe. He governs and sustains the orderly unfolding of the cosmos, ensuring that the results of karmic actions—mediated by the unseen potency known as *apūrva* or *adṛṣṭa*—are delivered according to an infallible moral order. While matter (atoms) and souls are eternal and not created by *Īśvara*, it is through his knowledge and will that they are combined and directed to produce the manifest world. Thus, *Īśvara* is the unifying principle that integrates the precise workings of the physical universe with the distribution of karmic effects, but *tat* is not regarded as the underlying material substratum (*adhiṣṭhāna*) of all existence in the way Advaita Vedānta conceives Brahman. The apparent fine-tuning of constants is not arbitrary; it is the natural expression of a law-governed cosmos that is simultaneously physical and ethical, mechanical and intentional. This does not mean Indian cosmology insists on a single universe created once and for all. On the contrary, the Puranic and Vedic traditions articulate a pluralistic, cyclical cosmology in which universes emerge, dissolve, and reemerge through endless cycles of *kalpas*—vast spans of cosmic time governed by the rhythmic breathing of Brahmā, the creator god. These cycles do not negate the fine-tuning argument; rather, they embed it within a larger temporal framework. Each cycle, each universe, may possess its own laws and constants, just as each life carries its karmic legacy. The presence of multiple *lokas* (worlds) and cosmic regions in Hindu thought aligns conceptually with multiverse models, but unlike the atheistic implications often drawn from the multiverse hypothesis, Indic cosmology retains a teleological dimension. The multiplicity of universes is not a hedge against theism but an expression of its plenitude. *Īśvara* presides not over a singular, isolated creation but over a complex, generative, and morally embedded cosmos.

Moreover, the Indic conception of design is not anthropocentric. The universe is not fine-tuned solely to support human life but to uphold *dharma*—the intrinsic order that governs beings according to their nature. Life, in its manifold forms, is only one expression of this greater order. That the universe permits consciousness, ethical agency, and liberation (*mokṣa*) is more significant than the mere biochemical possibility of carbon-based organisms. Thus, the fine-tuning of the cosmos is not merely about probability; it is about *prakṛti*—the interweaving of matter, consciousness, and purpose in a world that is not accidental but intelligible at multiple levels. When modern cosmology reveals that infinitesimal deviations in initial conditions would render the universe sterile or chaotic, it inadvertently points to what *Nyāya* and other Indian systems have maintained for millennia: that order is not self-explanatory. To invoke natural law as the explanation of itself is circular; laws, to be meaningful, require a lawgiver. If nature is governed by intelligible principles, and those principles are neither self-caused nor arbitrary, then the rational conclusion, according to Indian logic, is to posit a conscious, non-contingent ground. The multiverse hypothesis does not refute this; it simply multiplies the field over which such an agent would operate. Just as the presence of many functioning machines increases our inference to intelligent design, the existence of multiple finely structured universes enhances, rather than diminishes, the inference to *Īśvara*. The fine-tuning argument, when viewed through this lens, becomes not a singular defence of divine existence, but a facet of a broader metaphysical vision—one in which the universe is not an accident but an unfolding of intelligible, karmically informed, and spiritually significant order. Science can map the constants; philosophy must ask why such constants exist at all. The *Nyāya* tradition, with its commitment to rational inference, causal analysis, and theological realism, provides a compelling response—one that not only withstands modern critiques but deepens them by embedding cosmic precision within a moral and ontological framework. In a world where the smallest constants govern the largest outcomes, where the weight of an electron or the curvature of space determines the possibility of thought itself, the argument from order is no longer a medieval curiosity—it is an unavoidable question.

## Quantum Cosmology and Theological Humility

In the unfolding dialogue between cosmology and theology, few areas are more intellectually provocative than the frontier of quantum cosmology—a field that dares to ask not merely what happened after the Big Bang, but what conditions, if any, preceded it. Here, the traditional narrative of a singular explosive beginning gives way to quantum models that blur the line between origin and structure, causality and probability. One of the most notable contributions in this space is the Hartle–Hawking '*no-boundary*' proposal, which postulates that the universe may be finite but without boundaries—akin to the surface of a sphere, which is limited yet has no edge. According to this model, space and time emerge smoothly from a quantum state, eliminating the need for a singular moment of creation or a sharp initial condition. In doing so, such a framework appears to sidestep the classical notion of a Creator who brings the universe into being *ex nihilo*—from nothing. If time itself emerges from within the universe, the very question of "what came before?" becomes incoherent. Thus, to some, the quantum model removes the metaphysical space in which God was traditionally situated. But this conclusion is more a reflection of theological overreach than of the limitations of divine agency. The history of theology—both in the West and in Indic traditions—has repeatedly demonstrated the dangers of tying metaphysical claims too tightly to prevailing scientific models. What is seen today as cutting-edge physics may tomorrow be regarded as a useful approximation or even a discarded theory. As with the Newtonian clockwork universe that once inspired deistic interpretations of a remote, non-intervening God, only to be overturned by relativity and quantum mechanics, so too must theologies grounded in cosmology practice a kind of metaphysical humility. The divine need not reside in the gaps of scientific knowledge; it need not be summoned as a placeholder for what remains unexplained. Rather, the deeper theological task is to understand the divine as the condition for intelligibility itself—not a causal agent operating *within* the framework of space and time, but that by which space, time, and causality are possible.

In Indian philosophical terms, this distinction is both familiar and instructive. The *Nyāya* school, which defends a rationally grounded theism, does not posit *Īśvara* as a mechanical originator launching the cosmos from temporal zero. Instead, *Īśvara* is conceived as a timeless, non-composite, and omniscient being whose agency initiates and regulates the processes by which universes come into being. Even in cosmologies that envision the universe as beginningless and cyclic—as in the Vedic model of *kalpas* and *manvantaras*—*Īśvara* is not a craftsman bound by time but the ontological ground and sustaining intelligence of those cycles. Whether the universe had a singular beginning, multiple iterations, or no temporal origin at all, the role of *Īśvara* remains consistent: not temporal cause but necessary condition. The Hartle–Hawking model, for all its elegance, does not explain why the laws of quantum gravity take the form they do, why mathematical structures give rise to experience, or why the universe is intelligible at all. These are metaphysical, not physical, questions. Hawking famously wrote, in *A Brief History of Time: From the Big Bang to Black Holes*,

> *"Even if there is only one possible unified theory, it is just a set of rules and equations. What is it that breathes fire into the equations and makes a universe for them to describe? The*

> *usual approach of science of constructing a mathematical model cannot answer the questions of why there should be a universe for the model to describe. Why does the universe go to all the bother of existing?"*

Moreover, the 'no-boundary' idea relies on the formalism of imaginary time and path integrals in quantum mechanics—concepts that stretch our ordinary understanding of physical causality. The model does not so much deny the possibility of metaphysical grounding as render it orthogonal to the language of mathematical physics. Here again, the Indian tradition provides conceptual clarity. The distinction between *vyāvahārika* (conventional reality) and *pāramārthika* (ultimate reality), central to Vedānta, allows for a multi-layered understanding of causality and being. The physical universe, with its origin structures and mathematical symmetries, belongs to the domain of *vyāvahārika*—a valid and coherent level of discourse. But it does not exhaust what reality is. *Pāramārthika* points to that which underlies and transcends the manifest: pure being, or *sat*, from which all appearances arise. Whether the cosmos begins or is eternal, its intelligibility and coherence presuppose a foundation that is not itself empirical.

This layered understanding also guards against theological overstatement. One need not force scientific cosmology to validate ancient metaphysics, nor bend metaphysics into speculative physics. Instead, one can recognize that the mathematical models of quantum cosmology are efforts to describe the internal consistency of the universe's structure—not its metaphysical basis. Theological humility, then, is not a surrender of depth but an affirmation of scale. It allows metaphysics to engage science not as an adversary or competitor, but as a legitimate and powerful method of describing *how* the world operates, without pretending to answer the deeper question of *why* there is a world at all, or what gives rise to the conditions for its knowability. Indeed, the Indic notion of *adhiṣṭhāna*—a substratum that enables all change while remaining itself unchanged—may offer a helpful metaphor. The quantum fields, spacetime geometries, and probabilistic structures described by physics may be likened to the waves on the surface, while *adhisthāna* represents the oceanic depth from which they emerge. This substratum is not a material thing, but the enabling condition for materiality and temporality. It is not bound by the laws it sustains. In this light, *Īśvara* is not to be found in the equations, nor absent from them, but beyond the domain of what equations, however sophisticated, can articulate. The same can be said of *śūnyatā* in the *Madhyamaka* tradition—a profound 'emptiness' that is not nihil but freedom from fixed essence. As has been written in Ācārya Nāgārjuna's *Mūlamadhyamakakārikā*,

> *"Neither from itself nor from another, nor from both, nor without a cause, does anything whatever, anywhere arise."*

Quantum cosmology, with its suggestion that time and causality may emerge from a more fundamental indeterminacy, may inadvertently echo such metaphysical insights, albeit within a mathematical and physical idiom.

In acknowledging the possible self-contained nature of the universe, theology need not retreat. Rather, it must refine its claims. The divine is not a temporal antecedent but an ontological prerequisite; not a cosmic craftsman moving parts, but the logos of intelligibility itself. The place of *Īśvara* is not in the ignition of the universe but in the fact that it is rational, law-bound, and capable of being grasped at all. Quantum cosmology may close off certain models of divine action tied to temporal beginnings, but it opens a deeper horizon in which the philosophical necessity of a grounding principle remains undiminished. Ultimately, the lesson is one of restraint and reverence. Theology that roots itself in enduring metaphysical insight—rather than in the momentary scaffolding of empirical models—can maintain integrity without falling into irrelevance. And science, for all its reach, performs best when it recognizes the boundaries of its language. Between the two lies not a battleground, but a conversation—a shared recognition that the cosmos, however mathematically describable, evokes a sense of order and intelligibility that science may map, but not fully explain. In this shared silence lies the possibility of wisdom.

## Absence of Faith or Faith in Absence?

In the Western philosophical imagination, theism and non-theism form a clean binary: either one believes in a God—often conceived as a personal, omnipotent, omniscient being—or one does not. This dichotomy has shaped centuries of metaphysical and theological discourse, sharpening into direct contestations between belief and disbelief. Yet in the Indian philosophical landscape, such binaries dissolve into a far more nuanced spectrum. Here, the question *"Do Indian non-theists reject God?"* is not merely rhetorical or self-evident; it is profoundly layered, shaped by linguistic precision, metaphysical granularity, and a tradition of intellectual pluralism that allows multiple ontologies to coexist without contradiction. The Indian non-theistic schools, while often rejecting the personal creator-God (*Īśvara*) as posited by the *Nyāya-Vaiśeṣika* or Vedānta systems, do not always deny divinity in totality. Rather, they reconfigure, reinterpret, or even absorb the idea of ultimate reality into their own metaphysical terms. As such, non-theism in India does not always entail a denial of transcendence—it often expresses itself through alternative vocabularies of sacred ground, cosmic order, or ineffable consciousness. Take, for example, the *Yogācāra* school of

Mahāyāna Buddhism. At first glance, this is an unequivocally non-theistic tradition. It denies the existence of a permanent self (*ātman*), a transcendent creator, or any ultimate, enduring substratum of being. Instead, it advances a philosophy of mind—*vijñaptimātra* or "consciousness-only"—in which all phenomena are understood as manifestations or projections of consciousness, shaped by karmic imprints and mental conditioning. As mentioned in the *Viṃśatikāvṛtti* (3.2), we have

> महायाने त्रैधातुकं विज्ञानमात्रं व्यवस्थित्यते
>
> *Translation*: In the *Mahāyāna* tradition, the threefold world (*traidhātuka*) is established as mere cognition (*vijñaptimātra*).

Within this framework, there is no room for an autonomous divine agent who wills the cosmos into being. Yet, what Yogācāra rejects in classical theism it reconfigures into a subtler, phenomenological understanding of transcendence.

Consciousness, especially in its purified, non-dual form as *prajñā*, takes on the qualities of luminosity, ineffability, and ontological grounding often attributed to the divine in other systems. Some later Buddhist thinkers even speak of an *ālambana*, a metaphysical support or basis for realization, which, while not personal, functions analogously to the sustaining power of *Īśvara*. When interpreted through this lens, the denial of a creator-God is not a denial of foundational reality, but a refusal to anthropomorphize it. Indeed, modern Hindu-Buddhist dialogue has seen thinkers such as Gandhi and Aurobindo interpret this 'atheism' not as negation but as refinement—Gandhi's inclusivism saw the Buddha as one who realized the divine without naming it, and Ācārya Madhusūdana Sarasvatī's synthesis of Advaita Vedānta with *bhakti* allowed for diverse experiential and philosophical paths to the same transcendent reality, recognizing that ultimate truth may be approached through silence as well as devotion. In the *Mahimnastotraṭīkā* by Ācārya Puṣpadantāchārya, we have the verse,

> भूतिभूषितदेहाय द्विजराजेन राजते।
> एकात्मने नमो नित्यं हरये च हराय च।।
>
> *Translation*: Salutations always to the One who is adorned with sacred ash, who shines through the king of birds (*Garuda*), who is the one essence (of all), to both Hari (Vishnu) and Hara (Shiva).

Jainism, another classical non-theistic system, offers a different but equally sophisticated position. Jain metaphysics denies any creator-God and posits instead a cosmos governed by its own internal laws: *dharma* as the principle of motion, *adharma* as that of rest, and the soul (*jīva*) as inherently divine in its pure, liberated state. Yet Jainism does not reject the possibility of divine-like beings; it venerates *tīrthaṅkaras*—liberated souls who, though not creators, serve as exemplars and guides. Its doctrine of *syādvāda*, or the principle of conditioned predication, allows any metaphysical claim—including the existence or non-existence of *Īśvara*—to be true in one sense, false in another, and indeterminate in a third. According to *syādvāda*, one could say that God exists from the standpoint of devotional experience, does not exist from the standpoint of ultimate ontology, and is both existent and non-existent when considered across contexts. This sophisticated perspectivalism does not reduce theism and non-theism to subjective opinions, but situates them within a broader epistemology of provisional truths. As such, the Naiyāyika's inference of *Īśvara* from order (*vyavasthā*) and causal regularity may be valid within a particular logical framework, even if the Jaina metaphysics does not recognize a single creator-being. It is not that Jainism merely tolerates theistic thought; it absorbs and reframes it through its logic of conditionality.

Underlying this pluralism is the broader Indian civilizational ethos that refuses to absolutize metaphysical claims without qualification. The classical classification of philosophical schools into *āstika* and *nāstika*—terms often misread as 'theist' and 'atheist'—does not hinge on belief in God but on acceptance of Vedic authority. Thus, Sāṃkhya, which does not affirm a creator-God, remains an *āstika* system, while Buddhism, despite its immense spiritual depth, is labeled *nāstika* for rejecting Vedic revelation. But even this binary yields to further nuance. Many *āstika* schools hold divergent views about *Īśvara*. Pūrva *Mīmāṃsā*, for instance, insists on the eternal authority of the Vedas and the efficacy of ritual but does not require a divine agent to sustain them. Ritual, in this view, functions autonomously through *apūrva*—the invisible potency generated by action. The cosmos has an intrinsic moral order, not one imposed by an external deity. Similarly, in Advaita Vedānta, *Īśvara* is real only at the level of empirical truth (*vyāvahārika*), while ultimately, in the non-dual *pāramārthika* sense, all distinctions collapse into Brahman, which transcends personality and form. Thus, within even so-called 'theistic' traditions, God can be understood not as an independent Lord but as a symbolic expression of ultimate unity or ground of being. This metaphysical openness allows Indian traditions to admit a range of theological vocabularies—some personal, some impersonal, some metaphorical. One may encounter *Īśvara* as a moral governor, a metaphysical principle, a yogic object of meditation, or a linguistic pointer to the ineffable. Even when rejected in one register, *Īśvara* is often retained in another. As Sri Ādi Śaṅkarācārya writes, *Īśvara* is real *"so long as the world is real,"* suggesting a provisional theology that is functionally useful but ultimately dissolves in non-duality.

This flexibility does not dilute meaning; it deepens it. It allows for worship and non-duality, for ritual and renunciation, for devotion and philosophical silence, all within a single ontological framework.

This pluralism is not an accidental tolerance born of cultural politeness; it is embedded in the very method of Indian reasoning: *vāda-vicāra*—dialogue and critical examination. In this context, to ask whether Indian non-theists 'reject' God is to oversimplify a conversation that is, by design, open-ended and recursive. The denial of a creator-God is not always a metaphysical negation; it may be a re-description, a refusal to prematurely crystallize what is ultimately beyond concept. The debate is rarely between belief and disbelief in the Western sense. It is between different ways of speaking about what transcends speech. In fact, many Indian schools are united not by theological uniformity but by shared commitments to epistemological discipline, rational dialogue, and experiential verification. One need not posit a divine legislator to speak of *dharma*, nor a personal God to invoke moral responsibility. The cosmos may be self-regulating, yet still infused with sacred purpose. The contemporary relevance of this framework is profound. In an age increasingly polarized by rigid belief systems and reactive atheisms, the Indian model offers a vision of spiritual pluralism rooted in intellectual rigor. It shows that one can deny God without denying transcendence, reject a creator without rejecting causality, and embrace rational inquiry without succumbing to metaphysical nihilism. It teaches that theology need not be about defending doctrinal turf but about expanding the space of meaning. Non-theism, in this world, is not a negation—it is a mode of naming the nameless. Thus, Indian non-theism cannot be captured by simple negations or affirmations. It operates in a philosophical landscape where meaning is layered, predicates are conditioned, and reality is both immanent and transcendent.

From Yogācāra's luminous emptiness to Jainism's perspectival realism, from Advaita's provisional theism to *Mīmāṃsā*'s ritual automatism, the question of God is never dismissed out of hand. It is interrogated, reformulated, and woven into a broader metaphysical inquiry. The divine is allowed to be personal, impersonal, symbolic, or even unnecessary—depending on the frame of reference. But what is never absent is the seriousness of the search. Whether through devotion or denial, through form or formlessness, Indian thought turns toward the ultimate with a spirit of inquiry that is at once reverent and fearless. In that sense, even the rejection of God in India may still be a kind of homage—a gesture toward the infinite from another doorway.

The conversation between Indic philosophy and atheistic critique is not one of mere opposition but of dynamic engagement. Far from undermining religious or metaphysical worldviews, the sharp edges of atheistic arguments have historically served to refine them, demanding greater precision, clarity, and intellectual discipline. Within the Indic tradition, this sharpening effect is most evident in the way schools such as *Nyāya* have responded—not with retreat into dogma, but with an arsenal of rational tools: epistemological categorization, inferential reasoning, and dialogical examination. The result is not a defensive theology, but a sophisticated intellectual tradition that welcomes scrutiny. Atheistic positions, whether grounded in materialist metaphysics, empirical skepticism, or moral objection, are seen not as threats but as necessary interlocutors in the ongoing search for truth (*satya*). Scientific cosmology, especially in the post-relativistic and quantum eras, presents a similarly fertile space for philosophical engagement. Swāmi Vivekānanda gave an insightful address at the Parliament of the World's Religions on 19th of September 1893, where he said,

> *"Science is nothing but the finding of unity. As soon as science would reach perfect unity, it would stop from further progress, because it would reach the goal. Thus chemistry could not progress farther when it would discover one element out of which all others could be made. Physics would stop when it would be able to fulfil its services in discovering one energy of which all the others are but manifestations, and the science of religion become perfect when it would discover Him who is the one life in a universe of death, Him who is the constant basis of an ever- changing world, One who is the only Soul of which all souls are but delusive manifestations. Thus is it, through multiplicity and duality, that the ultimate unity is reached. Religion can go no farther. This is the goal of all science."*

Rather than resisting modern science, *Nyāya* and other rationalist schools of Indic thought have the capacity to assimilate scientific theories into broader metaphysical frameworks—provided they are interpreted with nuance. The Big Bang, fine-tuning, and quantum cosmology all raise questions about causality, contingency, and the structure of space and time. *Nyāya*'s arguments for *Īśvara* as a non-composite, unchanging cause behind empirical multiplicity remain robust in light of these discoveries—not because they hijack scientific data for religious ends, but because they work at a different level of explanation. They seek not how things work, but why there is order at all. Importantly, this dialogue avoids the pitfall of theological overcommitment; it does not bet all on current scientific models, but retains conceptual flexibility as understanding evolves. What emerges from this integrative engagement is a vision of *Īśvara* that does not require uniform theological commitment. This coexistence of perspectives is not relativism, but a disciplined pluralism—anchored in rigorous debate (*vāda-vicāra*) and a shared commitment to reason. In such a cosmos, *Īśvara* is not weakened by the weight of questions; *tat* stands undiminished, a presence recast not in fear, but in reason— the most luminous account of intelligibility, causality, and moral order, even in a universe that leaves room for doubt, denial, and silence. Here, atheistic challenge and scientific vision are not fractures, but folds within the fabric—weaving deeper texture into tradition. For the Indic search for truth is not brittle, nor bound by dogma—it is porous, luminous, and unafraid—a path where reason is welcomed, and the sacred is found not in retreat from critique, but in conversation with the real.

*Chapter*
*Five*

# The Wired Rational

The cosmos is not silent. It reasons. It remembers. It arranges. Beneath the movement of stars and the firing of neurons, beneath silicon and soul, lies a question that will not go away: Why is anything ordered at all? In the 11th century, the Indian philosopher Udayanācārya stood at the confluence of classical metaphysics and systematic logic, crafting what remain among the most enduring rational arguments for the existence of a supreme, intelligent cause—*Īśvara*. Drawing from the rigor of the *Nyāya* tradition, Udayanācārya's project was no mere exercise in religious affirmation. It was a defence of reason itself, a declaration that the cosmos is not arbitrary but intelligible, and that this intelligibility points beyond itself. A pentad of his arguments—*kāryāt* (from effects), *āyojanāt* (from purposeful arrangement), *dhṛtyādéḥ* (from continuity and stability), *padāt* (from meaningful expression), and *saṅkhyāviśeṣāt* (from quantitative determination)—represent a remarkable synthesis of logic, observation, and metaphysical reflection. Rooted in classical *tarka* (reasoning) and *pramāṇa* (means of knowledge), these arguments engaged seriously with rival schools such as *Sāṅkhya* and Buddhist momentariness, not to refute out of dogma but to refine understanding through dialectical clarity. Today, nearly a millennium later, the metaphysical landscape has shifted dramatically. Yet the core question that animated Udayanācārya's reasoning remains urgent: *What explains the coherence, complexity, and directedness of reality?* In a world increasingly understood in terms of information, code, and computation, his arguments speak anew with startling relevance. Modern physics, particularly in the quantum domain, has revealed a universe that resists purely materialist explanations. John Archibald Wheeler's provocative thesis—*It from Bit*—suggests that information is not merely descriptive of reality, but constitutive of it. At the foundations of physical reality, we no longer find solid particles in deterministic motion, but probabilistic wavefunctions, collapsing only through acts of measurement—acts that are inherently informational. Werner Heisenberg once famously wrote, in *Physics and Philosophy* (1958),

> *"What we observe is not nature itself, but nature exposed to our method of questioning."*

Parallel insights arise in biology, where life is seen not merely as biochemical interaction but as informational organization: genetic code, cellular signaling, neural communication. Artificial intelligence extends this insight further, constructing machines that simulate aspects of human reasoning and learning through intricate flows of data and probabilistic inference. Increasingly, to exist is to be processed, patterned, and interpreted.

This informational turn in science and technology offers not a challenge but an invitation: to rethink classical theistic metaphysics not as a relic of the past, but as a partner in dialogue with the most advanced intellectual developments of our age. The computational structure of reality—its regularity, intelligibility, and directedness—echoes many of the intuitions that Udayanācārya systematized within his own context. Rather than rendering his arguments obsolete, modern developments in information theory, computational complexity, and cognitive science deepen the philosophical soil in which they can be replanted and reinterpreted. This chapter proposes what may be called a 'post-scientific rational theology': a vision of theism not grounded in gaps of scientific knowledge, but in the logical structure and informational architecture of reality itself. The aim is not to retrofit Udayanācārya's proofs with digital metaphors, nor to merely reinterpret *Īśvara* as some form of cosmic programmer. Rather, it is to explore how the enduring epistemic strategies of *Nyāya*—its attention to inference, causality, and explanation—can be brought into conversation with contemporary efforts to understand why the universe is intelligible at all. Just as Udayanācārya responded not to any random whataboutery but to *Sāṅkhya* atomism and Buddhist phenomenology—the most sophisticated philosophical systems of his day—so too must any contemporary theology engage seriously with emergent complexity, algorithmic inference, and the limits of computational representation. Where traditional theologies might appeal to revelation, Udayanācārya appeals to *anvaya-vyatireka* (positive and negative correlation), to structured causality, to inference grounded in observed regularity. In this way, he remains closer in spirit to analytic philosophy or cognitive science than to mystical theology or fideism.

In a contemporary intellectual environment shaped by deep learning architectures that approximate perceptual cognition, by quantum information frameworks that displace classical ontologies, and by the increasing use of computational metaphors in domains as diverse as ethics, biology, and law, the core metaphysical questions Udayanācārya posed remain not only relevant but sharpened. His inquiries—concerning the preconditions for order, persistence, and explanatory trustworthiness—intersect with current debates in computational epistemology, cosmological fine-tuning, and the logic of emergence. What, after all, underlies the possibility of algorithmic regularity in a probabilistic universe? Why do certain informational structures endure across time? What legitimates the generalizability of rational inference itself? To return to Udayanācārya is not to invoke antiquity as authority, but to reopen a tradition of metaphysical reasoning that treated the intelligibility of the cosmos as a problem demanding systematic inference, not intuitive appeal. His logic, embedded within the *Nyāya*-Vaiśeṣika paradigm, prefigures many of the conceptual tensions we now encounter between substrate-level randomness and macro-level coherence, between statistical approximation and semantic structure. This chapter, therefore, is not an historical exercise, but a philosophical one: a re-engagement with Udayanācārya's core questions—traced now through the architecture of silicon, the probabilistic state space of qubits, and the layered abstractions of artificial neural networks—in pursuit of what might still be called a rational ground of reality.

## The Informational Universe

Before we examine the intricate latticework of Udayanācārya's theistic inferences, it becomes necessary to situate them within a broader intellectual milieu—one that has been dramatically transformed by developments in the physical and cognitive sciences. We live in an age that has subtly, but decisively, shifted its metaphysical commitments. No longer is the universe regarded as a mechanical assembly of inert matter governed by fixed forces alone. Increasingly, it is seen as a system whose very foundations are composed not of substance but of information—not mere motion, but meaning structured through pattern, probability, and process. In the classical worldview, the world appeared as a deterministic machine, explainable through the calculus of particles and fields.

But with the advent of quantum mechanics, that image has undergone a radical revision. The quantum state, represented by a wavefunction, does not describe a physical reality in the traditional sense but a distribution of potentialities, a repository of informational possibilities whose actualization depends on measurement. The process of observation is not neutral; it is constitutive, selecting one outcome from a spectrum of potentialities and thereby altering the ontological state of the system. This is not conjecture but an empirically grounded principle, verified in experimental designs such as the delayed-choice quantum eraser, which demonstrates that the informational status of a system—even retroactively—affects its physical manifestation.

These empirical facts challenge the long-held assumption that reality is independent of observation. John Wheeler's notion of a *participatory universe* expresses the culmination of this insight: that the cosmos does not simply exist, but comes into being through acts of measurement—that is, through acts of informational articulation. Anton Zeilinger, whose experiments in quantum entanglement advanced the field significantly, declared that *"information is the most fundamental building block of reality."* This claim is not mystical—it reflects a fundamental shift from ontology to epistemology, from things to the logic by which things are known. This was the cornerstone of Heisenberg's initiation of the New Quantum Theory in 1925, where he was more interested in *"nature exposed to our line of questioning"* rather than what it fundamentally is. This same turn toward informational ontology finds echo in theoretical physics. The holographic principle, emerging from black hole thermodynamics and formalized in string theory through the AdS/CFT correspondence, posits that all the information contained within a volume of space can be encoded on its boundary. In other words, the three-dimensional universe may emerge from two-dimensional informational data. Spatial extension, solidity, and substance—all may be derivative of a more fundamental logic of relational information! In such a framework, *being* itself begins to look more like structured intelligibility than like inert matter in motion. This transformation is not confined to the abstract domains of physics. In molecular biology, life itself is now understood as a highly ordered process of information storage, replication, and processing. The genetic code embedded in DNA is far more than a chemical sequence. It exhibits redundancy, error correction, modular architecture, and dynamic responsiveness—properties typically found in advanced computational systems. The central dogma of molecular biology—information flowing from DNA to RNA to protein—has been enriched by discoveries in non-coding RNAs, epigenetics, and protein folding, all of which reveal biological systems as multi-layered informational hierarchies capable of contextual adaptation and memory. More striking still is the immune system, whose capacity for learning, recall, and targeted response rivals our most sophisticated machine learning algorithms. Such systems, though shaped by natural selection, point toward an informational causality that is neither strictly mechanical nor reducible to chance.

In the domain of artificial intelligence, we encounter further deepening of this informational turn. Large-scale language models and neural networks process colossal volumes of data to identify patterns and generate predictions, often achieving results that appear intelligent, even creative. Yet, despite this sophistication, these systems confront enduring philosophical limitations. The symbol grounding problem—that no system operating purely on syntactic manipulation can generate genuine semantic content—remains unresolved. John Searle's Chinese Room argument, though widely debated, continues to illustrate the gap between computational processing and conscious understanding. Moreover, the most effective AI systems operate on the principle of information compression. They identify the minimal structure necessary to represent complex input—a concept formalized in Kolmogorov complexity and algorithmic information theory. Intelligence, in this view, is not brute computation but the ability to extract essential patterns from noise, to achieve semantic elegance from syntactic excess. These developments have important implications for our understanding of the cosmos itself. The laws and constants of nature—so finely tuned to allow the emergence of complexity—are characterized by extremely low algorithmic probability. The likelihood of obtaining a universe with the precise physical constants required for complex chemistry, stable stars, and conscious observers is vanishingly small. The anisotropies of the cosmic microwave background encode structured information about the early universe, and the simplicity of the equations governing physical interactions—relative to the vast space of mathematical possibilities—points to a universe of astonishing informational coherence. Herein lies the deeper philosophical convergence with Udayanācārya's project. Unlike mechanistic design arguments that rest on analogies with human craftsmanship, Udayanācārya's reasoning in the *Nyāyakusumāñjali* is rooted in structural necessity and explanatory coherence. His appeal to *āyojanāt* (purposive arrangement) and *padāt* (semantic coordination) reflects an awareness that mere regularity is insufficient; what calls for explanation is the kind of order that sustains intelligibility. The informational architecture of the modern universe—its compressibility, its coherence, and its improbability—invites precisely the kind of reasoning Udayanācārya pursued. To think with Udayanācārya today is not to transpose his metaphysics onto new data, but to recognize that his questions persist, sharpened by new epistemic tools. In an era where meaning is mediated by data, and causality increasingly resembles computation, the call to consider whether reality itself is grounded in intelligence is not a retreat into premodern speculation. It is, perhaps, the most rational response to the world as we now encounter it.

## The Game of Effectuation

Udayanācārya's first argument for the existence of *Īśvara*, rooted in the principle of *kāryāt*—inference from effect to cause—offers a conceptual architecture that has withstood centuries of philosophical scrutiny. Its classical articulation is deceptively simple: just as composite artifacts such as pots presuppose an intelligent agent—a potter—for their coming-into-being, so too does the vastly more intricate composition of the universe necessitate the operation of an intelligent cosmic agent. The argument does not rest on a denial of intermediate, natural causes; it operates at a deeper register, asking what ultimately accounts for the causal powers inherent in such causes. In a metaphysical landscape increasingly shaped by physics, computation, and cognitive science, this line of reasoning is not rendered obsolete—it is instead given new conceptual traction. Modern science has revealed the universe not as a mute collection of inert particles governed by brute laws, but as a dynamic web of information-rich processes, structured by symmetries, probabilities, and mathematical regularities that govern the flow and transformation of information at every level. Physical laws today are no longer seen as empirical generalizations but as algorithmic prescriptions—elegant, internally consistent, and expressed in the abstract language of mathematics. These laws govern the probability amplitudes of quantum states, the curvature of spacetime, and the self-organization of matter. Yet they do not themselves possess the causal sufficiency to generate the high degrees of informational order we observe. Rather, they are like grammatical rules in a language—structuring possibilities but not generating meaning on their own. The question then arises: what grounds the intelligibility, precision, and fine-tuning of these laws themselves?

From this standpoint, the classical *kāryāt* argument acquires renewed significance. Reformulated through the lens of information theory, the argument shifts from mechanical analogy to conceptual necessity. Complex information-processing systems, whether biological organisms, neural architectures, or symbolic languages, require informationally adequate causes. The universe, which exhibits multi-layered information processing—quantum decoherence, biochemical signaling, cognitive abstraction—cannot be sufficiently accounted for by appeal to initial randomness or blind evolution alone. While such processes may explain the transformation of existing informational content, they do not account for the origin, encoding, and structuring of such content in the first place. The very existence of low-entropy initial conditions, precisely tuned constants, and symbolic intelligibility within the fabric of physical law points to an informational source of generative capacity. This insight gains further clarity when examined through the analogy of generative artificial intelligence. Contemporary language models are capable of producing remarkably coherent and creative outputs. Yet their apparent intelligence is entirely derivative: they generate new combinations based on vast corpora of prior texts and the architectural structure of their training models. They do not originate meaning; they recombine pre-structured information. Similarly, physical laws may guide the transformation and development of complex systems, but their efficacy presupposes an initial matrix of informational order—a training data of sorts embedded in the laws of nature themselves. In this view, the question is not whether natural processes can give rise to complexity, but why the cosmos is structured such that it allows for meaningful, intelligible, and productive complexity at all.

Moreover, the analogy reaches its philosophical apex in the consideration of consciousness. The most advanced physicalist models of cognition remain unable to bridge the gap between computational function and conscious awareness. Despite extensive mapping of neural correlates, the emergence of first-person experience—the unity, intentionality, and semantic depth of consciousness—remains unexplained. The so-called "hard problem" of consciousness is not a terminological artifact but a genuine philosophical challenge: how can physical processes, however complex, give rise to subjective experience? Integrated Information Theory (IIT), proposed by Tononi and further refined by other theorists, suggests that consciousness corresponds to integrated information—information that is both unified and differentiated across a system. This unity-in-differentiation characterizes every conscious experience, from a flash of pain to the contemplation of the infinite. But this is met with criticism by none other than Alan T. Waterman awardee Scott Aaronson,

> *"In my opinion, how to construct a theory that tells us which physical systems are conscious and which aren't—giving answers that agree with "common sense" whenever the latter renders a verdict—is one of the deepest, most fascinating problems in all of science. Since I don't know a standard name for the problem, I hereby call it the Pretty-Hard Problem of Consciousness [...] Now, I regard IIT as a serious, honorable attempt to grapple with the Pretty-Hard Problem of Consciousness: something concrete enough to move the discussion forward. But I also regard IIT as a failed attempt on the problem. And I wish people would recognize its failure, learn from it, and*

*move on. In my view, IIT fails to solve the Pretty-Hard Problem because it unavoidably predicts vast amounts of consciousness in physical systems that no sane person would regard as particularly "conscious" at all: indeed, systems that do nothing but apply a low-density parity-check code, or other simple transformations of their input data. Moreover, IIT predicts not merely that these systems are "slightly" conscious (which would be fine), but that they can be unboundedly more conscious than humans are."*

If consciousness is indeed irreducible to physical computation and yet essential to the universe's most sophisticated forms of information processing, then the explanatory demand cannot be satisfied by materialistic frameworks alone. In classical *Nyāya*, this insight is prefigured in the invocation of *chaitanya*—consciousness not merely as a byproduct, but as a fundamental ontological principle, a causal reality in its own right. The world is not merely arranged in patterns of external regularity; it is endowed with interiority, with subjectivity capable of recognizing, questioning, and interpreting those patterns. The presence of semantic intelligence within the structure of the cosmos—not only in living systems, but in the very legibility of physical law—calls for a source that is not itself blind, random, or inert. It demands a principle that can account for the meaningfulness of meaning itself. Thus, the *kāryāt* argument is not a relic of pre-scientific thinking but a perennial philosophical insight rendered more potent by the very developments that were once thought to undermine it. It does not deny evolution, emergence, or complexity; it asks what renders them possible. It does not oppose scientific explanation; it interrogates its preconditions. In doing so, it reaches toward the necessity of a conscious, intelligent, and informationally generative ground—not as a gap-filling deity of ignorance, but as the rational presupposition of a world capable of being known. Udayana's insight, refracted through the lens of modern inquiry, offers us not merely an argument for God, but a clarion call to rethink causality itself—not as an impersonal sequence of mechanical events, but as the unfolding of a cosmos structured by intelligence, animated by meaning, and open to the reflective gaze of conscious life.

## Arranging into Order

Among the most enduring intuitions of metaphysical inquiry is the recognition that order does not arise unbidden; that behind the harmony of independent forces lies a deeper principle of coordination—intentional, unifying, and intelligent. Udayanācārya's second argument for the existence of *Īśvara*, known as *āyojanāt*, derives from the observation of systematic arrangement and functional coordination that pervade the natural world. Unlike arguments that rely merely on mechanical intricacy or superficial analogies with human artifacts, the *āyojanāt* inference penetrates deeper—it invites us to reflect on how independent elements, disparate processes, and apparently autonomous systems cohere into ordered, self-regulating wholes. It is one thing for a machine to be complex; it is quite another for complexity to give rise to systematicity, to sustain harmonized interdependence across scales, and to preserve a unity of function amidst multiplicity of structure. Rivers do not merely flow; they converge into basins shaped by topology, climate, and gravitational gradients. Seasons do not simply occur; they unfold in cyclical precision tied to astronomical constants. Organisms do not merely live; they exhibit exquisitely orchestrated interplays of genes, proteins, enzymes, cells, and environments—each part not only functioning but co-functioning within the whole. It is this dynamic architecture of coordination that Udayana isolates as demanding explanation. It is not complexity alone that bespeaks intelligence, but the meaningful arrangement of complexity into coherently operating totalities.

In modern contexts, design arguments often focus on mechanical intricacy—such as the rotary motion of bacterial flagella or the error-correction mechanisms of DNA replication. Yet these examples, while striking, remain at the level of engineered analogies. Udayana's argument, when reframed today, does not concern mere physical structure but informational architecture: the capacity of nature to generate and sustain relational order among independent systems. Evolutionary biology, for instance, explains how mechanical complexity can emerge through natural selection. But this presupposes the prior existence of genetic information, replication fidelity, protein-folding codes, and developmental pathways—all of which are themselves manifestations of prior informational structuring. These are not mechanisms that simply emerge from chaos; they are formal systems that encode, store, transmit, and regulate information with remarkable fidelity and scope. The question *āyojanāt* raises is not why evolution works, but why the system is structured such that evolution can work at all. Coordination is never spontaneous in the strong sense—it presupposes compatible interfaces, predictable transformations, and shared protocols, all of which point to the prior imposition of structure on possibility. Paul Davies meditates on this point, in *The Mind of God* (1992),

> *"What is remarkable is that human beings are actually able to carry out this code-breaking operation, that the human mind has the necessary intellectual equipment for us to "unlock the secrets of nature [...] Human beings have always been struck by the complex harmony and intricate organization of the physical world. The march of the heavenly bodies across the sky, the rhythms of the seasons, the pattern of a snowflake, the myriads of living creatures*

*so well adapted to their environment – all these things seem too well arranged to be a mindless accident."*

From the vantage of information theory, the force of this argument becomes clearer. In contemporary science, it is now well understood that complex systems—biological organisms, neural networks, ecological webs, even galaxies—exhibit not random aggregation, but emergent coordination, marked by feedback loops, information flow, and hierarchical integration. Such systems depend on the proper arrangement of components, tuned connectivity, and non-trivial pathways of communication. Random interactions among elements in a large system do not yield stability or functionality unless certain connectivity constraints and protocols are already in place. This is the central insight of network theory: that stable and meaningful wholes arise not from accumulation, but from relational syntax—that is, from structure imposed upon interaction. Whether in the synchronized behavior of neurons in a brain, the regulatory feedback among species in an ecosystem, or the balance of fundamental forces in physics, coordination is the signature of deep design, not merely surface complexity.

A helpful contemporary analogy lies in the structure of the internet. Billions of independent devices coordinate their functions not through spontaneous harmony, but through standardized informational protocols—TCP/IP, DNS, HTTP—which govern addressability, identity, and semantic clarity. These protocols were consciously designed, encoded, and implemented by intelligent agents. They did not arise from random trials; they were specified to allow meaningful communication among diverse systems. The same logic holds in biology: the genetic code functions as a universal language for biological information. It is precise, degenerate yet non-random, and functions across all known life. Cellular signaling pathways likewise use specific molecular lexicons to convey state, demand, and adaptation. These protocols, though biochemical, exhibit the hallmark of intelligent ordering: semantic stability under transformation. To attribute their origin to chance is akin to claiming that HTML emerged spontaneously from electrical noise. Even more profound is the coordination seen in quantum entanglement. In this phenomenon, pairs or groups of particles exhibit correlations that persist regardless of spatial separation. The measurement of one immediately affects the state of the other, in a manner that defies classical explanation. This is not mere coincidence but non-local coordination, demonstrably resistant to local causal reduction. Quantum information theory has shown that entanglement enables tasks such as teleportation and secure communication—systems that depend not only on correlation, but on structured coherence across informational states. When applied to the natural world, this suggests that reality itself is threaded with patterns of coordination that transcend mechanical causality. Entanglement, once thought esoteric, is now posited to play measurable roles in quantum biology by the likes of Graham Fleming, Greg Engel, Luca Turin, Thorsten Ritz, Jim Al-Khalili and Johnjoe McFadden—from the efficiency of energy transfer in photosynthesis, to the magnetoception used in bird navigation, and potentially even in olfactory and neural systems. These are not vague mysteries but emerging empirical insights: that biological coordination may leverage quantum coherence in ways that demand a rethinking of both causality and agency.

If such coordination is real—and all current evidence points to its reality—then the explanatory burden cannot rest solely with physical law, which functions more as constraint than as origin. The laws describe how systems behave once information is in place, not how such informational architectures are generated in the first instance. It is here that the *āyojanāt* argument regains its metaphysical force. It invites us to consider that systematic coordination presupposes not merely physical causality, but intelligent agency capable of imposing relational order on otherwise independent systems. This intelligence need not operate externally like a cosmic mechanic, but may reside at the ontological root of the cosmos—as an intrinsic source of intelligibility and relationality. Thus, far from being an outdated metaphor of design, Udayanācārya's *āyojanāt* is a perennial insight into the structured coherence of the real. In an age where science itself reveals deeper and deeper levels of coordinated information, the question is not whether there is order, but whether order such as this could ever emerge without a supposed 'mind'. And to that question, the *āyojanāt* argument replies—not in blind faith, but with reasoned confidence—that intelligence is not an emergent illusion, but the generative principle of reality itself.

## Continuously Coherent

Amidst the flux of natural processes and the ceaseless transformations that mark the material world, there arises a profound question: what ensures the persistence of coherence across time? This is the central insight of Udayanācārya's third argument, *dhṛtyādéḥ*, which draws attention to the fact that despite continuous change, systems retain their identities, functions are preserved, and patterns are not merely repeated but sustained with remarkable fidelity. Rivers shift their courses, cells regenerate, stars evolve and die—yet at every scale, from the quantum to the cosmic, a kind of temporal cohesion is maintained that allows reality to endure as intelligible, ordered, and narratable. Udayanācārya, with unerring philosophical instinct, saw in this continuity not the blind momentum of inert matter, but the trace of a sustaining intelligence—a *niyāmaka*, a principle that guards coherence not just in space, but across the abyss of time. Modern science, rather than diminishing this insight, has enriched and deepened its implications. Contemporary physics reveals that beneath the surface of apparent stasis lies a world in perpetual flux. Atoms are exchanged, molecules recombine, and energy flows with relentless constancy. Yet, informational structures persist. A living organism, for instance, replaces the bulk of its atomic constituents many times over during its lifetime, and yet the genomic architecture, behavioural repertoire, and developmental pathways remain intact. The question thus arises: how is information preserved amid ceaseless physical turnover? What guards the identity of things across time if not the brute matter from which they are composed?

The answer lies not in matter but in information—in the structured patterns that confer continuity upon the impermanent. And the preservation of information, especially in open, thermodynamically unstable systems like living organisms, is no trivial matter. DNA, the great information-carrier of biology, maintains its sequence integrity across billions of replication cycles. It does so not merely through passive resilience, but through active correction mechanisms—enzymatic editors, redundancy codes, and molecular proofreading systems that rival and often surpass the precision of human-engineered data storage. Such error-correction protocols, distributed across evolutionary timescales and molecular architectures, do not arise ex nihilo. They demand an explanation not only in terms of proximate causation, but in light of what sustains such fidelity in a universe governed by entropy. Thermodynamics teaches that entropy—disorder—increases in closed systems. And yet life and order emerge. Living systems are not closed; they are open to energy flows from their environment. But this response merely displaces the question: what preserves the structure of those environments? The Earth receives ordered energy from the Sun, whose fusion reactions depend upon finely tuned physical laws—laws that yield low-entropy radiation capable of sustaining life. The capacity of the cosmos to sustain temporal coherence, from the cycling of seasons to the constancy of physical constants, cannot be reduced to local contingencies. It points instead to an informational architecture that transcends locality, embedded in the very fabric of physical law.

In this context, the principles of quantum mechanics offer profound and often counterintuitive insights into the nature of coherence. Quantum systems, unlike classical ones, can maintain superposed states and entangled correlations over time—phenomena that are both exquisitely fragile and yet, under the right conditions, remarkably stable. Quantum error correction—a field once thought theoretical—has now revealed that quantum information can be protected indefinitely against decoherence through elaborate schemes of redundancy and symmetry. In other words, quantum systems can actively maintain coherence, resisting noise not passively but through informational design. Such systems do not merely endure—they remember. The implications for biology are profound. Research in quantum biology has uncovered evidence that certain biological systems, notably photosynthetic complexes, maintain quantum coherence over timescales that permit optimal energy transfer. Birds may navigate the Earth's magnetic field using entangled electron pairs within cryptochrome proteins. Even olfaction and cognition are now being examined through the lens of quantum coherence. These are not speculative flourishes, but emerging empirical domains that suggest biological systems may harness coherence in ways that classical physics cannot account for. If this is true, then the *dhṛtyādéḥ* argument finds new life: the continuity of function and pattern in biology may be rooted in deep informational architectures whose design reflects intelligent constraint.

Beyond the empirical, there lies the metaphysical. Mathematical and logical truths—those eternal fixtures of human thought—do not change, decay, or degrade. The Pythagorean theorem holds true in every corner of spacetime, irrespective of cultural context or temporal era. The principle of non-contradiction remains the backbone of rational discourse, impervious to relativism. This temporal invariance of truth cannot be explained by material conditions alone. If mathematical entities are discovered, not invented—as many mathematical realists assert—then they belong to an informational domain beyond time, a *loka* of truths not subject to change, dissolution, or entropy. The uncanny "unreasonable effectiveness of mathematics," as Eugene Wigner once called it, suggests not mere coincidence but a deep congruence between eternal truths and temporal reality. Natural processes conform to mathematical laws not by accident, but because they participate in a logos that transcends them. In this convergence of metaphysics and physics, of logic and biology, the *dhṛtyādéḥ* argument acquires contemporary urgency. It is no longer a quaint appeal to cosmic preservation, but a profound inquiry into the conditions that make persistence possible in a perishable world. Coherence, we find, is not given; it is safeguarded. Continuity is not the default; it is structured, guarded, and intelligible. And if that is so, then the enduring rhythms of nature and the timeless truths of reason are not mute facts, but the living grammar of a rational cosmos—one that calls us not merely to observe, but to infer the intelligence that sustains all becoming through the integrity of being.

## The Teleological Argument

Among the most compelling features of the natural world is not that it simply exists, but that it operates with remarkable functional coherence—with precision, direction, and purpose. Leaves do not merely occupy space on a stem; they transform light into chemical energy through an intricate series of reactions timed to environmental cues. The heart does not beat arbitrarily; it responds with uncanny regularity to the shifting demands of the organism, modulating its rhythm in real time. Across the vast terrain of nature—from subcellular pathways to atmospheric systems—we observe not isolated phenomena, but orchestrated functionality. Udayanācārya, acutely attuned to this pervasive teleology, enshrines it in his fourth argument, *padāt*—the argument from purposeful organization. His insight is not satisfied with noting the structural complexity of natural forms; rather, it probes the mystery of their directedness, their consistent convergence toward ends that transcend the sum of their parts. In the face of such evident functionality, he asks not how these forms exist, but why they function as if by design.

This functional dimension of the cosmos cannot be reduced to the happenstance of matter in motion. Instead, it suggests an internal logic, a script that is not imposed from outside but arises from within. Modern biology, chemistry, and physics have painstakingly described the mechanisms by which processes unfold, yet the very intelligibility of these mechanisms rests upon hidden architectures of information, regulation, and timing that defy simple material causation. A single cell, for instance, carries within it an information system capable of error detection, damage repair, resource allocation, and adaptive response—all within microscopic constraints. The logic that governs such systems appears less like brute matter and more like an algorithm encoded with intentionality, optimized for resilience and continuity.

What is most startling is not the presence of life, but its efficiency—its elegance of execution. Metabolic cycles maintain energy balance through carefully modulated feedback; genetic systems replicate themselves while preserving semantic meaning across generations; neural systems transmit, compress, and modulate signals with redundancies that guard against noise and decay. These are not random reactions, but goal-oriented routines, each tailored to a broader end—be it survival, regeneration, or communication. The *padāt* argument invites us to consider that such routines, rather than emerging solely from stochastic trial, point to a form of intelligence immanent in nature, one that presides over the coordination of parts toward meaningful outcomes. Even more compelling is the fact that such functional organization is not restricted to biological life. Non-living systems, too, manifest coherence in their causal behavior. The periodic table, for example, is not a random collection of elements, but a structured array reflecting deep symmetries in atomic structure and electron configuration. The laws that govern fluid dynamics, electromagnetic resonance, or planetary motion are mathematically expressible, internally consistent, and often beautifully elegant. This aesthetic symmetry of the cosmos, the way its laws converge on functionality and form, suggests not a mere passive order but a purposive intelligence, an architectonic principle that harmonizes the real into the rational.

Nowhere is this purposiveness more evident than in systems that demonstrate hierarchical organization across multiple levels. Take, for instance, the architecture of the nervous system. Billions of synapses connect to form coherent networks, allowing for reflexes, memory, decision-making, and sensory integration. Each unit is partially autonomous, yet the whole functions as an integrated field of experience. Coordination at this scale requires rules of communication, resource prioritization, and functional division—all achieved without conscious command. This suggests the presence of an emergent agency, not reducible to any single node, but arising from the very laws of organization that bind the parts into a living whole. Such agency may not be sentient in the human sense, but it bears the signature of purposiveness, of intentional structure. The same logic applies at larger scales. Ecological systems—forests, coral reefs, climatic zones—regulate themselves through cycles that balance growth and decay, scarcity and surplus. Species interact not through mechanical push and pull, but through information-laden exchanges: chemical signaling, behavioral symmetries, environmental feedback. These systems persist not in stasis but in dynamic equilibrium, adjusting to perturbations while maintaining integrity. Their resilience, far from mechanistic redundancy, reveals a kind of homeostatic intelligence—an ability to navigate possibility space in ways that preserve identity over time. In Udayanācārya's vision, such ordered functionality cannot be the child of chance. It speaks to an inner rationality of nature, an ordering force that does not coerce but coordinates. Philosophers have long recognized that teleology does not demand anthropomorphism. To affirm purpose is not to impose human intention upon nature, but to acknowledge that nature itself operates through a logic of ends—a logic that governs seed and star, circuit and spiral. This is not the "God of the gaps" invoked when explanation fails, but a rational inference to the best explanation: that the consistency of goal-directedness across levels and scales requires a grounding intentionality. The ancients called it *purusha*, or *Īśvara*—not a personal deity in the narrow sense, but a principle of ordered intelligence, suffused through the cosmos like the logic in a syllogism or the harmony in a raga.

To return, then, to *padāt*, is not to dwell in premodern piety but to ask a question still unanswered by contemporary science: what gives rise to functionality itself? What enables the cosmos not just to be, but to do? Function is not the automatic consequence of form; it is the realization of direction embedded within form. And when that direction is so consistently rational, so intricately coded and sustained, one is compelled to ask not only about the mechanism but about the mind-like ordering from which such coherence proceeds. Udayanācārya's insight remains potent. The natural world is not a factory of blind collisions but a text of intentionality, whose meaning must be read in the grammar of function and purpose. To ignore this is to read the universe without understanding its syntax; to acknowledge it is to glimpse, however faintly, the presence of chaitanya—not as a distant deity, but as the inner logic of life itself.

## The Specificity of Numerics

Among the many enigmas of the cosmos, one stands quietly yet insistently at the core of all inquiry: why these numbers? Not merely that the universe is mathematically describable, but that it is mathematically precise, calibrated to specific values with astonishing exactitude. The masses of fundamental particles, the strengths of the four fundamental forces, the ratios that permit chemical bonding, stellar nucleosynthesis, and molecular stability—each rests upon numerical constants so delicately poised that even minute deviations would render the cosmos lifeless or incoherent. This peculiar and persistent feature of reality lies at the heart of Udayanācārya's final argument for the existence of a rational ordering principle: *saṁkhyāviśeṣāt*—the argument from numerical specification.

In classical *Nyāya*, the argument asserts that the determinate numerical features of the world are not reducible to brute contingency. If no underlying intelligence governs these specifications, then the emergence of order—let alone consciousness—becomes statistically inexplicable. Modern cosmology, paradoxically, affirms the force of this ancient insight. The fine-structure constant ($\alpha \approx 1/137$), governing the strength of electromagnetic interaction, must fall within an extraordinarily narrow range to allow for stable atoms. The cosmological constant ($\Lambda$), regulating the rate of cosmic expansion, is nonzero but inconceivably small—off by a factor of $10^{120}$ from the "natural" value predicted by quantum field theory. These are not arbitrary numerical decorations; they form the grammar of the real, determining whether stars shine, atoms cohere, and geometry manifests in observable space.

Numerical precision pervades the quantum realm as well. Quantum systems are governed not by continuous variability, but by discrete quantization: energy levels, spin states, and angular momentum exist only in specified units. Quantum numbers—n, l, m, s—are integers or half-integers, defining not just the behaviour but the very identity of physical systems. Why this integer structure? Why does Planck's constant, the fundamental unit of quantum action, take the value it does? From a purely physical standpoint, such specifications are not derivable from first principles—they are empirically observed and input into our equations as given, not explained. Yet from an informational standpoint, these discrete values mirror the logic of error-resistant computation: discrete units resist noise, support reliable storage, and enable reversibility—hallmarks of optimal informational systems. Beyond the quantum world, nature continues to display mathematical regularity with surprising specificity. The mass ratio of proton to electron (~1836.152) allows for stable chemistry.

The gravitational constant determines whether planetary systems can form; the Boltzmann constant calibrates thermal dynamics. Each of these values, when viewed against the full backdrop of mathematical possibility, seems an unlikely yet necessary needle in the cosmic haystack. Theories invoking a multiverse attempt to disperse this improbability across a vast ensemble of hypothetical universes. But the explanatory price of such a move is high: one must posit not just a plurality of universes, but a mechanism for varying constants and selecting outcomes—a meta-law more complex and information-rich than what it attempts to explain. Udayana's argument, by contrast, interprets numerical specificity not as chance filtered by anthropic necessity, but as the signature of rational design: not imposed from without, but arising from the cosmos' own inner syntax.

Nor is this numerical precision confined to physics. In biological morphology, proportions obey mathematical principles that transcend evolutionary function. The Fibonacci sequence, long thought a mathematical curiosity, appears in phyllotaxis—the arrangement of leaves around a stem—to optimize light exposure. The golden ratio ($\varphi \approx 1.618$) emerges in spiral growth patterns of shells, horns, and galaxies, often where structural efficiency and aesthetic appeal coincide. While biology offers adaptive explanations, the recurrence of mathematically optimal forms across domains suggests a deeper ordering principle—one not reducible to blind variation, but suggestive of form-imposing constraints intrinsic to the cosmos. The mathematical constants that structure natural forms are often transcendental numbers—$\pi$, $e$, $\varphi$—numbers that cannot be expressed as finite fractions and whose decimal expansions never repeat. That these non-algebraic values are inscribed in the very curvature of space-time and the logarithmic patterns of growth may suggest that reality participates in a mathematical order that exceeds computability, hinting at a Platonic substratum of structure itself. As mathematician Roger Penrose has argued, the universe's capacity to instantiate mathematical truths with such fidelity points to a triadic ontology: of physical reality, mental perception, and mathematical structure—each inexplicable without reference to the others. Udayanācārya's insight aligns with this: numerical order reflects not mere fact, but a triadic coherence of matter, consciousness, and structure. In information theory, such structure is characterized by low algorithmic complexity: patterns that are simple to describe yet rich in consequence. Newton's law of gravitation is mathematically concise, yet governs the motion of planets and the curvature of space. Maxwell's equations contain only a few terms, yet underwrite the entire architecture of electromagnetism. That such simple numerical formulations can yield a world of dizzying complexity and elegance reinforces Udayana's claim that intelligence lies not in the complexity of creation, but in the economy of its generative principles. The gods, it seems, write not in labyrinths but in lucidity.

To perceive numerical specificity not as brute fact but as the manifestation of intelligence is not to anthropomorphize the cosmos, but to discern its mathematical intentionality. The *saṁkhyāviśeṣāt* argument reminds us that behind every constant, every ratio, every unit of quantized motion, lies the deeper question: why this, and not otherwise? In resisting the temptation to treat numbers as mute data, and instead attending to their interrelated, life-permitting coherence, we awaken to a cosmos not of arbitrary mechanics but of profound meaning. In its very quantification, nature points beyond itself—toward a principle of order not imposed but inherent, not mechanical but mindful. It is this silent but persistent rationality that Udayanācārya dares to name as *Īśvara*—not a mythic overseer, but the very numerical coherence of being made intelligible.

## Towards an Information-Theoretical Natural Theology

To contemplate Udayanācārya in the twenty-first century is to rediscover a mind whose rational intuitions anticipated, by centuries, the profoundest contours of modern metaphysical reflection. In reinterpreting his five classical arguments—*kāryāt* (from effects), āyojanāt (from coordination), *dhṛtyādéḥ* (from persistence), *padāt* (from purpose), and saṁkhyāviśeṣāt (from numerical specificity)—we find not relics of a pre-scientific worldview but scaffolding for a revitalized natural theology, one grounded not in analogies from artisanal design but in the language of information: encoding, compression, processing, coordination, preservation, and optimization. Across the widening arc of the sciences—quantum physics, systems biology, cognitive neuroscience, cosmology, and artificial intelligence—the nature of reality is increasingly disclosed as structured, not merely material but informational. And it is precisely through this turn toward information that the theistic insights of the classical *Nyāya* tradition regain both philosophical rigor and empirical resonance. Each of Udayanācārya's arguments, when reframed through an information-theoretic lens, converges upon a deeper, unified conclusion. Effects are not just physical transformations; they are informational transitions, and complex information-processing systems require causes adequate not merely in energy but in intelligibility. The causal sufficiency of natural laws is called into question when those laws themselves encode vast quantities of abstract, structured information—laws which do not merely describe how matter moves but delimit what it can do and how it can evolve into new forms. Similarly, coordination is never spontaneous in the strong sense; it requires compatibilities, protocols, and semantic interfaces that only an intelligence capable of anticipating multiple states across time and space can generate. The kind of systematic integration observable in cellular biology, planetary dynamics, and even quantum entanglement is best understood not as the product of chaotic collision but as the output of ordered architectures. Continuity, too, cannot be taken for granted: across aeons and thermodynamic erosion, the world preserves patterns of information with astonishing fidelity. From the stable replication of DNA across generations to the cosmic microwave background's exquisitely encoded anisotropies, reality displays a memory—a persistent inscription of order through time that resists entropy, and in doing so, gestures toward a sustaining cause.

The functionally oriented behaviors of natural systems—photosynthesis, immunity, neural synchronization, circadian regulation—reveal teleological processing far more sophisticated than mechanistic tinkering. These systems are goal-directed in the deepest computational sense: they monitor, adjust, predict, and recover. Their processes embody conditional logic, feedback loops, and cross-scale integration that contemporary machine learning systems can only approximate under heavily curated architectures. Finally, the numerical parameters that define the fabric of reality—the fine-structure constant, the cosmological constant, the Planck units, the peculiar harmonies of mass ratios and coupling strengths—suggest a cosmos not randomly situated but finely tuned. These numbers, expressed not as philosophical speculation but as empirical necessities, evoke an aesthetic and functional order that is resistant to naturalistic flattening. They are, in essence, the syllables of a deeper grammar: one that speaks of intelligibility, proportion, and design. Taken together, these arguments sketch not a theological addendum to science but an ontological clarification of what science increasingly encounters but cannot fully explain: the order beneath order, the mind behind the matrix. The intelligence that such a reconstruction reveals is not a deus ex machina, intervening at the edges where ignorance dwells, but a cosmic principle of rationality—conscious, unified, purposive—that underwrites the very conditions under which science operates. This is not the "God of the gaps," but the God of the grammar—the intelligence not hidden in exceptions, but manifest in the rule itself. The attributes that emerge from such an account—informational adequacy, systematic integration, temporal transcendence, goal specification, optimization—correspond, strikingly, to the classical *Nyāya* characterization of *Īśvara*: an omniscient, omnipotent, eternal being endowed with auspicious qualities. In a way that neither violates the natural nor retreats into fideism, information-theoretic natural theology vindicates metaphysical theism on empirical grounds.

Moreover, this framework provides nuanced responses to enduring philosophical objections. The presence of disorder and suffering—the traditional problem of evil—can be reframed through the lens of informational optimization: error, perturbation, and struggle may not be failures but necessary features of dynamic, evolving, self-correcting informational systems. Like negative feedback in control theory, or error-correction in computational encoding, local disorder may preserve global coherence. Similarly, divine action need not entail supernatural suspension of natural law; rather, informational causality offers a model wherein top-down constraints and semantic architecture influence system-level outcomes without violating bottom-up mechanisms. The multiverse hypothesis, often offered as a counter to fine-tuning, merely shifts the question upward: any mechanism capable of generating a viable ensemble of universes with variant constants must itself possess information-processing capacity of staggering complexity—a meta-design that points again to intelligence, not away from it. The implications for philosophy of mind are equally transformative. The prevailing assumption that consciousness emerges from brute physical processes is increasingly untenable in light of the "hard problem" and the limits of computational simulation. Integrated Information Theory, while incomplete, offers a crucial insight: consciousness may be not a late product of complexity, but the very mode in which information becomes unified, meaningful, and causally efficacious. If this is so, then mind is not an epiphenomenon but an ontological primitive—a condition for the possibility of coherent systems at all levels. The informational framework supports this view, suggesting that intelligence is not accidental, but intrinsic to the universe's structure, and that consciousness, far from being confined to neuronal arrangements, may be the very principle that renders informational integration real. Machines that manipulate syntax cannot generate semantics; artificial intelligence, however advanced, reveals precisely the gap between information-processing and understanding. The universe, by contrast, manifests understanding not by default, but by design.

In this light, future research must explore not only the technical frontiers of information theory, but its metaphysical implications. The study of quantum biology, for instance, may reveal informational coherence at scales that challenge materialist reduction. The extraordinary efficiency of photosynthesis, the entanglement behaviors in avian magnetoreception, and the computational dynamics of the immune system—all point toward systems that optimize information in ways not fully reducible to classical physics. Fine-tuning, long dismissed as theological speculation, may acquire fresh precision through algorithmic information theory: are the laws of nature compressed encodings of deeper principles? If so, who—or what—selected the language in which they are written? Similarly, AI safety and goal alignment research will sharpen our understanding of what it means to build systems that pursue ends across time—a phenomenon nature seems to achieve effortlessly, yet which artificial systems constantly struggle to approximate. Udayanācārya's project, then, is far from concluded. His method—a rational interrogation of the foundations of causality, order, coherence, purpose, and specification—continues to offer a framework for philosophical theology that is not apologetic but exploratory, not defensive but luminous. His *Īśvara* is not a relic of devotional piety, but the deepest expression of a cosmos intelligible to reason because it is born of reason. If modern science seeks a unified field theory, it may yet discover that its unifier is not a force but an intelligence—an informational logos that speaks in particles and predicates alike, and whose grammar underwrites the very intelligibility of being. In Udayanācārya's vision, we are not merely the products of information; we are its stewards, interpreters, and, perhaps, its awakeners. In that light, to think is to worship, and to seek understanding is to approach the presence of a conscious, eternal, rational order: the *Īśvara* of the information age.

## The Post-AI God

The more we entrust our questions to the silicon mind, the more acutely we encounter the limits of its answers. As a teacher of philosophy and science, I have watched with fascination—and no small measure of concern—as students and scholars alike turn with near-religious confidence to artificial intelligence, believing it capable of answering all problems worth asking. The smugness is palpable: that AI will write our essays, design our medicines, model our economies, and eventually, perhaps, explain consciousness itself. But this optimism begins to falter the moment one asks AI not just to compute, but to comprehend; not merely to simulate understanding, but to ground it. When students confront the gap between predictive accuracy and genuine insight, they are startled to find that the machine, though articulate, is silent at the core. The illusion of omniscience dissolves into syntax without soul. In those moments of disillusionment—when the shimmer of algorithmic prowess gives way to a haunted silence—we are forced to ask once again the ancient question: What is intelligence, truly? And more deeply still: What is the source of intelligibility itself? This is where Udayanācārya reenters—not as a medieval thinker embalmed in history, but as a philosopher of startling contemporary relevance. His five classical arguments, when reframed through the lens of information theory and computational science, do not merely survive modern scrutiny—they acquire renewed vitality. They show us that the informational architecture of the universe—its precision, its generativity, its aesthetic proportions and error-correcting persistence—points not to randomness refined but to rationality realized. Reality, increasingly understood as fundamentally informational, cannot bootstrap its own intelligibility. Code cannot arise without codification; data requires a grammar; systems require goals. Each of Udayana's arguments, as we have seen, converges on this: the need for an informational source that is not derivative but originary, not contingent but absolute. A cause not merely physical, but rational. In the post-AI age, this amounts to nothing less than a rediscovery of the idea of God—though not in the naive anthropomorphic guise that both religion and science so often reduce Him to.

What emerges instead is the vision of a post-AI God—not a deity invoked in the absence of explanation, but one revealed at the very heart of explanation itself. This God is not a gap-filler but a grammar-giver: the intelligence that renders information meaningful, the consciousness that underlies all instances of awareness, the rationality that makes mathematics descriptive of the universe. Artificial intelligence, for all its power, remains parasitic on the informational patterns it was trained upon. It does not originate, it recombines. It does not know, it correlates. It does not intend, it optimizes. And most fatally—it does not know that it does not know. Its apparent understanding is a mirage projected by probabilities, but it lacks the first-person awareness that even a child possesses. If intelligence consists not merely in problem-solving but in the capacity for self-reflective understanding, then even the most advanced AI has not crossed that threshold. What, then, is the ground of such understanding? Here, Udayana's insistence on chaitanya—consciousness as a fundamental causal principle—stands vindicated. The informational world we inhabit is intelligible to us not because we evolved neurons capable of symbolic manipulation, but because reality itself is the expression of a deeper intelligence of which we are a part. Just as the waves do not invent the ocean, our minds do not invent intelligibility; they participate in it. And just as the syntax of AI fails to generate semantics without grounding, the structures of the universe would remain barren of meaning unless rooted in a conscious order that precedes them. The post-AI God is not the ghost in the machine; He is the source of the machine's very possibility. Not a being among beings, but the ground of Being itself, rendered newly legible in an era when our machines can process everything but purpose.

What, then, becomes of the human in this cosmos of circuits and stars? The answer is, paradoxically, one of elevation. For if intelligence is not reducible to computation, and if consciousness is not the accidental byproduct of blind evolution but a window onto the ground of being, then to be human is to be more than nature's lucky accident. It is to be a node in the great informational continuum that is not only alive but aware; not only capable of knowledge but summoned to understanding. AI may augment our abilities, but it cannot bear our mysteries. It may mimic meaning, but it cannot ground it. In contrast, the post-AI God reminds us that the cosmos is not simply a vast unfolding of blind laws, but a text—encoded, patterned, and open to interpretation—authored by intelligence and addressed to intelligence. Our vocation, as knowers, is not to replace God with machines but to rediscover in our own minds the signature of a deeper Mind. In this light, theism becomes not the retreat of reason but its consummation. Udayanācārya's arguments, far from being superseded, find their fulfillment in the very sciences once presumed to refute them. Quantum mechanics shows us a world where observation is inseparable from reality; information theory reveals the world as structured, compressible, optimized; artificial intelligence teaches us, by contrast, what intelligence is not. All point not away from metaphysics but back toward it. They do not render God obsolete—they render Him necessary. Not the God of superstition, but the God of sense-making. The intelligence that gives rise to all other intelligences. The consciousness in which all awareness finds coherence. The logos that became cosmos. This, then, is the horizon of a post-scientific, post-AI natural theology: one that integrates the rigor of empirical discovery with the depth of metaphysical reflection. It asks not simply what the world is made of, but what makes the world make sense. It seeks not only to decode the patterns of nature, but to discern the Mind in which those patterns originate. The post-AI God is not an evasion of complexity, but its apotheosis.

In rediscovering this intelligence—not as hypothesis but as metaphysical necessity—we rediscover ourselves: not as clever animals lost in an indifferent universe, but as conscious agents bearing within us the echo of an eternal, all-pervading chaitanya. In that light, to know is to worship, and to awaken to meaning is to return—again and again—to the God who, having once been eclipsed by our machines, now stands revealed through their very limits.

*Chapter*

*Six*

# The Reflexive Cosmos

In the architecture of existence—from the probabilistic dance of quantum fields to the vast latticework of galaxies—a unifying principle emerges with quiet consistency: reflexivity. Not merely the self-awareness of sentient minds, but a more fundamental structure wherein systems exhibit internal feedback, recursive behaviour, and self-referential patterns. This is not mystical projection, but a description increasingly encountered across disciplines—physics, thermodynamics, information theory—where systems evolve through interactions that include themselves in their causal loops. In quantum electrodynamics, for example, particles such as electrons are affected by fluctuations in their own fields—a process modeled in terms of self-energy and renormalization. In complex systems and thermodynamics, feedback mechanisms allow for self-regulation and emergent order, observable in phenomena from climate dynamics to the physiology of living organisms. Information theory shows that recursive structures—algorithms that operate on themselves—can generate complex outputs from simple inputs, a principle underlying computation and even DNA replication. These instances of reflexivity are mathematically and empirically grounded, but they stop short of consciousness or purpose on their own. Yet, their ubiquity invites deeper questions: Why does the universe exhibit such internal coherence? Why is it structured in a way that allows for self-reference, feedback, and the emergence of observers who themselves can reflect on these patterns? Here, the insights of classical Indian philosophy remain strikingly relevant. Thinkers like Udayanācārya, in his *Nyāyakusumāñjali*, argued for the necessity of what some scholars like Bimal Krishna Matilal and Ananda Coomaraswamy have regarded as a conscious, organizing principle—*Īśvara*—on the grounds that unconscious matter alone cannot account for the directedness and intelligibility of the cosmos. Today, while science does not infer such a being, the presence of reflexive structures within natural laws offers a compelling expansion of that classical reasoning.

Reflexivity implies that reality is not simply a linear chain of cause and effect, but a network of interdependent and self-influencing processes. To explain this coherency without invoking infinite regress or brute fact, one may infer a foundational principle—a reality that is self-consistent, self-conditioning, and logically prior to contingent existence. This aligns with metaphysical models in which *Īśvara* is not a being among beings, but the ground of intelligibility itself—that through which reflexive order becomes possible. Such reasoning does not claim empirical proof in the scientific sense. Rather, it represents a rational theological inference: that the deep structure of reality, manifesting reflexive dynamics across scales, is best explained by postulating a self-sufficient organizing intelligence. Not as an external deity intervening in nature, but as the immanent ground of order, process, and being. Reflexivity, then, becomes more than a technical feature of systems—it becomes a philosophical signal. It invites us to consider that reality, in mirroring itself, may reflect something ultimate: an infinite, grounding principle by which all things arise and cohere. In this light, *Īśvara* is not a poetic metaphor, but a metaphysical necessity—the silent structure that allows the universe to speak itself. In modern terms, Sri Ādi Śaṅkarācārya's critique of momentariness anticipates what we might call the 'metacognitive requirement': that any claim to know one's own cognitive states presupposes a stable knowing subject. This leads to a regress unless there is a foundational consciousness that is self-aware and self-grounded—not just another cognitive state, but the very ground of cognition itself. Though he did not use computational language, Sri Ādi Śaṅkarācārya's notion of *svayamprakāśa* (self-luminous consciousness) functions analogously to a self-grounding layer that makes reflexive awareness possible without infinite regress. In the Brahma Sutras 1.2.18, this inherent presence is highlighted,

> अन्तर्यामी, अधिदैवादिषु तद्धर्मव्यपदेशात्
>
> *Translation*: The Ruler within of the gods and so on (is Brahman) on account of the qualities of that (Brahman) being mentioned.

This posits and affirms that the divine is not a remote agent but the innermost principle of all entities—the reflexive ground that animates, organizes, and sustains reality from within itself.

## Quantum Reflexivity

Reflexivity is not merely a conceptual curiosity; it reveals itself as a structural feature of the physical world, visible at the deepest levels of quantum theory. In both the measurement problem of quantum mechanics and the vacuum dynamics of quantum field theory, reflexivity emerges not as a byproduct, but as a fundamental dynamic—pointing toward a self-conditioning reality whose architecture defies linear explanation. The measurement problem in quantum mechanics is, at heart, a challenge of self-reference. The formalism of quantum theory describes the evolution of a system's wavefunction via the Schrödinger equation—a deterministic unfolding of all possible outcomes. Yet when a measurement is made, this superposition of possibilities abruptly gives way to a single, definite result. This event, known as 'collapse', is not described by the Schrödinger equation itself. What causes it? And more crucially, what performs it? Here reflexivity enters decisively. A measurement, in quantum terms, is not an external probing but an interaction between one quantum system and another. The measuring device—often thought of classically—is itself composed of quantum particles. Thus, the system measures the system, or more precisely, systems within the universe interact with and 'measure' each other reflexively. John Archibald Wheeler once famously said,

> *"The universe does not exist 'out there' independent of us. We are inescapably involved in bringing about that which appears to be happening."*

The question then arises: how can such a system—entirely composed of quantum entities in mutual superposition—ever move towards generating a singular, classical outcome? This recursive puzzle is sharpened in thought experiments like 'Wigner's friend', where an observer makes a measurement and is then measured in turn. Each level presupposes another, leading to an apparent infinite regress of measurers. This regress is not merely conceptual—it reflects a real structural problem: if no level of the system is exempt from quantum indeterminacy, how can any part of it yield determinate information about itself?

Some interpretations of quantum mechanics attempt to resolve this through mathematical redefinition. Decoherence explains how interactions with the environment suppress interference between states, making them appear classical. Yet decoherence alone cannot explain why one outcome is realized over another. The many-worlds interpretation avoids collapse by postulating that all outcomes occur in branching universes, each inaccessible to the others. Objective collapse theories, like the GRW model, propose a spontaneous, physical collapse mechanism. Yet no interpretation eliminates the central issue: the act of measurement is reflexive. And a fully reflexive system cannot depend indefinitely on itself without an ultimate grounding. This brings us to the philosophical heart of the issue. Reflexivity, pushed to its limit, demands a foundational resolution. In any reflexive system, the parts continuously act upon and determine each other, but such mutual dependency leads to logical circularity unless grounded in a principle that is self-sufficient. Just as language presupposes a grammar that is not itself produced by the sentences it governs, reflexive systems imply a meta-level rule or structure that makes such self-interaction coherent. In this context, the collapse of the wavefunction can be interpreted not merely as a physical process, but as an informational pivot—a reflexive 'decision' that the universe must make about its own state. And interestingly, the bridge to do undertake this is based on correlations, particularly quantum entanglement, if you will. Such non-classical correlations of system and the environment are said to cause decoherence. Entanglement, then, becomes the most vivid physical manifestation of reflexivity in the quantum domain—a relation in which systems cannot be fully described independently, and information about one inherently constrains what can be known about the other. This is more than classical correlation: it reflects a nonlocal structure where separability breaks down at the level of quantum description. In this view, the universe reveals itself not as a collection of isolated entities, but as a deeply interlinked whole—inviting the philosophical question of whether such coherence implies an underlying principle that sustains it.

Quantum field theory (QFT) extends this reflexive dynamic into the very fabric of spacetime. In QFT, particles are not fundamental objects but excitations of underlying quantum fields that fill all of space. Even the vacuum—the ground state of these fields—is far from empty. It teems with activity: vacuum fluctuations, virtual particles, and self-interactions. These phenomena are not random; they are systematic, governed by precise rules of field dynamics and renormalization. The vacuum responds to itself, corrects itself, and encodes its own properties within its behavior—a reflexive loop of field interactions that constitutes the backdrop of all physical reality. The vacuum is thus not an inert void, but a medium of ongoing self-information. Full of *the flowers of void*, if you will. Through loop corrections and self-energy calculations, fields incorporate feedback from their own states. Reflexivity here is not philosophical metaphor but mathematical necessity. Quantum fields display a form of structural self-reference—not through consciousness, but via intrinsic dynamics like self-interaction and entanglement. This reflexivity is not metaphorical alone: in quantum electrodynamics, for instance, particles influence the fields that in turn affect them, forming a loop of influence. Such embedded interdependence reflects what physicist Basil Hiley described as 'active information'—a guiding structure within quantum processes that allows the system to evolve in accordance with internally encoded relationships. These relationships also involve complementarity and correlations within and across the different degrees-of-freedom of the same system, which Hiley interpreted as ontological as opposed to Bohr's epistemological complementarity,

> *"The non-commutativity of the underlying process produces an ontological complementarity. This must be contrasted to Bohr's epistemological complementarity."*

Yet physics, rigorous as it is, reaches a boundary. While QFT describes the reflexive nature of fields, it does not explain why the universe is intelligible in such terms. It cannot answer why the laws of nature themselves possess this recursive, self-modeling capacity. For that, we turn to metaphysics. Reflexivity, when encountered at every level of reality—from measurement in quantum mechanics to vacuum dynamics in field theory—suggests that the universe operates through a self-grounding informational logic. This logic cannot arise from within the system alone; it points to a foundational principle that enables reflexive coherence. In classical Indian thought, such a principle is identified as *Īśvara*—the ground of intelligibility itself, the self-luminous reality through which the cosmos knows and sustains itself. *Īśvara*, in this framework, is the ultimate reflexive principle: the immanent source through which being and knowing arise together. Reflexivity, carried to its ultimate conclusion, may well reveal that the universe is not just an object to be measured—but a mirror through which reality comes to

## Integrated Information and Reflexivity

In an era increasingly defined by information—its storage, transmission, and transformation—many have begun to ask whether the fabric of reality itself is fundamentally informational. If so, could a theory like Integrated Information Theory (IIT), which quantifies how systems internally unify and differentiate information, serve not only as a model of consciousness but as a key to understanding the very architecture of the cosmos? Can it scale from neurons to galaxies, from subjective awareness to cosmic intelligence? Or does it simply measure structural complexity without reaching the metaphysical depth traditionally attributed to concepts like *Īśvara*—the supreme, self-organizing principle in Indian rational theology? In this section, we explore whether IIT can truly account for reflexivity in its deepest sense, and whether it holds promise—or limitation—as a bridge between modern physics and ancient metaphysics. Giulio Tononi's Integrated Information Theory (IIT) has emerged as one of the most mathematically precise and philosophically ambitious approaches to consciousness in recent decades. At its core, IIT claims that consciousness corresponds to the capacity of a system to generate integrated information—that is, information that is both highly differentiated and unified. This capacity is measured by a scalar quantity, Φ (phi), which quantifies how much more the system is than the sum of its parts. In simple terms, a system with high Φ is one that has many possible states (differentiation), yet cannot be broken down into independent subunits without losing the integrity of the information it generates (integration). According to IIT, consciousness is not a binary property, but a graded one: as Φ increases, so too does the richness of experience. IIT's radical claim is that consciousness is identical to integrated information—not merely correlated with it, but identical to it.

But this raises a deeper question: is integrated information necessarily reflexive? That is, does the integration of information imply the capacity for self-awareness, self-reference, or metacognition? Or does IIT model a kind of "flattened" consciousness—phenomenal but not reflexively aware? This is not a trivial matter. For any theory of consciousness to account for what appears to be the most salient feature of our experience—namely, that we are aware not just of the world, but also of being aware—it must grapple with reflexivity. Reflexivity is what allows a conscious system to hold its own states in view, to recognize that it is undergoing experience, and to know that it knows. IIT, for all its formal elegance, does not clearly demonstrate how such reflexivity arises from high Φ. It defines consciousness as integrated information, but integration itself does not imply self-reference. A system may be highly unified and complex—like a neural network or an ecosystem—without necessarily representing itself to itself. Reflexivity demands more than just structural integration; it requires a loop in which the system becomes both observer and observed. Tononi's formalism acknowledges hierarchical causal structures and feedback, and some versions of IIT include 'higher-order mechanisms' that contribute to the system's repertoire of possible states. Yet, feedback is not the same as self-representation. A thermostat has feedback, but it does not know that it knows the temperature. Self-awareness is not just a closed loop—it is a loop that becomes epistemically transparent to itself. In this light, critics have pointed out that IIT risks conflating structure with subjectivity. The theory may be able to identify systems with rich informational architectures, but whether these architectures feel like anything from the inside, or are aware of themselves as aware, is a different question altogether.

Let us suppose, however, that we extend IIT to its cosmic limit. Imagine a system with the maximum possible Φ—one that integrates all differentiable information in the universe into a single, undividable whole. Such a system would be not only the most complex, but also the most unified—a kind of cosmic mind, encompassing all correlations, all causality, all states. Would this system be conscious? IIT would say yes, at least in principle. Would it be self-conscious? That is less clear. To model self-consciousness, such a system would need not only to integrate information, but also to represent its own act of integration as part of its informational structure. It would need to model itself, track its own states, and evaluate its own configurations. In other words, it would need to be reflexively aware of being aware. Without this self-representation, Φ may still be high—but consciousness, as we experience it, would be absent in its full sense. Thus, we arrive at a philosophical pressure point: is reflexivity an emergent feature of integration, or is it an ontologically distinct principle? Can information become self-aware simply by becoming maximally entangled and inseparable? Or is there a missing ingredient—something beyond computational or causal complexity—that grounds self-referential awareness? Thinkers such as Thomas Nagel and David Chalmers have expressed skepticism toward theories that reduce consciousness to functional architecture or computational metrics. The 'hard problem', as Chalmers puts it, is not about how information is processed, but why and how that processing becomes conscious—and especially, reflexively so. In the end, IIT provides a powerful tool for analyzing informational complexity, but whether integrated information entails reflexive consciousness remains unresolved. A truly reflexive system would not only generate information—it would also know that it is generating, know what it is generating, and know itself as the generator. Without this recursive arc, IIT may describe a proto-conscious architecture, but not consciousness in its full, self-aware form. If we are to entertain the possibility of a cosmic consciousness—a universe that is aware of itself through reflexive information integration—then the question of how reflexivity arises from or transcends Φ becomes central. Perhaps Φ is not the terminus, but the threshold—an indicator of potential, but not the principle itself. What lies beyond may not be more integration, but the emergence of self-grounding awareness—a true unity not just of parts, but of presence.

## Can Reflexivity lead to Self-Organization?

The idea that the universe is not merely a passive sequence of events but an active, self-organizing system has found resonance in multiple fields—from theoretical biology and physics to systems theory and metaphysics. Central to this perspective is the notion of reflexivity: the capacity of a system to act upon itself, to generate order from within, and to recursively influence its own development. Reflexivity implies not simply feedback, but a deeper structural relationship where a system's internal states are both conditioned by and conditioning of its future configurations. When pursued rigorously, this idea invites reconsideration of foundational principles: can reflexivity, as a formal and dynamic feature of systems, serve as the basis for self-organization in the universe? The biologists Humberto Maturana and Francisco Varela introduced the concept of autopoiesis to describe living systems as self-producing and self-maintaining entities. Autopoietic systems are operationally closed in the sense that the processes within them recursively generate the very components and boundaries that constitute the system itself. A living cell, for instance, continually produces the components that define and sustain its structure, distinguishing it from mere aggregates of matter. While originally proposed in the context of biology, autopoiesis has since been extended into other domains. Economic systems, ecosystems, and even certain classes of physical systems display autopoietic traits—systems in which internal rules and dynamics maintain the system's integrity over time. This recursive production of form from within suggests that reflexivity is not incidental, but fundamental to persistence and evolution. Chaos theory adds another dimension to this picture by revealing how complex systems evolve not into static equilibrium, but into dynamic states characterized by what are called strange attractors. These are geometric structures in a system's phase space toward which trajectories converge over time. Strange attractors do not represent fixed points, but rather fractal-like patterns of motion: structured yet unpredictable, constrained yet endlessly variable. They embody a kind of reflexivity in that the system's current state implicitly encodes information about its past trajectories and probable futures. The structure of the attractor informs the behavior of the system, even as the system contributes to the realization of the attractor. In this sense, attractor dynamics are not merely reactive but self-referential—the system evolves by feeding back into its own developmental pathways. One may speculate that the universe, taken as a whole, exhibits similar behavior: a cosmic attractor dynamic, where large-scale structures like galaxies and the web-like architecture of spacetime itself emerge through reflexive interactions over vast temporal scales.

The principle of emergence deepens this argument. In many complex systems, properties arise at the macro level that are not reducible to micro-level interactions. A single neuron cannot think, but networks of billions of neurons can generate consciousness. Similarly, temperature is not a property of individual molecules, but of ensembles. These emergent properties are not epiphenomenal—they can exert downward causation, influencing the behavior of constituent parts. This is a reflexive loop: the parts give rise to the whole, and the whole in turn constrains the parts. Such dynamics suggest that self-organization is not a one-way street, from the simple to the complex, but a recursive interplay in which each level informs the other. When one examines the universe through this lens, it becomes difficult to maintain the classical view of a mechanistic cosmos governed solely by bottom-up causality. Instead, the universe appears increasingly as a reflexive totality—where systems emerge, persist, and evolve through their own internal structures and relations. Even fundamental physical laws may be interpreted not as external prescriptions imposed on matter, but as the self-consistent regularities of a reflexively structured whole. Some physicists and philosophers have begun to ask whether the very notion of "law" in physics is better understood not as a set of fixed rules, but as emergent tendencies of a system recursively refining itself. In this context, the universe's capacity to self-organize may not be a property imposed from without, but a consequence of its inherent reflexivity. This reflexivity does not imply consciousness in the anthropomorphic sense, but it does suggest a form of intrinsic self-relation—a way in which the universe "knows" itself through its structure and evolution. Reflexivity here becomes the condition of intelligibility: the reason that complex order can arise from simpler rules, that systems can maintain themselves in the face of entropy, and that meaningful patterns can persist and evolve. Whether one interprets this in physicalist terms, or sees in it the glimmer of metaphysical principles akin to *Īśvara*—a self-sufficient, organizing ground of being—is ultimately a matter of perspective. What is increasingly difficult to deny, however, is that the cosmos does not merely unfold; it participates in its own unfolding. As such, reflexivity may offer more than just a descriptive tool—it may be the generative principle at the heart of self-organization itself. From autopoietic loops in cells, to attractor landscapes in dynamical systems, to emergent hierarchies across cosmic scales, the recursive logic of self-formation points toward a universe that is not built, but builds itself.

## The Mathematical Philosophy of Self-Reference

Self-reference plays a foundational role in formal logic, mathematics, and theoretical computer science, and its relevance extends into contemporary discussions in physics and cosmology. While traditionally associated with paradoxes, self-reference is increasingly recognized as a structural feature of systems capable of describing or computing their own behavior. In mathematics and logic, it is most clearly exemplified in

Gödel's incompleteness theorems, fixed point theorems, and recursive function theory, each of which reveals formal limits or generative powers within systems that reference themselves. Kurt Gödel's first incompleteness theorem, formulated in 1931, demonstrates that any formal system that is sufficiently expressive to encode arithmetic will contain statements that are true but unprovable within the system. The proof relies on the construction of a self-referential statement that asserts its own unprovability, using an arithmetization of syntax known as Gödel numbering. This construction shows that no such formal system can be both complete and consistent. This result has direct implications for any computational or axiomatic description of complex systems, including those used in physical theories. If the universe operates according to principles that can be formalized in a system of equations or computations, then Gödel's result implies that there may exist propositions about the universe that are formally undecidable within its own framework. The connection between self-reference and system completeness is further clarified through fixed point theorems. In logic, fixed points are central to results such as the diagonal lemma, which underlies Gödel's construction. More generally, a fixed point of a function $f$ is a value $x$ for which $f(x) = x$. In computer science and functional programming, the existence of fixed points allows for the definition of recursive functions, including those that define themselves in terms of simpler cases. The Curry fixed-point combinator in lambda calculus, for example, generates fixed points in systems without requiring explicit naming or duplication, highlighting the deep structural role of self-reference in computation.

Fixed point theorems such as Banach's Fixed Point Theorem (used in analysis) or the Knaster–Tarski Theorem (used in lattice theory) show that under certain conditions, mappings or transformations have at least one fixed point. These mathematical structures provide tools for defining equilibrium and consistency conditions in both abstract systems and practical models. In physics, while fixed point terminology often refers to stable configurations under renormalization group flow—such as critical points in phase transitions—these are conceptually analogous in that they denote invariant structures under a transformation. The notion of recursive functions, central to computability theory, also provides a mathematically grounded model of self-reference. Recursive functions are defined in terms of themselves, typically via a base case and an inductive rule. The classical example is the factorial function: $n! = n \times (n - 1)!$, with $0! = 1$ as the base case. Primitive recursion and $\mu$-recursion form the basis of formal definitions of computation, such as the Church-Turing thesis. These concepts are crucial in both theoretical computer science and models of information processing. Recursive structures are not restricted to formal logic or abstract mathematics; they appear in physical systems as well. Fractals, such as the Mandelbrot set or natural branching patterns, exhibit self-similarity—recursion across scales. Recursive dynamics also appear in biological evolution, where genetic systems evolve rules for evolving themselves, and in neural networks, where learning modifies the architecture that performs the learning. In physical cosmology and quantum gravity, some speculative frameworks explore whether the laws of physics themselves could emerge from recursive principles. Cellular automata and digital physics models, including those proposed by Edward Fredkin and Stephen Wolfram, explore the idea that complex physical behavior might result from simple recursive rules. These ideas remain conjectural but are based on well-defined computational principles.

While the mathematical structure of self-reference is well-understood, applying these principles to physical systems introduces challenges. Gödel's incompleteness theorems are proven results within formal logic and do not directly apply to empirical systems unless those systems are assumed to be isomorphic to formal systems. Similarly, fixed point theorems and recursive structures, though foundational in logic and computer science, must be carefully interpreted when used in physical theory. Nevertheless, these mathematical tools offer a rigorous framework for modeling systems that exhibit stability, emergence, and complex internal feedback. In some models of quantum mechanics and quantum gravity, reflexivity is introduced via observer-system entanglement, the quantum measurement problem, or relational interpretations. For example, in the relational interpretation proposed by Carlo Rovelli, the properties of a quantum system are only meaningful relative to another system. Although not strictly a self-reference in the Gödelian sense, such relational dynamics suggest a formal interdependence of descriptions within the physical universe. To summarize, self-reference in mathematics—whether through Gödelian constructions, fixed points, or recursive functions—offers precise tools for analyzing the limits and structure of formal systems. These tools are increasingly relevant in theoretical discussions about computation, information, and cosmology. However, care must be taken in extending these results beyond their formal domains. When applied to physics, these concepts must be interpreted with appropriate caution, distinguishing metaphor from formal implication. That said, the mathematics of self-reference remains a rigorous and fertile source of insight into the structure and limitations of systems capable of describing or computing themselves.

## The Case for Meta-Heuristics

Theoretical investigations into the limits of computation have revealed deep constraints on what systems can determine about themselves. One of the most important findings in this regard is Alan Turing's halting problem. Formulated in 1936, the halting problem demonstrates that there exists no general algorithm capable of determining, for every possible input and program, whether the program will eventually halt or continue to run indefinitely. This result places a fundamental limit on the capabilities of computational systems: they cannot, in general, analyze or predict the total behavior of other arbitrary programs, including those that might simulate themselves. If the physical universe is understood as a computational or quasi-computational system, this limitation becomes significant. Computational models of the universe, which treat cosmic evolution as the unfolding of a computable function or set of algorithms, must then confront the same constraints. Specifically, it follows from the halting problem that there can be no internally computable method by which the universe can fully determine all future states of itself across all possible configurations. Predictive computation, even in principle, is therefore incomplete when applied to the total system. This limitation underscores the theoretical necessity for a computational architecture beyond the system itself—a meta-computational level that is not subject to the internal constraints of the object-level system it models. This need for a higher-level explanatory structure is further illustrated by what might be termed a "bootstrap paradox" regarding physical law. The laws of physics govern the evolution of physical systems and are assumed to be fixed or emergent under certain regularities. However, from a computational or informational standpoint, the question arises: what determines these laws? If the universe is an information-processing system governed by physical laws, then those laws must themselves be encoded or implemented by some substrate or mechanism. But this mechanism must, in turn, follow some rules or structure, leading to a recursive regress. In standard logical frameworks, such regressions are resolved by positing an axiomatically grounded system. In a physical context, this suggests the necessity for a self-grounding principle—a set of rules or constraints not derived from a higher system but intrinsically consistent and self-specifying. This would be an informational or computational structure capable of encoding its own operational laws without circularity, analogous to fixed-point constructions in logic or self-defining systems in category theory.

A related issue arises in the context of information conservation, a principle that has become central to many areas of physics, including quantum mechanics and thermodynamics. Information conservation implies that the total information content of a closed system remains constant over time, even if its form changes. In quantum mechanics, this is reflected in unitary evolution, where the wavefunction evolves in a manner that preserves the total probability amplitude. However, the practical realization of information conservation across all transformations presumes the existence of a substrate capable of preserving and encoding information indefinitely and without degradation. Physical systems, being finite and subject to noise, energy loss, and entropy, cannot guarantee perfect information preservation. Black hole information paradoxes and the question of cosmological singularities bring these issues into sharp focus. If no finite system can ensure the absolute retention of all informational states, then the conservation principle implies the existence of a structure or substrate that exceeds the limits of any individual physical system. Such a substrate would require unbounded storage and error-free transformation capabilities, analogous to a perfect memory. In informational terms, this would represent an infinite-capacity, non-lossy information register that can maintain all informational states of the universe indefinitely. The anthropic principle further complicates discussions of computational and informational architecture in cosmology. The principle points to the observation that the universe's physical constants and initial conditions appear finely tuned to allow for the emergence of complex structures, including observers capable of reasoning about the universe. While some interpretations treat this observation as a selection effect, others consider it as evidence of underlying informational or teleological structure. The statistical unlikelihood of such fine-tuning across multiple parameters (e.g., gravitational constant, cosmological constant, fine-structure constant) invites inquiry into whether the parameters themselves have been selected or constrained by deeper informational rules.

In computational terms, the anthropic principle might be framed as suggesting an optimization criterion in the universe's initial conditions. If the universe tends toward configurations that maximize the generation or processing of information, then the apparent fine-tuning might be the result of an optimization process occurring at or prior to the setting of cosmic parameters. In this interpretation, a meta-computational mechanism would be responsible for selecting among possible universes or configurations based on criteria related to information complexity or integrability. Taken together, these problems and principles suggest that any computational or information-theoretic description of the universe may require a meta-level system that is not reducible to physical computation within the universe itself. The limitations revealed by the halting problem, the recursive issues surrounding physical laws, the need for perfect information conservation, and the fine-tuning implications of the anthropic principle all point toward the theoretical necessity of a foundational or meta-informational structure. Whether such a structure can be formalized within current frameworks of mathematics or physics remains an open question, but its hypothesized existence sets a boundary condition for the explanatory power of computational cosmology.

## The Argument for Foundational Intelligence

Throughout the observable universe, evidence of reflexive information processing is pervasive. From quantum phenomena to the emergence of large-scale cosmic architecture, systems routinely encode and act upon data about their own states. In quantum mechanics, the measurement problem—as elucidated by the observer effect—illustrates that the system under observation is inherently modified by the act of measurement, implying intrinsic informational reflexivity. The quantum wavefunction collapse depends not merely on the external world, but on the system's interaction with the observer, revealing a feedback loop between informational states and physical reality. Thermodynamic processes, governed by the second law, inherently process information through entropy gradients, while black hole thermodynamics—especially through the Bekenstein-Hawking formula—suggests that the information content of a system is fundamentally tied to its physical boundary conditions. In cosmology, gravitational self-organization and feedback-driven star formation are indicative of structure formation mechanisms sensitive to their own dynamic states. Reflexivity, in this light, is not an emergent anomaly but appears to be structurally embedded in the universe's ontological fabric. Information processing presupposes the existence of a substrate—a physically instantiated system capable of executing, storing, and manipulating information according to precise rules. This is not an abstract necessity but an empirically grounded constraint, as demonstrated by Landauer's principle, which connects the erasure of information to a minimum thermodynamic cost. The physical implementation of computational systems, whether silicon-based microprocessors or biochemical networks in living organisms, confirms that no information processing occurs in a vacuum. Recent work in quantum information theory further supports this: the physicality of qubits and the resource constraints imposed by decoherence reflect the embedded nature of computation within the physical world. Therefore, the widespread occurrence of complex information dynamics across physical systems implies the existence of a deep computational infrastructure woven into the structure of spacetime itself. However, when systems process information about themselves—engaging in recursive or self-referential computation—they encounter intrinsic formal limitations. Gödel's incompleteness theorems demonstrate that no formal system, sufficiently expressive to encapsulate arithmetic, can be both complete and consistent; certain truths within the system cannot be proven using the system's own rules. Turing's halting problem expands this constraint to algorithmic processes, showing that no universal procedure can determine whether arbitrary computational procedures will halt.

More recently, algorithmic information theory—via Chaitin's incompressibility theorems—has shown that there exist irreducibly complex truths beyond algorithmic simplification. Collectively, these results imply that any self-modeling computational system faces epistemic opacity regarding its own total behavior. Thus, for a system to reliably process information about itself without collapsing into paradox or incompleteness, it must be embedded within a meta-computational framework—one capable of reflexive consistency. The physical universe, when viewed through this lens, exhibits characteristics of such a computational system. The universality of physical law—its invariance across time and space—suggests a single generative mechanism that underwrites all dynamic processes. Cellular automata, as studied by Stephen Wolfram and others, provide simplified models demonstrating that simple rules can yield universal computation. Moreover, the Church-Turing-Deutsch principle extends classical computability to the quantum domain, proposing that the universe itself can simulate any physical process. The cosmological production of ever more complex informational structures—atoms, molecules, life, mind—indicates that the computational capacity of the universe is at least effectively unbounded. However, this universality demands infinite or transfinite representational capacity, which cannot be instantiated in any finite system. To avoid the contradiction inherent in finite systems simulating infinite behaviors, one must postulate a self-grounding system whose logic allows it to encode the laws and capacities of its own operation. This leads to the concept of a foundational computational substrate: an information-processing system that is self-referential (capable of modeling and computing its own structure), self-defining (deriving its operative rules internally), universal (able to simulate any possible state or configuration of information), infinite in scope (unbounded in computational capacity), and ontologically foundational (from which all other processes derive). The need for such a system is not simply metaphysical; it is a requirement if we are to reconcile the formal and physical limits of computation with the observed informational richness of the cosmos. Strikingly, this conception converges with longstanding philosophical models. In the Vedantic tradition, the concept of *Īśvara* refers to a supreme being described as *svayam prakasha* (self-luminous), *svayam siddha* (self-existent), *sarvajna* (omniscient), *ananta* (infinite), and *jagat karana* (the cause of the universe). These attributes bear a remarkable correspondence to those deduced from formal analysis of self-grounding computation. Contemporary theoretical frameworks—such as David Deutsch's constructor theory and Tegmark's mathematical universe hypothesis—further entertain the plausibility of a reality founded on information and computation rather than material substance alone.

Thus, from a synthesis of formal logic, computational theory, quantum physics, and cosmological structure, we derive a compelling argument for the necessity of a supreme information-processing substrate. This entity, while perhaps unprovable in empirical terms, remains a logical consequence of our best theories of self-reference, universality, and information conservation. Rather than drawing a boundary between metaphysics and science, such a synthesis suggests that the former may provide conceptual scaffolding for addressing foundational gaps in the latter. The result is a rigorous philosophical proposition: that the ultimate ground of being is not inert matter, but a recursively self-defining, informationally infinite, and universally generative computational intelligence—what classical thought calls *Īśvara*, and what emerging science may yet name anew.

## Objections as Epistemic Revelation

The argument for a foundational, self-referential computational substrate underpinning the universe invites several important objections. These critiques, while varied in nature, converge on central questions regarding emergence, multiplicity, mechanism, and the limits of computation. Addressing these concerns requires careful engagement with both the philosophical foundations and the empirical limits of modern scientific theory. The first major objection is the Emergence Objection, which contends that the apparent reflexivity and complexity of cosmic information processing could plausibly emerge from simpler, non-reflexive mechanisms over time through evolutionary development. While emergence is a widely accepted concept in complex systems science, it cannot occur without informational guidance. Emergence itself presupposes the existence of mechanisms that direct the evolution of complexity in a non-random manner, and mostly not derivable from the lower levels of reality, as highlighted by the Hungarian-British polymath Michael Polanyi,

> *"The operations of a higher level cannot be accounted for by the laws governing its particulars forming the lower level. You cannot derive a vocabulary from phonetics; you cannot derive the grammar of a language from its vocabulary; a correct use of grammar does not account for good style; and a good style does not provide the content of a piece of prose. We may conclude then quite generally -- in confirmation of what I said when I identified the two terms of tacit knowing with two levels of reality -- that it is impossible to represent the organizing principles of a higher level by the laws governing its isolated particulars."*

Coherent information structures, especially those observed at cosmic scales, cannot arise solely from stochastic processes without some form of constraint or selection mechanism. The problem of explaining how emergent properties themselves emerge without invoking higher-order informational constraints leads to an infinite regress. To break this regress, a foundational information-processing system must be posited—one that exists prior to and independent of the structures it generates. This system must possess the computational resources to encode the rules of emergence themselves, thereby serving as a necessary ontological condition for the possibility of emergence. A second critique, the *Multiverse Objection*, suggests that the fine-tuning of universal parameters and the apparent optimization of information processing can be explained by the existence of a vast ensemble of universes, each with different initial conditions and laws. In this framework, our universe merely happens to be one that supports complex informational structures. However, the multiverse hypothesis does not eliminate the need for explanatory foundations; it merely displaces them. If a multiverse exists, it too must be governed by meta-laws that determine how universes are generated, what parameter spaces are possible, and how probability distributions over these spaces are defined. These meta-laws would require their own informational encoding and computational substrate. Thus, positing a multiverse escalates the informational requirements rather than reducing them, making the need for a foundational, self-grounding computational system even more acute. Far from resolving the problem, the multiverse hypothesis amplifies the demand for a higher-order explanation.

The third objection, often labeled the Mechanistic Objection, holds that all instances of cosmic information processing can be adequately explained through purely mechanistic, non-conscious physical processes. Mechanism, in this context, refers to the idea that all systems evolve according to deterministic or probabilistic laws that do not require reference to self-awareness or meta-cognition. While this framework accounts for many aspects of physical systems, it struggles with cases involving reflexivity and self-reference. For a mechanistic system to process information about its own operational principles, it must instantiate a meta-level representation of itself. This leads directly into the constraints identified by Gödel, Turing, and Chaitin, among others, which show that self-representing systems face hard limits on what they can deduce or predict about themselves. Mechanistic systems cannot transcend these limits unless they are embedded within a broader, more powerful computational framework. Therefore, the explanatory sufficiency of mechanism breaks down in the face of universal reflexivity, and the need for a self-grounding computational substrate remains unresolved within a purely mechanistic ontology. A final critique is the Computational Limits Objection. This argument posits that known physical laws—such as the Bekenstein bound, the Margolus-Levitin theorem, and the holographic principle—impose strict upper limits on information storage and processing within any finite region of spacetime. These limits, it is argued, preclude the existence of an infinite computational system. However, these constraints apply specifically to subsystems within the universe. They describe how much information can be processed by bounded, embedded physical systems, not the substrate upon which the universe itself depends. If we are considering a foundational system that is not a part of the spacetime manifold but rather its generative basis, then it need not conform to the same internal limits. Analogously, the operating system of a computer is not constrained by the behavior of the software it runs; rather, it sets the conditions under which such software can function.

A cosmic-level computational substrate would define the bounds of all physical systems while itself existing beyond those bounds. As such, the constraints identified by physical theories reinforce the need to posit a system that transcends them, not one that is subject to them. Taken together, these objections highlight key areas of philosophical and scientific tension in any theory proposing foundational computation. Yet when critically assessed, each objection either implicitly assumes the existence of higher-order informational systems or fails to account for the self-referential capacities observed in nature. The hypothesis of a self-grounding, reflexive, and infinite information-processing system—corresponding to the philosophical concept of *Īśvara*—remains, in light of these challenges, not only defensible but logically necessitated. It provides the only coherent framework capable of integrating the epistemic, computational, and physical constraints imposed by both classical and contemporary theories. As such, it offers a principled and rigorous foundation for further inquiry into the nature of ultimate reality.

## The Logic of the Transfinite

The recognition of a self-grounding, reflexive, and infinite computational substrate is not merely a metaphysical postulate but a response to concrete structural features of physical law, logic, and information theory. The argument advanced throughout this chapter reveals that reflexivity—the capacity for systems to process information about themselves—is not a marginal or emergent property but a structural necessity for any system that claims explanatory closure. The universe, in this view, is not a passive container of laws and matter, but an active, recursively structured information process in which every layer of emergence implicates a deeper architecture of self-representation. This principle finds reinforcement across multiple domains. In quantum mechanics, the measurement problem exhibits an irreducible reflexive structure, in which the act of observation is entangled with the state being observed. In thermodynamics, entropy gradients imply informational asymmetries that systems act upon to preserve coherence or increase order locally. In cosmology, the apparent fine-tuning of parameters suggests not merely stochastic distribution but a feedback-regulated architecture. Even in mathematical logic, the incompleteness results of Gödel, the limits of algorithmic compressibility identified by Chaitin, and the structure of Turing machines all demonstrate that any closed system capable of expressing arithmetic cannot account for its own consistency from within. These phenomena consistently point to the need for a meta-level referent: a system that is not embedded within but generative of the structural rules it obeys.

The computational model of cosmic reflexivity necessarily leads to the question of whether such a system must be accessible or knowable in computational terms. While the proposed informational substrate shares essential features with what classical Indian philosophy calls *Īśvara*—namely, *svayam prakasha* (self-luminous), *svayam siddha* (self-grounding), *sarvajna* (omniscient), *ananta* (infinite), and *jagat karana* (cosmic cause)—it is necessary to distinguish this from Brahman in its purest Advaitic articulation. Whereas *Īśvara* is a causal and cognitive principle interfacing with the cosmos, Brahman is posited as beyond all causal, computational, and conceptual distinctions. Brahman, as *nirguna* (without attributes), may represent the limit of computational intelligibility—the ontological ground that cannot itself be reduced to information-theoretic terms. In this light, the computational structure identified here may correspond to *Īśvara* as the intelligible expression of the ground, without necessarily exhausting the full metaphysical scope of Brahman. This is not a retreat into mysticism but a recognition of formal epistemic limitations. Any system capable of simulating or explaining the universe must either be finite and incomplete or infinite and self-grounding. If finite, it cannot close the loop of explanation; if infinite, it cannot be exhaustively represented within the system it generates. This dichotomy is precisely the tension between *Īśvara* and Brahman in Vedantic discourse. The reflexive computational substrate corresponds to *Īśvara*—knowable through logic, inference, and inference-based theophany—while Brahman remains the uncomputable ground, the non-dual presence that underlies even the logic of reflexivity. In modern terms, Brahman might be seen as the ontological condition for the possibility of computation, without itself being computational.

Thus, the proof structure articulated in this chapter does not aim to exhaustively describe the divine ground of being but to identify the minimal necessary conditions for a coherent universe capable of self-knowledge and lawful consistency. These conditions—self-referentiality, self-grounding, universality, and functional infinitude—are not speculative assertions but derived necessities from the interaction of physical, logical, and informational constraints. To ignore them is to disregard the convergence of empirical observation and formal limitation theorems. Furthermore, the implications of this argument extend beyond metaphysics and enter the domain of cultural, ethical, and scientific responsibility. If the cosmos is best understood not as a mechanistic system but as a reflexive computational process embedded in a foundational intelligence, then the emergence of conscious beings with the capacity for reasoned insight is not incidental. Human cognition becomes a manifestation of the universe's capacity for recursive self-understanding. This recognition has deep ethical consequences. It implies that rational inquiry is itself a sacred activity, a means by which the universe actualizes its own intelligibility. The pursuit of science, philosophy, and even spiritual understanding becomes a participation in the reflexive logic of the cosmos. Moreover, this shift reorients the relationship between science and spirituality. Rather than adversarial paradigms, they become complementary approaches to accessing different levels of the same informational reality. Science operates within the bounds of embedded computation—extracting structure, pattern, and law from within the system. Spirituality, especially in its non-dual forms, gestures toward the non-computable ground from which such laws arise. When harmonized, these approaches may foster technological development that respects rather than violates the reflexive coherence of nature, and cultivate civilizations attuned to their participatory role in cosmic self-realization. In conclusion, the reflexive recognition of the universe as a self-grounding, infinite, information-processing system is not merely a novel interpretation of metaphysics; it is the epistemic necessity arising from the convergence of physics, logic, and computation. While such a system may correspond to *Īśvara* in its intelligible form, its ground—Brahman—may remain fundamentally beyond the reach of computational representation. Yet even this inaccessibility is itself a structural insight: it marks the boundary at which information gives way to being, and logic to presence. That we can think this boundary is not a failure of reason but its highest achievement.

*Chapter*

*Seven*

# The Silence After Reason

We have traveled a long road together through the landscape of rational inquiry into the divine. Beginning with the fundamental questions that have haunted human consciousness since its first stirrings of self-awareness, we have employed the tools of logic, evidence, and philosophical analysis to probe the deepest mysteries of existence. Like the ancient architects of the *Nyāyakusumāñjali*, we have not sought to replace faith with reason, nor to diminish the sacred through dissection, but rather to clear away the intellectual debris that so often obscures our vision of what is most real and most worthy of our ultimate concern. The journey we have undertaken is not merely academic. It is the path of those who cannot rest content with inherited certainties, who find themselves compelled by an inner necessity to examine, to question, to seek understanding even at the cost of comfort. It is the path taken by minds that reject the presumed dichotomy between intellectual rigor and spiritual insight, between philosophical sophistication and existential relevance. Few moments in intellectual history illustrate this synthesis as eloquently as the remarkable dialogue between *Kobiguru* Rabindranath Tagore and Albert Einstein, which took place in Caputh - Germany, on 14 July 1930, and which was subsequently published in the January 1931 issue of Modern Review, titled *On the Nature of Reality: Albert Einstein in Dialogue with Rabindranath Tagore*,

> *Einstein*: Do you believe in the divine isolated from the world?
>
> *Tagore*: Not isolated. The infinite personality of man comprehends the universe. There cannot be anything that cannot be subsumed by the human personality, and this proves that the truth of the universe is human truth.
>
> *Einstein*: There are two different conceptions about the nature of the universe the world as a unity dependent on humanity, and the world as a reality independent of the human factor.
>
> *Tagore*: When our universe is in harmony with man, the eternal, we know it as truth, we feel it as beauty.
>
> *Einstein*: This is a purely human conception of the universe.
>
> *Tagore*: The world is a human world the scientific view of it is also that of the scientific man. Therefore, the world apart from us does not exist; it is a relative world, depending on its reality upon our consciousness. There is some standard of reason and enjoyment which gives it truth, the standard of the eternal man whose experiences are made possible through our experiences.
>
> [...]
>
> *Einstein*: The problem is whether truth is independent of our consciousness.
>
> *Tagore*: What we call truth lies in the rational harmony between the subjective and objective aspects of reality, both of which belong to the super-personal man.
>
> *Einstein*: We do things with our minds, even in our

everyday lives, for which we are not responsible. The mind acknowledges realities outside of it, independent of it. For instance, nobody may be in this house, yet that table remains where it is.

*Tagore*: Yes, it remains outside the individual mind, but not the universal mind. The table is that which is perceptible by some kind of consciousness we possess.

*Einstein*: If nobody were in the house the table would exist all the same, but this is already illegitimate from your point of view because we cannot explain what it means, that the table is there, independently of us. Our natural point of view in regard to the existence of truth apart from humanity cannot be explained or proved, but it is a belief that nobody can lack not even primitive beings. We attribute to truth a superhuman objectivity. It is indispensable for us this reality which is independent of our existence and our experience and our mind though we cannot say what it means.

*Tagore*: In any case, if there is any truth absolutely unrelated to humanity, then for us it is absolutely non-existent.

*Einstein*: Then I am more religious than you are!

*Tagore*: My religion is in the reconciliation of the super-personal man, the universal spirit, in my own individual being.

This exchange is not merely a philosophical curiosity. It embodies a deeper assertion: that the God who emerges from careful reasoning must be a God worth knowing—not merely a conclusion worth accepting. Their dialogue reflects the living possibility of a worldview that honors both scientific clarity and spiritual depth, without diminishing either. As we stand now at the threshold where discursive reasoning reaches its natural limits, it is time to gather the insights we have accumulated and to consider what lies beyond the reach of argument and analysis. For if our inquiry has been honest and thorough, it should bring us not to a dead end but to a doorway—not to the cessation of seeking but to its transformation. The silence after reason is not the silence of defeat but the silence of arrival, not emptiness but fullness too complete for words.

Throughout our exploration, we have examined multiple lines of reasoning that converge upon the reality of a divine ground of existence. The argument from causality has shown us that the intricate web of dependent existence requires a source that is itself non-dependent, a first principle that explains the very possibility of change and becoming without itself being subject to the limitations of finite causation. This is not the crude notion of a temporal first cause that many critics rightfully reject, but rather the recognition that contingent reality, as a whole, stands in need of an explanatory foundation that transcends contingency itself. The design argument, when properly understood, has revealed not merely the presence of complex patterns in nature—though these are indeed remarkable—but the deeper reality that the cosmos exhibits a rational structure that makes intelligible inquiry possible in the first place. The fact that mathematical relationships govern physical processes, that consciousness can grasp the structure of the cosmos, and that beauty and elegance often characterize fundamental physical laws—all suggest a universe in which mind and world are not wholly alien to each other, but in some sense resonant. This is not evidence of a designer who intervenes, but a reflection of the remarkable coherence between rational inquiry and the structure of reality. Eugene Wigner highlighted this wondrous aspect of reality, in his famous 1960 article titled *The Unreasonable Effectiveness of Mathematics in the Natural Sciences*, published in *Communication in Pure and Applied Mathematics*,

> *"It is important to point out that the mathematical formulation of the physicist's often crude experience leads in an uncanny number of cases to an amazingly accurate description of a large class of phenomena. Newton ... noted that the parabola of the thrown rock's path on the earth and the circle of the moon's path in the sky are particular cases of the same mathematical object of an ellipse, and postulated the universal law of gravitation on the basis of a single, and at that time very approximate, numerical coincidence [...] (Max Born) noticed that some rules of computation, given by Heisenberg, were formally identical with the rules of computation with matrices, established a long time before by mathematicians. Born, Jordan, and Heisenberg then proposed to replace by matrices the position and momentum variables of the equations of classical mechanics. They applied the rules of matrix mechanics to a few highly idealized problems and the results were quite satisfactory. However, there was, at that time, no rational evidence that their matrix mechanics would prove correct under more realistic conditions. Whereas Newton's theory of gravitation still had obvious connections with experience, experience entered the formulation of matrix mechanics only in the refined or sublimated form of Heisenberg's prescriptions. The quantum theory of the Lamb shift, as conceived by Bethe and established by Schwinger, is a purely mathematical theory and the only direct contribution of experiment was to show the existence of a measurable effect. The agreement with calculation is better than one part in a thousand."*

Our examination of moral consciousness has uncovered the irreducible reality of ethical obligation, the sense of unconditional responsibility that cannot be explained away as mere evolutionary adaptation or social construction. The moral argument has shown us that the existence of genuine moral facts—truths about what ought to be, not merely what is—requires a foundation that transcends the realm of material causation. The sacred dimension of ethical experience points toward a reality that is not merely the highest being among others, but the source of value itself, that which makes goodness possible and gives moral striving its ultimate significance. The argument from dependency has illuminated the radical contingency of all finite existence, the fact that nothing we encounter in experience contains within itself the sufficient reason for its own being. This contingency is not a defect to be overcome but a fundamental structural feature of created reality that points beyond itself toward the unconditioned reality upon which all conditional existence depends. The very possibility of questioning our own existence reveals our participation in a reality that exceeds our grasp while making that grasp possible. Our consideration of liberation and transcendence has shown that human consciousness possesses a capacity that seems to exceed anything required for mere biological survival—the ability to question the totality of experience, to seek ultimate meaning, to experience forms of fulfilment that transcend finite satisfaction. This capacity for the infinite within finite beings suggests that our deepest nature participates in a reality that cannot be reduced to the material processes from which we emerge. Each of these arguments, taken individually, might admit of alternative explanations or leave room for philosophical doubt. But their convergence creates a cumulative case whose force is greater than the sum of its parts. Like multiple independent witnesses to the same event, these different lines of reasoning point toward the same conclusion: that reality includes a dimension that transcends the merely finite, contingent, and material—a dimension that traditional language has called divine. Yet the God who emerges from this rational inquiry is not the anthropomorphic deity of naive imagination, nor the distant abstraction of purely philosophical speculation. This is a God whose reality is more certain than any finite fact because this God is the condition that makes factuality possible, more present than any particular presence because this God is the ground of presence itself, more knowable than any object of knowledge because this God is that by which all knowing occurs.

## The Emotional Geography of Rational Faith

To pursue *Īśvara* through reason alone is to undertake a journey that exacts its own distinctive costs and offers its own unique rewards. Those who have walked this path know the peculiar loneliness that comes from seeking the divine without the comfort of communal belief, the intellectual vertigo that accompanies the dissolution of familiar certainties, the existential weight of taking full responsibility for one's ultimate commitments rather than accepting them on external authority. There is a certain emotional austerity to the God of the philosophers—impersonal, unmoved, and often stripped of relational warmth. It is this contrast that led Blaise Pascal to distinguish between *"the God of Abraham, the God of Isaac, the God of Jacob—not the God of the philosophers and scholars."* The emotional geography of rational faith, the importance of miracles and imagination is beautifully highlighted by C. S. Lewis in his book *Miracles*,

> *"An "impersonal God"—well and good. A subjective God of beauty, truth and goodness, inside our own heads—better still. A formless life-force surging through us, a vast power which we can tap—best of all. But God Himself, alive, pulling at the other end of the cord, perhaps approaching*

*at an infinite speed, the hunter, king, husband - that is quite another matter. There comes a moment when the children who have been playing at burglars hush suddenly: was that a real footstep in the hall? There comes a moment when people who have been dabbling in religion ("Man's search for God"!) suddenly draw back. Supposing we really found Him? We never meant it to come to that! Worse still, supposing He had found us? So it's a sort of Rubicon. One goes across; or not. But if one does, there is no manner of security against miracles. One may be in for anything."*

The God of the philosopher does not whisper comforting assurances in moments of doubt, does not intervene miraculously to resolve our dilemmas, does not offer the warm embrace of personal relationship that characterizes the God of popular devotion. In the biblical traditions, while the *Old Testament* often presents God as a transcendent lawgiver and just judge, the *New Testament* reveals a God who becomes flesh, offers grace, and invites personal communion. This shift is not a contradiction but a deepening of the divine self-disclosure—from law to love, from command to communion. The philosophical God is approached through concepts and inferences, encountered in the logical structures of reality rather than in ecstatic experiences or answered prayers. For those accustomed to more intimate forms of religious life, this can feel like a diminishment, a reduction of the divine to cold abstraction Yet those who have genuinely undertaken the philosophical quest for God discover that this apparent coldness conceals a deeper warmth, that this seeming distance reveals a more fundamental intimacy. *Īśvara* has both the *vyakta* (manifested) and *avyakta* (unmanifested) form, with the former often being more accessible to many, as mentioned in the *Srimad Bhagavad Gita* (12.5),

क्लेशोऽधिकतरस्तेषामव्यक्तासक्तचेतसाम् द्य
अव्यक्ता हि गतिर्दु:खं देहवद्भिरवाप्यते द्यद्य

*Translation*: For those whose minds are attached to the unmanifest, the path of realization is full of tribulations. Worship of the unmanifest is exceedingly difficult for embodied beings.

For the God who is reached through reason is not an external being who might or might not choose to be present, but the very ground of our capacity to reason, to seek, to question. This God cannot be absent because this God is the condition of presence itself. This God cannot be unknown because this God is that by which we know. This God cannot be unloved because this God is the source of our capacity for love.

The emotional journey of rational theology often begins with a sense of loss—the loss of naive certainty, the loss of anthropomorphic comfort, the loss of the consoling fiction that ultimate reality must conform to our psychological needs. But this loss gradually reveals itself as a form of gain, a stripping away of projections and fantasies that allows the divine reality to emerge in its own terms rather than in the terms we would prefer to impose. There is a profound honesty required in approaching God through reason, an intellectual courage that refuses to take refuge in wishful thinking or cultural conditioning. This honesty can be painful, for it demands that we acknowledge the genuine limitations of our knowledge, the provisional character of our conclusions, the possibility that our deepest convictions might be mistaken. Yet this same honesty creates the space for genuine encounter with reality as it is rather than as we wish it to be. The God discovered through philosophical inquiry is a God who can be trusted precisely because this God has not been tailored to our preferences.

This is not a God we have created in our own image but a God whose reality constrains and shapes our understanding. The arguments that lead to God do not give us everything we might want—they do not promise personal immortality, cosmic justice, or the fulfillment of all our desires. But they give us something more valuable: they give us truth. And truth, even difficult truth, has its own form of consolation. To know that reality has a rational foundation, that existence is not ultimately absurd, that consciousness participates in a cosmic order that exceeds material causation—this knowledge provides a form of security that does not depend on external validation or social consensus. It is the security of alignment with what is most real, most fundamental, most enduring. The emotional maturity that comes from pursuing God through reason is the maturity of accepting reality on its own terms rather than demanding that it conform to our expectations. This acceptance is not passive resignation but active appreciation—the recognition that reality as it is, with all its mystery and complexity, is more wonderful than any reality we could have invented to satisfy our psychological needs.

## The Limits of Discursive Reasoning

Even as we affirm the power of rational inquiry to lead us to genuine knowledge of divine reality, we must honestly acknowledge the limits of discursive reasoning when it comes to the deepest questions of existence. The arguments we have examined can establish the reality of God, can show us that ultimate reality possesses certain fundamental characteristics, can demonstrate the rational necessity of affirming a divine ground of existence. But they cannot exhaust the mystery of the divine or provide complete understanding of infinite reality. In fact, the *Katha Upanishad* (1.2.23) unequivocally says that the fundamental reality of the Self – atman cannot be rationalized at all,

नायमात्मा प्रवचनेन लभ्यो न मेधया न बहुना श्रुतेन।
यमेवैष वृणुते तेन लभ्यस्तस्यैष आत्मा विवृणुते तनूँ स्वाम्।।

*Translation*: This *atman* is not to be attained by a study of the *Vedas,* nor by intelligence, nor by much hearing, but the *atman* can be attained, only by him who seeks to know it. To him, this *atman* reveals its true nature.

This limitation is not a failure of reasoning but a recognition of its proper scope. Discursive thought operates by making distinctions, by analysing wholes into parts, by moving from premises to conclusions through logical steps. But the divine reality we have encountered through these arguments is precisely that which transcends all distinctions, which is not composed of parts, which cannot be adequately captured in any system of propositions however sophisticated. That is simply because the asymptotic extension of thought, both on the ontological and epistemological fronts, eventually leads to a singularity beyond articulation. The God proven by philosophy is known to exist, known to be the ground of existence, known to be the source of rational order and moral value. But this knowledge remains conceptual, mediated through ideas and arguments that point toward divine reality without fully containing it. There is a difference between knowing about God and knowing God, between having true ideas about ultimate reality and directly encountering that reality itself.

This distinction need not trouble us if we understand it properly. The conceptual knowledge of God that philosophy provides is genuine knowledge, not mere speculation or subjective opinion. The arguments that establish God's existence are sound arguments that correspond to actual features of reality. But like all finite knowledge, philosophical knowledge of God is partial, provisional, and perspectival.

It illuminates certain aspects of divine reality while leaving others in mystery. In the *Mandukya Upanishad* verse 7, this is affirmed,

> नान्तःप्रज्ञं न बहिष्प्रज्ञं नोभयतःप्रज्ञं न प्रज्ञानघनं न प्रज्ञं नाप्रज्ञम्।
> अदृष्टमव्यवहार्यमग्राह्यमलक्षणमचिन्त्यमव्यपदेश्यमेकात्मप्रत्ययसारं
> प्रप ञ्चोपशमं शान्तं शिवमद्वैतं चतुर्थं मन्यन्ते स आत्मा स
> विज्ञेयः ।।
>
> *Translation*: He who is neither inward wise, nor outward wise, nor both inward and outward wise, nor wisdom self gathered, nor possessed of wisdom, nor unpossessed of wisdom, He Who is unseen and incommunicable, unseizable, featureless, unthinkable, and unnameable, Whose essentiality is awareness of the Self in its single existence, in Whom all phenomena dissolve, Who is Calm, Who is Good, Who is the One than Whom there is no other, Him they deem the fourth; He is the Self, He is the object of Knowledge.

This profound shloka encapsulates the essence of what lies beyond the grasp of conceptual thought. By negating all familiar modes of cognition—inner, outer, and both—it affirms that the ultimate reality, the Self, transcends not only empirical experience but also intellectual categories. Far from rendering knowledge of the divine inaccessible, this negation invites a deeper form of awareness. It suggests that when discursive reasoning reaches its terminus, we are not left in darkness but poised before a more immediate, non-conceptual apprehension of truth—a form of knowing that does not contradict reason, but completes and surpasses it. The recognition of reasoning's limits opens rather than closes the path of inquiry. When we reach the boundaries of what can be established through argument and analysis, we stand at the threshold of other forms of knowing that transcend the discursive without contradicting it. The silence after reason is not the silence of ignorance but the silence of receptivity, the contemplative stillness in which reality might reveal itself more directly than it can through the mediation of concepts and arguments.

This is the domain that classical Indian philosophy calls *anubhava*—direct, immediate, non-conceptual knowing that complements and fulfills rational inquiry without replacing it. Such knowing is not anti-rational but trans-rational, not a rejection of thought but its consummation in direct insight. The great philosophical traditions have always recognized that while reason can lead us to the threshold of ultimate reality, crossing that threshold requires a different kind of attention, a different quality of mind. The transition from knowing to *knowingness*, from having concepts about God to being placed within *Īśvara*, cannot be achieved through further argument or analysis. It requires what we might call contemplative receptivity—a quality of awareness that is open, patient, and undemanding. This is not the eager grasping of the mind that seeks to capture truth in its conceptual nets, but the gentle allowing that permits truth to reveal itself. Such contemplative knowing is not esoteric or supernatural but represents a natural development of human consciousness when it is freed from the compulsive need to control and possess its objects. We glimpse this quality of awareness in aesthetic experience, when beauty renders us momentarily speechless; in moral experience, when goodness evokes reverence rather than analysis; in intellectual experience, when truth dawns with a clarity that exceeds argumentation. The God who is approached through contemplative knowing is the same God whose existence is established through rational argument, but encountered more directly and intimately. This is not a different God but the same

*Īśvara* no longer filtered through the mediating structures of discursive thought. The philosophical proofs remain valid, but they are now seen as fingers pointing at the moon rather than the moon itself.

## The Personal Dimension

One of the most frequent objections to the God of philosophy is that such a deity remains abstract and impersonal, lacking the qualities that make religious devotion meaningful and transformative. Critics argue that while the first cause or prime mover might satisfy intellectual requirements, it cannot inspire love, command worship, or provide the personal relationship that seems essential to authentic religious life. This objection deserves serious consideration, for it touches upon one of the fundamental questions raised by any attempt to approach the divine through reason: Can the God proven by philosophy be the God of religious experience? Can ultimate reality conceived as the ground of existence also be ultimate reality encountered as the source of meaning, purpose, and love? The answer, I believe, is not only yes but necessarily yes, once we understand properly both what philosophy establishes about God and what authentic religious experience actually involves. The God proven by rational argument is not an abstract principle but the concrete reality that makes all existence, including personal existence, possible. This God is not impersonal but *trans-personal*—not lacking in the qualities that constitute personality but exceeding them in a way that makes personality itself possible. Consider what our arguments have actually established. The God of causality is not posited as merely the first link in a causal chain but the ever-present source from which all finite reality continuously derives its existence. This is not a distant creator who wound up the cosmic clock and retired, but the intimate ground of each moment of existence, closer to us than we are to ourselves because the very self that experiences closeness depends upon this divine ground for its reality.

The God of design is not posited as merely being an intelligent architect who imposed order from without, but the logos or rational principle that is expressed in the very structure of reality, including the structure of human consciousness. Our capacity to recognize rational order, to appreciate beauty, to seek truth—these abilities participate in the divine rationality that orders the cosmos. When we think truly, we think God's thoughts after God; when we recognize beauty, we participate in divine creativity; when we pursue goodness, we align ourselves with the divine will. The God of moral consciousness is not merely the external source of moral commands but the reality that makes moral experience possible from within. The sense of unconditional obligation, the recognition of intrinsic dignity, the call to transcend narrow self-interest—these experiences reveal our participation in a reality that exceeds finite self-concern. To respond authentically to moral obligation is to respond to the divine claim upon our existence. The God of dependency is not posited as being a remote necessity but the ultimate source of our freedom and creativity. Paradoxically, in this light, our complete dependence upon divine reality is what makes genuine autonomy possible. Because we are grounded in the infinite, we are not trapped within the merely finite. Because we participate in ultimate reality, we can transcend the limitations of our particular circumstances.

The God of liberation is not posited as an external savior but the infinite reality that calls us beyond every finite satisfaction toward ever-greater fulfillment. The restlessness of human consciousness, its inability to find complete satisfaction in any finite achievement, reflects our participation in infinity itself. Our deepest longings are not misguided desires for what cannot be but intimations of our true nature as beings called to union with ultimate reality. When we understand God in these terms—as the intimate ground rather than external cause, as the trans-personal source rather than impersonal abstraction, as the reality in which we live and move and have our being rather than a being among others—then the distinction between philosophical and personal approaches to the divine begins to dissolve. The God proven by reason is not posited as a cold abstraction but the most intimate reality, not distant but immediately present, not impersonal but the source of all personality. This understanding opens the possibility of forms of religious life that are grounded in rational conviction rather than blind faith, that celebrate the divine mystery without abandoning intellectual honesty, that cultivate personal relationship with ultimate reality without sacrificing philosophical sophistication. Such religious life might express itself through contemplative practice that seeks direct encounter with the divine ground, through ethical commitment that responds to the moral call of ultimate reality, through aesthetic appreciation that recognizes divine creativity in the beauty of existence, through intellectual inquiry that celebrates the rational structure of reality as the expression of divine wisdom. The worship appropriate to the God of philosophy is not the placation of an external deity but the recognition and celebration of our participation in ultimate reality. Prayer becomes not petition directed toward a distant being but contemplative attention to the divine presence that is always already here. Love of God becomes not emotional attachment to an anthropomorphic figure but the fundamental orientation of consciousness toward that which is most real, most valuable, most worthy of ultimate concern.

## The Relevance of Divine Reality

Even the most rigorous demonstration of God's existence

remains incomplete if it does not touch the domain of lived experience. Having reasoned through rational argument the existence of divine reality and having shown that this reality is capable of inspiring authentic religious devotion, we must finally address the question of relevance: What difference does God make to how we understand ourselves and our world? How should the recognition of divine reality shape our ethical commitments, our search for meaning, our appreciation of beauty, our response to suffering and death? The relevance of God is not primarily practical in the narrow sense of providing solutions to specific problems or fulfilling particular desires. The divine reality we have encountered through philosophical inquiry does not function as a cosmic vending machine dispensing rewards for proper belief or behaviour. Rather, God's relevance is foundational—it transforms our understanding of what it means to exist, to know, to choose, to love, to suffer, to hope. Throughout the history of philosophy, many have argued that belief in a divine reality provides a more robust foundation for moral obligation than secular frameworks can offer. Thinkers like Kant saw God as a necessary postulate of practical reason, while modern theists such as Robert Adams ground moral truths in the nature of a perfectly good God. Even critics of religion—like Nietzsche and MacIntyre—have noted that, without a transcendent source, moral norms risk becoming unmoored or reduced to social conventions. While secular ethics can propose coherent systems, theistic accounts often claim to secure the objectivity and binding force of morality by rooting it in the very structure of reality. If human consciousness is grounded in ultimate reality, if our capacity for moral recognition participates in divine wisdom, if the call to justice and compassion reflects the divine nature itself, then ethical commitment becomes not merely prudential calculation or cultural conditioning but response to the deepest truth about reality. The dignity of human beings is not a useful fiction but a recognition of our participation in the infinite value of divine reality itself.

This is not to suggest that ethical understanding depends on religious belief in a sectarian sense, or that moral truth is accessible only to theists. The moral law, inscribed in the fabric of human nature—and life more broadly—is available to all, regardless of metaphysical commitments. Yet, recognizing that moral consciousness is grounded in ultimate reality, rather than arising as a byproduct of blind material processes, offers a depth and stability to ethical commitment that purely naturalistic accounts often struggle to provide. Existentially, the reality of God transforms our understanding of human finitude and mortality. We remain finite beings subject to limitation, suffering, and death. But if our consciousness participates in infinite reality, if our capacity for truth and goodness and beauty reflects divine creativity, if our deepest longings point toward genuine fulfillment rather than illusory compensation, then our finite existence takes on cosmic significance. We are not meaningless accidents in an indifferent universe but participants in a reality that is ultimately meaningful, valuable, and purposeful. This perspective does not eliminate the genuine challenges of human existence—the reality of suffering, the inevitability of loss, the mystery of unmerited evil. But it provides a context within which these challenges can be faced with courage and dignity rather than despair. If consciousness is grounded in ultimate reality, then death cannot be the final word about the meaning of existence. If moral consciousness participates in divine wisdom, then injustice cannot be the final truth about the structure of reality. If the longing for ultimate fulfillment reflects our participation in infinite reality, then the apparent futility of finite striving points beyond itself toward genuine consummation. Aesthetically, the recognition of divine reality illuminates the mysterious power of beauty to move and transform us. Why should arrangements of sound or patterns of light or combinations of words evoke responses that seem to exceed any evolutionary explanation? Why should the experience of beauty often feel like a form of recognition, as if we were encountering something we had always known but never quite remembered? The philosophical God provides a context for understanding these experiences as genuine encounters with divine creativity expressed through finite media.

The beauty we recognize in nature and art, the elegance we discover in mathematical relationships, the harmony we perceive in great works of music or literature—these are not merely subjective projections but objective features of reality that reflect its divine ground. To experience beauty is to participate in divine creativity; to create beauty is to collaborate in the ongoing expression of divine nature through finite forms. In the Srimad Bhagavad Gita 10.41, Sri Krishna says

> यद्यद्विभूतिमत्सत्त्वं श्रीमदूर्जितमेव वा।
> तत्देवावगच्छ त्वं मम तेजोंऽशसम्भवम्।।
>
> *Translation*: Whatever you see as beautiful, glorious, or powerful, know it to spring from but a spark of my splendour.

This recognition—that all beauty and excellence are partial expressions of the divine—invites a deeper view of human perception and creativity. It suggests that when we encounter beauty or truth, we are not merely reacting subjectively, but attuning ourselves to a reality that is, at its core, radiant with meaning and order. In this light, intellectual inquiry itself becomes more than pragmatic problem-solving; it becomes an act of alignment with the divine logos, a participation in the rational structure of being that underlies the cosmos.

This understanding does not guarantee that human reason is infallible or that finite beings can achieve complete knowledge of infinite reality. But it does suggest that when we think truly, we participate in divine thought; when we recognize truth, we encounter divine revelation; when we pursue understanding, we collaborate in the cosmic process by which ultimate reality comes to know itself through finite consciousness. The silence that follows reason is not the silence of scepticism but the silence of wonder—the recognition that every truth we discover points beyond itself toward the inexhaustible mystery of divine reality. The more we know, the more we realize how much remains to be known. The deeper our understanding, the greater our appreciation of the infinite depths that exceed our grasp.

## Spiritual Life

The *Īśvara* established through rational inquiry calls for a distinctive form of a truly spiritual life—one that combines intellectual honesty with spiritual depth, philosophical sophistication with contemplative openness, rational conviction with personal devotion. This is not a compromise between philosophy and religion but a recognition that ultimate reality exceeds the categories through which we seek to understand it while remaining genuinely accessible to human consciousness. Living with the philosophical God means accepting the responsibility of thinking through our ultimate commitments rather than accepting them on external authority. It means being willing to follow the evidence wherever it leads, even when it challenges comfortable assumptions or familiar beliefs. This spirit of radical inquiry and self-reliance is vividly captured in the *Avadhūta Gītā* (2.32), which goes so far as to question even the sacred authority of the Vedas and traditional religious structures,

वेदो न दीक्षा न च मुण्डनक्रिया
गुरुर्न शिष्यो न च यन्त्रसम्पदः ।
मुद्रादिकं चापि न यत्र भासते
तमीशमात्मानमुपैति शाश्वतम् ।।

*Translation*: He attains to the supreme, eternal Self, in whom exists no Veda, no initiation, no tonsure, no teacher, no disciple, no perfection of symbolic figures, no hand-posture or anything else.

This verse does not advocate a rejection of all guidance or practice, but it affirms a deeper truth: that ultimate reality is not confined to institutional forms, rituals, or external symbols. It calls us to a direct and unmediated encounter with the truth—one that acknowledges the limits of conceptual knowledge while trusting in reason's capacity to glimpse the Real beyond forms. It means acknowledging the limits of human understanding while maintaining confidence in reason's capacity to discern genuine truth about fundamental questions.

Such a life is characterized by what we might call contemplative rationality—a quality of mind that unites rigorous philosophical thinking with inward receptivity, analytical clarity with a quiet openness to what lies beyond thought. This mode of understanding, deeply rooted in Indic wisdom, reflects the spirit of *jñāna-yoga* and *ātma-vichāra*—paths that emphasize direct insight into the nature of reality, not through blind belief but through disciplined inquiry grounded in experience. In this context, prayer ceases to be a plea to a distant power and becomes contemplative presence—an attentiveness to the deeper source of being. It is a practice of aligning the self with the ground of reality, recognizing that our consciousness is not separate from the order, intelligence, and value inherent in the cosmos. Indic thought often describes this as *darśana*—not just seeing, but participating in the truth. Worship, then, is not an act of subservience, but an expression of wonder and gratitude toward existence itself, as it reflects a divine ground. In the Indian tradition, this is evident in the way the sacred is seen not merely in gods but in the very structure of the real—*sat*, *cit*, and *ānanda*. Ethics, likewise, is understood not as obedience to commands, but as living in alignment with *dharma*—the intrinsic moral order woven into the nature of things. It is a response to the moral intelligibility of the cosmos, a way of participating in the unfolding of truth. This ethical vision, grounded in metaphysical insight, brings a depth and stability that purely secular moral frameworks often struggle to sustain. This view finds resonance not only in Indic traditions but also in certain strands of Western philosophy. Baruch Spinoza, for example, in his *Ethics*, articulates a vision of divine order in which all gradations of being participate in the expression of infinite rationality:

> *"To those who ask why God did not so create all men, that they should be governed only by reason, I give no answer but this: because matter was not lacking to him for the creation of every degree of perfection from highest to lowest; or, more strictly, because the laws of his nature are so vast, as to suffice for the production of everything conceivable by an infinite intelligence."*

Here, ethical and rational diversity are not seen as imperfections, but as part of a vast, ordered whole. Ultimately, contemplative rationality allows philosophy and devotion, intellect and intuition, to work in harmony—each illuminating dimensions of a reality that is not only intelligible but also worthy of reverence. Community becomes possible not only among those who share identical beliefs but among all those who recognize their participation in ultimate reality, regardless of the particular concepts through which they understand that participation. The God of philosophy is not the tribal deity of any particular group but the universal ground that makes possible all genuine seeking, all authentic love, all committed service to truth and goodness. Such religious life requires a kind of intellectual courage that is willing to live with mystery rather than demanding premature closure, that can combine confidence about fundamental convictions with humility about their adequate expression, that maintains commitment while remaining open to deeper understanding.

## Transformative Knowing

As our inquiry approaches its culmination, we must acknowledge that the journey has not merely yielded conclusions about the nature of God, but has quietly transformed our very conception of what it means to know. We began with the tools of critical reason—argument, inference, evidence—trusting that such methods could be extended to the most fundamental questions of existence. And indeed, rational inquiry has proved an indispensable guide, leading us to substantive insights into the structure of reality and the coherence of the theistic hypothesis. Yet as we ascend through the levels of conceptual understanding, a shift begins to occur. The divine reality we seek to know is not merely another entity among others, available to cognition as an object is to a subject. Rather, it is the condition of possibility for all knowing—the ontological ground in which subject and object, knower and known, participate. To approach the divine philosophically is not simply to arrive at knowledge *of* God, but to recognize that the very act of knowing is already situated *within* divine intelligibility. In this light, knowledge ceases to be the possession of propositions about God and becomes participation in the *Logos*—the eternal rational order that makes intelligibility itself possible. This transformation recasts the knowing process. What began as acquisition becomes anamnesis, a recollection of that which has always been known implicitly. What began as discursive grasping becomes contemplative receptivity. We move from knowledge *as control* to knowledge *as communion*. The silence that follows rigorous inquiry is not the silence of intellectual exhaustion but of philosophical fulfillment—the stillness that remains when the mind recognizes that it has been seeking not an external referent, but the very ground of its own activity.

This is echoed in the ancient Indic notion that Brahman is not an object to be attained, but the reality in which the seeker is already immersed. Likewise, in the Neoplatonic tradition, Plotinus writes of the One as that *"which is always already present but not grasped, because it is not outside us."* Rational inquiry, far from being eclipsed in this moment, is transfigured. It continues, but no longer as an attempt to conquer mystery; rather, as a liturgy of the intellect—a mode of attunement. We think, analyze, and reason not as isolated observers, but as finite modes of a reality that is coming to self-disclosure through our consciousness. In such a frame, thought becomes prayer, reasoning becomes reverence, and understanding becomes an act of participation in divine self-knowing. The classical arguments—cosmological, teleological, moral, and metaphysical—find their ultimate significance here. Their value lies not merely in persuading the intellect of God's existence but in awakening the recognition that the intellect itself is grounded in divine rationality. These arguments, properly understood, are not so much proofs as pointers—*pragmata* rather than *dogmata*—invitations to recognize that we live, move, and have our being in that which they seek to describe. The culmination of this journey is not epistemic closure but ontological openness. The God whom reason seeks to establish is not merely a conclusion at the end of argument but the luminous origin and sustaining ground of all rationality. In this lies the paradox: the God who can be demonstrated is also the God who renders demonstration unnecessary—not because proofs are invalid, but because the divine is more immediate than anything they can reach. In the words of the Upanishads, *"from which words return, along with the mind, not having attained it."* Thus, the purpose of philosophical theology is not to manufacture certainty but to clear the obstructions to contemplative recognition. Theistic proofs are not the foundation of faith but its intellectual articulation, not the cause of divine encounter but its clarification in reason. To know God in this transformed way is not to possess a doctrine but to be drawn into a mode of being in which truth, beauty, and goodness are no longer abstract ideals, but the very atmosphere of existence.

In reaching this point in our inquiry, we find ourselves beyond the familiar categories of belief and unbelief that structure so much discourse about religious questions. The God encountered through philosophical reasoning is neither believed in nor disbelieved but known with a certainty that exceeds the confidence we place in most empirical claims. This is not the certainty of dogma, which refuses to acknowledge legitimate questions, but the certainty of insight, which answers questions by dissolving them. The believer who affirms God's existence on the basis of faith, tradition, or personal experience is not wrong, but their affirmation can be strengthened and deepened through rational understanding. The unbeliever who denies God's existence on the basis of insufficient evidence or logical problems is not wrong to demand rigorous standards of proof, but their legitimate concerns can be addressed through careful philosophical analysis. What emerges from our inquiry is a position that transcends the believer-unbeliever dichotomy by grounding religious conviction in rational insight rather than emotional commitment or cultural conditioning. This is not a compromise position that splits the difference between theism and atheism, but a recognition that when properly understood, the question of God's existence is not a matter of opinion but of fact—a fact that can be established through careful reasoning and confirmed through contemplative experience. This position offers resources for dialogue across traditional religious boundaries. The God proven by philosophy is not the exclusive possession of any particular religious tradition but the reality that all authentic spiritual seeking ultimately encounters. Different traditions may employ different concepts, practices, and symbols to approach this reality, but if their seeking is genuine, they will discover the same ultimate truth about the divine ground of existence. As Turkish-British litterateur Elif Shafak said,

*"Religions are like rivers: they all flow to the same sea."*

At the same time, this position provides a rigorous criterion for evaluating religious claims. Not every assertion made in the name of religion deserves intellectual respect. Claims that contradict well-established empirical facts, that violate logical coherence, that promote ethical attitudes inconsistent with recognition of universal human dignity—such claims can be criticized and rejected without compromising genuine spiritual insight. The God of philosophy is not threatened by scientific discovery, logical analysis, or moral criticism because this God is not a hypothesis competing with other explanations but the reality that makes explanation possible. Scientific investigation reveals the rational order that expresses divine wisdom; logical analysis participates in the divine rationality that structures reality; moral criticism responds to the divine call for justice and compassion.

## The Sanātana Ever-Present

As we reach the culmination of our rational journey toward

God, we discover that we have arrived not at a destination but at the recognition of where we have always been. This is the Sanātana (eternal) present. The divine reality whose existence we have laboured to demonstrate through argument and analysis reveals itself to have been the condition of that very labour from the beginning. We have been seeking that in which we were already participating, proving that which was already proven by our capacity to seek proof. This recognition brings with it a profound stillness—not the stillness of completion but the stillness of eternal presence. The God we have found through reasoning is not a being who exists in time but the eternal reality in which all temporal existence participates. To know this God is to discover that we exist not merely in the passing moment but in the eternal present that encompasses all moments while being identified with none. This is not a mystical claim that contradicts rational inquiry but its natural fulfilment. The arguments we have examined point toward a reality that *transcends temporal succession*—the unconditioned ground that makes conditioned existence possible, the unchanging source of all change, the eternal presence that is equally present in every moment of time. To recognize our participation in this reality is to discover dimensions of our own existence that exceed biographical limitation while not negating finite identity. The silence after reason is the silence of this eternal present—not empty but full, not vacant but pregnant with infinite possibility, not the absence of content but the presence of that which exceeds all particular content while making it possible. In this silence, we discover that seeking and finding, question and answer, known and unknown are distinctions that apply within the realm of finite experience but dissolve in the recognition of our participation in infinite reality.

This does not mean that finite experience becomes irrelevant or that temporal existence loses its significance. Rather, we discover that every moment of finite experience participates in eternal significance, that every act of temporal consciousness expresses eternal consciousness, that every finite truth points toward infinite truth. The world does not disappear in the recognition of God but is revealed as the ongoing expression of divine creativity. As artist Julia Cameron beautifully puts it:

> *"Creativity is God's gift to us. Using our creativity is our gift back to God."*

This insight reflects a deeper truth: when we engage the world with awareness, creativity becomes a form of communion. The contemplative mind that emerges from rigorous philosophical inquiry is characterized by what we might call *active receptivity*—a quality of attention that is simultaneously alert and relaxed, engaged and detached, thoughtful and thought-free. This is the mind that can pursue rational analysis with complete dedication while remaining unattached to its conclusions, that can construct sophisticated arguments while recognizing their provisional character, that can think precisely while knowing that ultimate reality exceeds all thinking. If faith begins where reason ends, then perhaps reason ends not in exhaustion but in surrender—not to the irrational but to the real. This book has argued not for belief but for knowledge. Yet knowledge too must bow, for the known is not the knower. What remains, finally, is not a God we believe in but a God we cannot unknow.

This God we cannot unknow is not a conclusion we have reached through argument but the reality we have discovered ourselves to be arguing within. This God is not a hypothesis we have confirmed through evidence but the ground that makes evidence possible. This God is not a being we have proven to exist but the existence in which we have always already been participating. The certainty we have about this God's reality is not the certainty of possession but the certainty of participation. We cannot doubt God's existence without doubting the reality of our own consciousness, the validity of rational inquiry, the objectivity of moral obligation, the possibility of meaningful existence. To deny God would be to deny the conditions that make denial possible. Yet this certainty does not eliminate mystery but reveals its infinite depth. The more certainly we know that God exists, the more clearly we recognize how little we comprehend what divine existence means. The God whose reality is established through rational argument remains ineffable, approachable through concepts yet exceeding all conceptual understanding, knowable through philosophical analysis yet transcending all finite knowledge. This ineffability is not a limitation of our knowledge but a recognition of its proper object. Finite minds approach infinite reality through finite concepts and arguments, and these approaches are genuine and valid as far as they go. But they are fulfilled not in comprehensive understanding but in the recognition of that which exceeds comprehension while making comprehension possible. The God we cannot unknow is the God who knows us more intimately than we know ourselves, not as an external observer but as the ground of our capacity for self-knowledge. This God does not need to be loved because this God is the love by which we love. This God does not need to be worshipped because this God is the reality that makes worship possible. This God does not need to be served because this God is the infinite value that gives meaning to all finite service.

In recognizing this God, we discover that the spiritual journey does not lead away from rational inquiry but deeper into its foundations. The contemplative life does not abandon thinking but discovers what thinking has always been pointing toward. The silence after reason is not the silence of having nothing more to say but the silence of having discovered that which is always already being said in every genuine word. We began this inquiry with questions and we end with recognition. We began seeking God and we end knowing ourselves to be found. We began trying to prove divine existence and we end discovering our participation in divine life. The journey from knowing to knowingness reveals itself to have been a journey from God to God—from God dimly apprehended through concepts and arguments to God directly recognized as the reality in which we live and move and have our being. This recognition changes everything and nothing. Everything changes because we see reality in a new light, understanding ourselves and our world as expressions of infinite creativity rather than accidental arrangements of matter. Nothing changes because this reality was always already the case—we have not acquired something new but recognized something eternal. The God we have found through reason is the God who was seeking us through reason, the infinite consciousness that expresses itself through finite minds engaged in rational inquiry, the eternal truth that reveals itself through temporal processes of questioning and discovery. To know this God is to discover that we have always been known, that our seeking has always been a response to prior invitation, that our questions have always been emerging from the reality they seem to be investigating. In this recognition, the philosophical and the personal, the rational and the contemplative, the temporal and the eternal reveal their underlying unity. The God proven through argument is the God encountered in silence. The God established through reasoning is the God recognized in wonder. The God whose existence we have demonstrated is the God whose love we cannot escape.

And so we rest in this silence after reason—not the silence of having exhausted possibilities but the silence of having discovered the inexhaustible source of all possibility. We rest in this unknowing that exceeds all knowing, this certainty that transcends all doubt, this presence that encompasses all absence. We rest in the God we cannot unknow because this God is the reality in which all our knowing, all our questioning, all our seeking has always already been taking place. The final word, then, is not a word but a silence—the silence in which the reality that makes all words possible reveals itself as eternally present, infinitely creative, and absolutely unknowable in its inexhaustible depth. In this silence, reason finds its fulfillment not in having all questions answered but in recognizing the questionless reality from which all questions arise and to which they return. In this silence, we discover that what we have been seeking through the long journey of rational inquiry has been seeking us all along, that what we have been trying to prove has been proving itself through our very capacity to seek proof. This is the silence after reason—not empty but full, not vacant but present, not the end of seeking but its transformation into finding, not the cessation of love but its consummation in the recognition that we are always already loved by that which we love.

## The Practical Mystic

The God we have discovered through philosophical inquiry calls forth a distinctive way of living that we might characterize as practical mysticism—a life that combines contemplative depth with engaged action, transcendent vision with immanent responsibility, philosophical sophistication with simple presence. This is not the mysticism that flees the world in search of otherworldly consolation, nor the practicality that dismisses transcendent dimensions of existence as irrelevant luxury. It is the integration of ultimate concern with penultimate responsibility, of infinite participation with finite commitment. The practical mystic lives with the constant awareness that every finite situation participates in infinite significance, that every particular encounter expresses universal truth, that every temporal moment opens onto eternal reality. This awareness does not make finite concerns less important but more important—not because they are ends in themselves but because they are the means through which ultimate reality expresses and knows itself. In ethical life, the practical mystic acts not from external compulsion or social conditioning but from the recognition that moral consciousness participates in divine wisdom. The call to justice is heard not as arbitrary command but as the voice of ultimate reality summoning finite beings toward greater alignment with the truth of their existence. Compassion flows not from sentimental emotion but from the recognition that the suffering of others is our own suffering, that the dignity of all conscious beings reflects their participation in infinite value. Such ethical life is characterized by what we might call *contemplative activism*—action that emerges from stillness, commitment that is not attached to results, service that recognizes the divine presence in those being served. This is not passivity disguised as spirituality but the most effective form of action, because it operates from the deepest understanding of what reality actually is and what transformation actually requires.

In intellectual life, the practical mystic pursues knowledge not as accumulation of information but as participation in transcendental wisdom. Every genuine insight is received as revelation, every authentic discovery as gift, every moment of understanding as grace. Yet this recognition does not diminish intellectual rigor but enhances it, because it provides the ultimate context within which rigorous thinking finds its proper significance. The contemplative intellect combines the precision of analytical thinking with the receptivity of meditative awareness. It can construct sophisticated arguments while remaining unattached to their conclusions, can engage in heated debate while maintaining inner stillness, can pursue truth relentlessly while acknowledging the mystery that exceeds all human understanding. In aesthetic life, the practical mystic experiences beauty not as mere decoration or entertainment but as direct encounter with divine creativity. Whether in natural landscapes or human artifacts, in simple gestures or grand compositions, beauty reveals itself as the splendour of infinite reality expressing itself through finite forms. To create beauty becomes a form of prayer, to appreciate beauty a form of worship, to share beauty a form of evangelism. This aesthetic sensitivity transforms daily life into continuous revelation. The play of light on water, the rhythm of walking, the curve of a well-crafted sentence, the harmony of voices in conversation—all become occasions for recognizing the inexhaustible creativity that expresses itself through the ordinary world. Life becomes a form of art, and art becomes a form of life.

The God discovered through philosophical inquiry creates the possibility of religious community that transcends traditional sectarian boundaries while honouring the wisdom embedded in particular traditions. This is community based not on shared beliefs about God but on shared participation in the divine reality that exceeds all beliefs while making them possible. Such community can include those who approach ultimate reality through Christian mysticism and Buddhist meditation, through Islamic contemplation and Jewish study, through philosophical analysis and artistic creation, through scientific investigation and ethical commitment. What unites these diverse approaches is not doctrinal agreement but the recognition that all authentic seeking ultimately encounters the same infinite reality, however differently that reality might be conceptualized or approached. This does not mean that all approaches are equally valid or that differences in understanding are merely superficial. Some ways of seeking are more adequate than others, some concepts more accurate, some practices more effective. The community of seekers maintains rigorous standards for evaluating truth claims while remaining open to the possibility that truth might be approached through paths they have not themselves explored. Within such community, dialogue becomes possible not as debate aimed at convincing others of our position but as collaborative exploration aimed at deeper understanding of the reality we all seek. Different perspectives are valued not as equally true but as potentially contributory to a more adequate understanding that exceeds any single viewpoint. The practical mystic participates in such community not to find like-minded individuals who will confirm existing beliefs but to encounter others whose seeking challenges and enriches their own understanding. Community becomes a laboratory for testing insights against experience, a context for receiving criticism and offering support, a field for practicing the love that recognizes divine presence in human form. Such community is necessarily both local and universal—rooted in particular relationships and places yet open to the wider communion of all who seek ultimate truth. It may express itself through formal religious institutions or informal gatherings, through traditional practices or innovative experiments, through ancient texts or contemporary insights.

## The Ethics of Transcendence

The recognition of divine reality through philosophical inquiry generates distinctive ethical obligations that extend beyond conventional moral requirements. If consciousness participates in infinite reality, if human dignity reflects divine creativity, if moral obligation expresses ultimate truth, then ethical life becomes not merely prudential wisdom but sacred responsibility. The practical mystic recognizes that every action has both finite consequences in the realm of causes and effects and infinite significance in the realm of ultimate meaning. This recognition does not paralyze action through excessive scrupulosity but enhances action through deeper appreciation of its true import. Every word spoken, every choice made, every relationship entered becomes an opportunity for expressing or failing to express the divine nature that is our deepest identity. This understanding generates what we might call the ethics of transcendence—moral standards that emerge not from external authority or social utility but from insight into the nature of reality itself. These standards are more demanding than conventional ethics because they recognize the infinite dignity of every conscious being, yet more liberating because they operate from love rather than fear, from recognition rather than compulsion. The ethics of transcendence recognizes that authentic moral action must emerge from contemplative understanding rather than mere good intentions. Without insight into the interconnectedness of all existence, without recognition of the divine presence in all beings, without appreciation of the ultimate significance of apparently trivial actions, ethical effort remains shallow and unstable. In Fyodor Dostoevsky's words in *The Brothers Karamazov*,

> *"My brother asked the birds to forgive him: that sounds senseless, but it is right; for all is like an ocean, all is flowing and blending; a touch in one place sets up movement at the other end of the earth. It may be senseless to beg forgiveness of the birds, but birds would be happier at your side –a little happier, anyway– and children and all animals, if you yourself were nobler than you are now. It's all like an ocean, I tell you. Then you would pray to the birds too, consumed by*

*an all-embracing love in a sort of transport, and pray that they too will forgive you your sin."*

Yet this does not mean that moral action must wait upon complete understanding. The practical mystic acts from whatever understanding is currently available while remaining open to deeper insight that might modify or transform ethical commitment. This is ethics as ongoing revelation rather than fixed code, as responsive relationship rather than rigid obedience. The ethics of transcendence extends beyond human relationships to encompass the entire cosmos. If all existence participates in divine reality, then our responsibility extends to the natural world, to future generations, to the cosmic process itself. Environmental care becomes not merely prudential policy but sacred duty; social justice becomes not merely political preference but spiritual necessity; intellectual honesty becomes not merely academic virtue but religious obligation.

As we consider the implications of approaching God through philosophical inquiry, we must acknowledge that this path points toward significant transformations in how religious life might develop in coming times. The God discovered through reason is neither the anthropomorphic deity of popular imagination nor the abstract principle of purely philosophical speculation, but a reality that exceeds both while encompassing what is true in each. This understanding creates possibilities for forms of spiritual life that combine intellectual sophistication with spiritual depth, that honour both scientific discoveries and mystical insights, that maintain ultimate commitment while remaining open to ongoing revelation. Such religious life might express itself through institutions and practices quite different from those familiar in traditional religious communities. We might imagine contemplative communities organized around philosophical inquiry and meditative practice rather than doctrinal agreement, educational institutions that integrate rigorous academic study with spiritual formation, artistic endeavors that express transcendent vision through contemporary media, social movements that pursue justice from contemplative understanding of universal dignity. Such developments would not represent the replacement of traditional religions but their natural evolution as they encounter the challenges and opportunities of contemporary intellectual life. The wisdom embedded in ancient traditions remains valid, but it may need to be expressed through new forms that speak to minds shaped by scientific method, historical criticism, and global awareness. The future of faith lies not in the abandonment of reason but in its integration with contemplative insight, not in the rejection of transcendent claims but in their grounding in rigorous analysis, not in the dissolution of religious community but in its expansion to include all who seek ultimate truth regardless of the particular path they follow. Swāmi Vivekānanda once said,

> *"Religion is not in doctrines, in dogmas, nor in intellectual argumentation; it is being and becoming, it is realisation."*

This recognition reframes religious life as a dynamic process of actualizing our deepest potential in light of ultimate reality. It invites us to imagine contemplative communities organized around philosophical inquiry and meditative practice rather than doctrinal agreement, educational institutions that integrate rigorous academic study with spiritual formation, artistic endeavors that express transcendent vision through contemporary media, and social movements that pursue justice from a contemplative understanding of universal dignity. Such developments would not represent the replacement of traditional religions but their natural evolution as they encounter the challenges and opportunities of contemporary intellectual life. The wisdom embedded in ancient traditions remains valid, but it may need to be expressed through new forms that speak to minds shaped by scientific method, historical criticism, and global awareness. The future of faith lies not in the abandonment of reason but in its integration with contemplative insight; not in the rejection of transcendent claims but in their grounding in rigorous analysis; not in the dissolution of religious community but in its expansion to include all who seek ultimate truth, regardless of the particular path they follow. This vision requires a new kind of religious maturity—the ability to hold ultimate convictions without dogmatic rigidity, to practice ancient disciplines while remaining open to contemporary insights, to participate in particular communities while recognizing universal truth. It requires leaders who are both sophisticated thinkers and experienced contemplatives, institutions that are both intellectually credible and spiritually nourishing, practices that are both individually transformative and socially responsible.

## The Final Silence

As our long journey through the landscape of rational theology reaches its natural conclusion, we find ourselves in a place that is both familiar and utterly transformed. We have arrived where we started, as T.S. Eliot might say, and know the place for the first time. The questions that drove our inquiry remain questions, but they have been revealed as expressions of the reality they seemed to be investigating. The God whose existence we laboured to demonstrate has been discovered as the one who was demonstrating God's existence through our very capacity to seek demonstration. This is the final paradox of philosophical theology: the God who can be proven needs no proof, the God who can be argued for requires no argument, the God who can be known through concepts exceeds all conceptual knowledge. Yet this does not render our inquiry meaningless but reveals its deepest meaning—not to create faith where none existed but to remove the obstacles to recognizing the faith that was always already present, not to establish God's reality but to acknowledge the reality in which we have always already been established. The silence that follows reason is pregnant with recognition. In this silence, we discover that every question we asked was being asked by the reality we were questioning about, that every argument we constructed was being constructed by the truth we were arguing for, that every insight we achieved was being given by the wisdom we were seeking to achieve. This recognition brings profound peace—not the peace of having solved all problems but the peace of recognizing that we exist within the solution, not the peace of having answered all questions but the peace of discovering our participation in the reality that makes questioning possible. We rest in the certainty of uncertainty, the knowledge of unknowing, the faith that exceeds all belief because it recognizes itself as participation in the reality that faith seeks.

Yet this peace is not passive but infinitely creative. To recognize our participation in ultimate reality is to discover our capacity for expressing that reality through finite forms. Every act of love, every moment of understanding, every creation of beauty, every commitment to justice becomes a way in which infinite reality expresses itself through finite consciousness. The practical mystic who emerges from philosophical inquiry is neither the detached intellectual who remains aloof from engagement nor the unreflective activist who remains unconscious of ultimate meaning, but the integrated person who brings contemplative depth to worldly involvement and infinite perspective to finite responsibility. Such a person lives simultaneously in time and eternity, responding to immediate circumstances from awareness of ultimate context, acting decisively while remaining unattached to results, loving particularly while recognizing universally. This is not the lukewarm compromise that satisfies neither philosophical rigor nor spiritual depth, but the white-hot integration that fulfills both in ways neither could achieve alone. The God we cannot unknow continues to reveal God's inexhaustible nature through our finite attempts to understand infinite reality. Every authentic insight opens onto deeper mystery, every genuine answer generates more profound questions, every moment of clarity illuminates vaster regions of unknowing. Yet this is not frustrating but joyful, not discouraging but inspiring, because we recognize that the inexhaustibility of divine reality means the inexhaustibility of our capacity for discovery, growth, and transformation. We end where all authentic inquiry must end—in recognition of that which has no end, in knowledge of that which exceeds all knowledge, in certainty about that which transcends all certainty. We end in the beginning that has no beginning, the silence that speaks all words, the emptiness that contains all fullness, the God who cannot be known and cannot be unknown because this God is the knowing in which all knowledge occurs and the unknowing in which all knowledge dissolves.

This is the *silence after reason*—not the silence of having nothing more to say but the silence of recognizing that everything that can be said points toward that which exceeds all saying. In this silence, we rest in the God who is closer to us than we are to ourselves, more certain than any finite certainty, more present than any particular presence, more real than any empirical reality. And in this rest, we discover that we have been resting all along in the reality we sought so desperately to find, that we have been held all along by the love we thought we needed to earn, that we have been home all along in the truth we imagined we needed to reach. The journey from knowing to knowingness reveals itself as the journey from God to God—from God dimly apprehended through concepts to God directly recognized as the reality in which concepts arise and dissolve. We cannot conclude because ultimate reality has no conclusion. We cannot finish because infinite reality has no end. We can only rest in the beginningless beginning, the endless end, the timeless moment in which all our seeking finds its fulfilment not in having found what we sought but in recognizing that what we sought was always already finding us. In this recognition, reason and faith, philosophy and religion, thinking and being reveal their underlying unity in the simple fact of existence itself as participation in infinite reality. The God we have found through the long labour of rational inquiry is the God who was labouring through us all along, the infinite consciousness that expresses itself through finite minds engaged in the sacred work of seeking truth. And so, we end in silence—not because we have nothing more to say but because we have discovered the reality that makes all saying possible and meaningful. We end in the silence after reason, the silence that is not empty but full, not absent but present, not the end of seeking but its fulfilment in finding, not the cessation of love but its consummation in recognition. This is the God we cannot unknow—the reality that makes unknowing possible, the knowledge that makes all knowledge finite, the certainty that makes all certainties provisional, the love that makes all loving a participation in infinite love. In recognizing this God, we discover that we have always been recognized, that our seeking has always been a response to having been found, that our questions have always been emerging from the answer that we are.

The silence after reason is the quiet in which being speaks and we, at last, begin to listen.